Pathways to Prosperity in Rural Malawi

DIRECTIONS IN DEVELOPMENT
Poverty

Pathways to Prosperity in Rural Malawi

Andrew Dabalen, Alejandro de la Fuente, Aparajita Goyal, Wendy Karamba, Nga Thi Viet Nguyen, and Tomomi Tanaka

WORLD BANK GROUP

Contents

Boxes

Figures

Tables

Acknowledgments

This book was prepared by a team led by Andrew Dabalen and Alejandro de la Fuente. Core team members included Aparajita Goyal, Wendy Karamba, Nga Thi Viet Nguyen, and Tomomi Tanaka. Overall guidance for this project was received by Pablo Fajnzylber and Laura Kullenberg. Peer reviewers for the report were Kathleen Beegle, Madhur Gautam, and Brian G. Mtonya.

Preliminary findings and recommendations from this book were presented to the core senior management team for Malawi in March 2016. Participants included Preeti Arora, Andre Bald, Bella Bird, Laura Kullenberg, Gayle Martin, and Yutaka Yoshino. The team thanks all of them for their comments and suggestions.

The team greatly benefited from conversations with and comments from Kate Ambler, Edward Archibald, Bob Baulch, Kathleen Beegle, Todd Benson, Blessings Nyanjagha Botha, Efrem Zephnath Chilima, Ivan Drabek, Time Hapana Fatch, Emanuela Galasso, Xavier Giné, Susan Godlonton, Jessica Goldberg, Hanan Jacoby, Priscilla Flaness Kandoole, Holger A. Kray, Praveen Kumar, Patience Masi, Brian G. Mtonya, Valens Mwumvaneza, Richard Record, Dena Ringold, Jean Saint-Geours, Ted Sitimawina, and Thomas Staiger.

The team also benefited from contributions on the Malawi Poverty Assessment produced by Serge Adjognon, Rui Benfica, Martin Cumpa, Francis Darko, Emanuela Galasso, Dean Jolliffe, Talip Kilic, Elizabeth Mata, Amparo Palacios-Lopez, and Ilana Seff. Useful inputs were also received from Narae Choi, Hanan Jacoby, Somik Lall, Rodney Lunduka, and Jacob Ricker-Gilbert.

The team also thanks Olivier Durand, Pablo Fajnzylber, Laura Kullenberg, Praveen Kumar, Robin Mearns, Vijay Pillai, and Richard Record for their participation at the inception meeting of this project. Peer reviewers at that time were Andrew Dabalen, Manuel Salazar, and Robert Townsend.

Last, the team thanks Martin Buchara for his formatting assistance. Alicia Hetzner edited this report.

About the Authors

Andrew Dabalen works on policy research analysis on poverty and social impact of policies, inequality of opportunity, program evaluation, risk and vulnerability, labor markets, and conflict and welfare outcomes. He has published a number of scholarly articles and working papers on poverty measurement, conflict, welfare outcomes, and wage inequality.

Alejandro de la Fuente is a senior economist at the World Bank's Poverty and Equity Global Practice. His current work involves providing policy advice and technical support to African governments on poverty analysis, food and nutrition security, program evaluation, and risk and vulnerability. Past engagements at the World Bank have involved working and leading projects on poverty, natural disasters, and weather insurance in countries in East Asia and Latin America and the Caribbean. Previous experience outside the Bank includes working for the Human Development Report Office at the United Nations Development Program, the International Strategy for Disaster Risk Reduction Secretariat, the Inter-American Development Bank, and various positions at the Ministry of Social Development and the Office of the President in Mexico. He holds a DPhil in development studies/development economics from Oxford University.

Aparajita Goyal is a senior economist in the Poverty and Equity Global Practice of the World Bank. Her current work focuses on policy advice and evaluation of microeconomic issues of development, with a particular emphasis on technological innovation in agriculture, access to markets, and intellectual property rights. Her research has been published in leading academic journals and has also been featured in popular press. At the World Bank, she has previously worked in the Development Economics Research Group, the Office of the Chief Economist for the Latin America region, and the Agriculture Global Practice since joining the Young Professionals Program. She holds a PhD in economics from the University of Maryland, an MSc from the London School of Economics, and a BA in economics from St. Stephen's College, University of Delhi, India.

Wendy Karamba is an economist in the Poverty and Equity Global Practice at the World Bank. She currently works on both operational and analytical activities on issues related to poverty and inequality in countries in Africa. Her research interests cover microeconomic development issues such as food and nutrition security, agriculture, gender, and poverty. She holds a PhD in economics from American University and a BA in economics and business administration from Westminster College, New Wilmington, Pennsylvania.

Nga Thi Viet Nguyen is an economist in the World Bank's Poverty and Equity Global Practice, where her work involves poverty analysis, policy evaluation, and the study of labor markets and human development. She was part of the core teams that produced the 2016 report *Poverty in a Rising Africa* and the 2013 book *Opening Doors: Gender Equality and Development in the Middle East and North Africa*. Her main research interest is empirical microeconomics with a focus on poverty and social impact, labor markets, and welfare outcomes.

Tomomi Tanaka is a senior economist in the Poverty and Equity Global Practice of the World Bank. Having trained in experimental economics, behavioral economics, and impact evaluation, she provides advice and support to African governments in designing surveys and assessing policy effectiveness. Before joining the World Bank, Tomomi was an assistant professor at Arizona State University, a specially approved associate professor at Keio University, and a research fellow of the Cabinet Office of the government of Japan. She has taught behavioral economics and game theory at the PhD level. Two of her articles have been published in the *American Economic Review*. She has also received the Enjoji Jiro Memorial Prize for the most promising young economists from Nikkei. She received her PhD in economics from the University of Hawaii and was a postdoctorate at the California Institute of Technology.

Abbreviations

ADMARC	Agricultural Development and Marketing Corporation
COMSIP	Community Savings and Investment Promotion (MASAF-supported)
CT	cash transfer
DHS	Demographic and Health Survey
EAGC	Eastern Africa Grain Council
EPA	extension planning area
FAOSTAT	Food and Agriculture Organization of the United Nations Statistics Division
FISP	Farm Input Subsidy Program
FY	fiscal year
GDP	gross domestic product
GIC	growth incidence curve
HIV/AIDS	human immunodeficiency virus/acquired immune deficiency syndrome
ID	identification
IHPS	Integrated Household Panel Survey
IHS	Integrated Household Survey
IHS2	Second Integrated Household Survey
IHS3	Third Integrated Household Survey
IHS4	Fourth Integrated Household Survey
IHST	inverse hyperbolic sine transformation
JCE	Junior Certificate of Education
LF	labor force
LIPWP	Labor-Intensive Public Works Program (Ghana)
MASAF-PWP	Malawi Social Action Fund–Public Works Program
MDG	Millennium Development Goal
MFI	microfinance institution
MGDS	Malawi Growth and Development Strategy

MGNREGS	Mahatma Gandhi National Rural Employment Guarantee Scheme
MK	kwacha
MPI	Multidimensional Poverty Index
MSCE	Malawi School Certificate of Education
NASFAM	National Smallholder Farmers Association of Malawi
NFSE	nonfarm self-employment
NPK	nitrogen, phosphorus, and potassium
NSSP	National Social Support Policy
ODA	official development assistance
OIBM	Opportunity International Bank of Malawi
OLS	ordinary least squares
OPV	open-pollinated variety
PPP	purchasing power parity
PSNP	Productive Safety Nets Program (Ethiopia)
PWP	public work program
R&D	research and development
RCT	randomized controlled trial
SACMEQ	Southern and Eastern Africa Consortium for Monitoring Educational Quality
SCTP	Social Cash Transfer Program
SFFRFM	Smallholder Farmers Fertilizer Revolving Fund of Malawi
SP	social protection
TIP	Targeted Inputs Program
WAP	working-age population
WRS	Warehouse Receipts System

Executive Summary

By most accounts, rural Malawi lacked dynamism in the past 15 years. Growth was mostly volatile, in large part due to unstable macroeconomic fundamentals evidenced by high inflation, fiscal deficits, and high interest rates. Poverty remained high and its pace of reduction slow compared with better performers in Sub-Saharan Africa such as Ethiopia, Ghana, Rwanda, and Uganda. Malawi's rural poor faced significant challenges in consistently securing enough food. Despite this difficult environment, there were areas of progress.

Over the past 15 years, gains in access to primary education were steady and positive. The proportion of rural households with school-age children attending school rose 4 percentage points between 2004 and 2010 to reach 57 percent and rose another 4 percentage points between 2010 and 2013. The proportion of households with a member who had completed primary school increased 7 percentage points—from 37 to 44 percent—between 2004 and 2010. Additional improvements occurred between 2010 and 2013, with that proportion increasing to 48 percent.

The incidence of child malnutrition trended downward. According to Demographic and Health Survey (DHS) data, between 2004 and 2015, stunting (a measure of long-term nutritional deprivation in children) in rural Malawi fell from 54 to 39 percent, while prevalence of underweight (ratio of weight to age), which measures short-term changes in child nutrition, dropped from 18 to 12 percent. Significantly larger declines in stunting than implied in the DHS are estimated from the Second and Third Malawi Integrated Household Surveys (IHS2 and IHS3, respectively) as well as from the 2013 Integrated Household Panel Survey (IHPS).

Under-five mortality also dropped. Because undernutrition is an underlying cause of child death, progress in reducing undernutrition has contributed to reaching the Millennium Development Goal (MDG) of reducing child mortality by two-thirds. Data from the DHS reveal that, between 2004 and 2010, deaths of children under five declined nationally from 133 to 112 per 1,000 live births and declined further between 2010 and 2015 to reach 64 deaths per 1,000 live births. Between 2004 and 2010, the greatest reduction in under-five mortality occurred in rural areas, where the number of deaths per 1,000 live births fell from 164 to 130. A downward trend also was observed in the prevalence, incidence, and deaths associated with human immunodeficiency virus/acquired immune deficiency syndrome (HIV/AIDS), malaria, and tuberculosis, particularly since 2000.

As a result of progress made in some health, nutrition, and education aspects, Malawi has partially or fully achieved four of eight of the MDGs, the set of targets for 2015 to address poverty in its many dimensions. These are MDG1c (reducing undernutrition), MDG2a (achieving universal primary education), MDG4 (reducing child mortality), and MDG6 (combating HIV/AIDS, malaria, and other diseases).

The proportion of the rural population suffering from overlapping deprivations in education (not completing primary education or school-aged children not attending school), health (under-five mortality and undernutrition) and living standards (lack of access to electricity, improved sanitation, and safe drinking water, as well as lack of ownership of different assets) declined between 2004 and 2013. The indicator used to track multiple deprivations (that is, multidimensional poverty) usually combines the head count of persons deprived in more than one dimension with the average number of deprivations among the deprived (referred as the intensity of deprivation). For rural Malawi, the decline in multidimensional poverty was due mainly to the reduction in the head count of persons deprived in more than one dimension, which fell 8 percentage points between 2004 and 2010—from 75 to 67 percent. The average intensity of deprivations also declined, but only by a small margin—around 3 percentage points.

Ongoing Challenges

Notwithstanding the improvements in nonincome dimensions of poverty, monetary poverty in rural Malawi remains pervasive. In 2010, on the basis of a basket of basic needs that costs MK 37,000 per person per year, more than half of the rural population stayed poor. Little over one-quarter lived in extreme poverty, defined as the inability to satisfy food needs. More worrisome is that the poverty head count in rural areas between 2004 and 2010 remained unchanged, at around 56 percent, and the share of the extremely poor rose from 24 to 28 percent. Figure ES.1 shows that the depth of poverty, which measures the average consumption shortfall of the poor from the poverty line, and its severity—measured by the poverty gap squared—also went up between 2004 and 2010. Finally, on the basis of the international poverty line of US$1.90 per person per day, Malawi's poverty rate in 2010 remained high—71 percent—and close to stagnant relative to 2004. The majority of these persons live in rural areas. Recent estimates on rural poverty that are based on a panel sample between 2010 and 2013 suggest a slight decline but invite caution (box ES.1).

Figure ES.1 Rural Poverty in Malawi, 2004–10

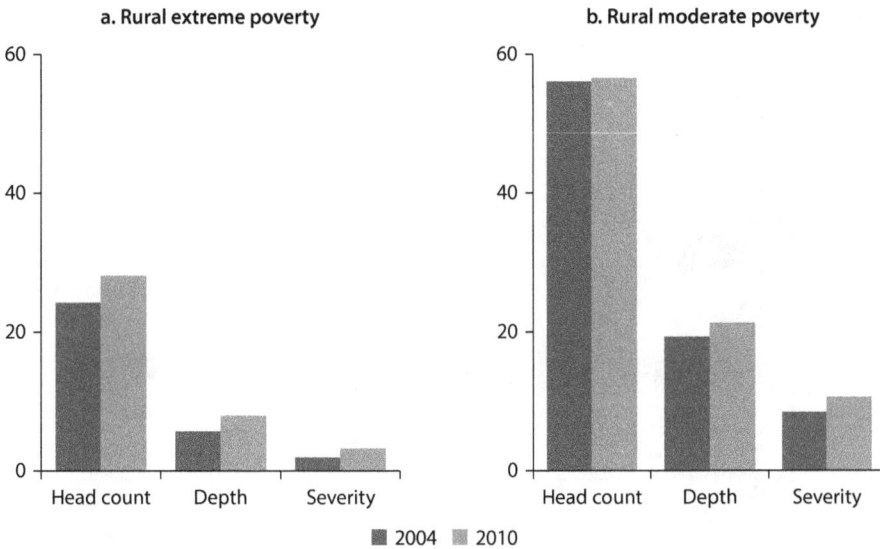

a. Rural extreme poverty

b. Rural moderate poverty

■ 2004 ■ 2010

Sources: Estimates are based on cross-sectional IHS2 and IHS3 data.
Note: IHS2 = Second Integrated Household Survey; IHS3 = Third Integrated Household Survey.

Box ES.1 Caution Regarding Any Recent Progress in Rural Poverty Reduction

While new official poverty estimates in Malawi since the IHS3 for 2010 will only become available with the Fourth Integrated Household Survey (IHS4) from 2016 to 2017, estimates from the most recent household survey—IHPS for 2013—which revisited some of the households interviewed in 2010, suggest that rural poverty may have dropped between 2010 and 2013. The depth and severity of poverty also fell (figure BES.1.1). The implied rate of poverty reduction—1 percentage point per year—though estimated for a short period of time, is similar to the regional annual average in Sub-Saharan Africa.

However, there are three reasons to be cautious about these recent results. First, substantial uncertainty surrounds the head count estimates, which, unlike measures of depth and severity, were measured with larger standard errors. Consequently, the rural drops in poverty were not statistically significant.

Second, the consumption data for households revisited in 2013 were collected during six months—April–November—during the nonlean season. Therefore, these data do not account for the lean months, when consumption typically drops and poverty increases.[a]

Third, any gains on poverty reduction were probably short-lived and potentially reversed by recent large-scale shocks—floods in 2015 and drought and floods in 2016. A study using the IHS3 panel and IHPS surveys in 2010 and 2013 found that shocks double the vulnerability to poverty. In 2010, when only household characteristics (number of members, location, and sociodemographic profile) were used to predict the likelihood of falling into poverty, 22 percent of households were expected to become poor in 2013. This proportion almost doubled to

box continues next page

Box ES.1 Caution Regarding Any Recent Progress in Rural Poverty Reduction *(continued)*

Figure BES.1.1 Rural Poverty Trends for Households in Malawi, 2010 and 2013

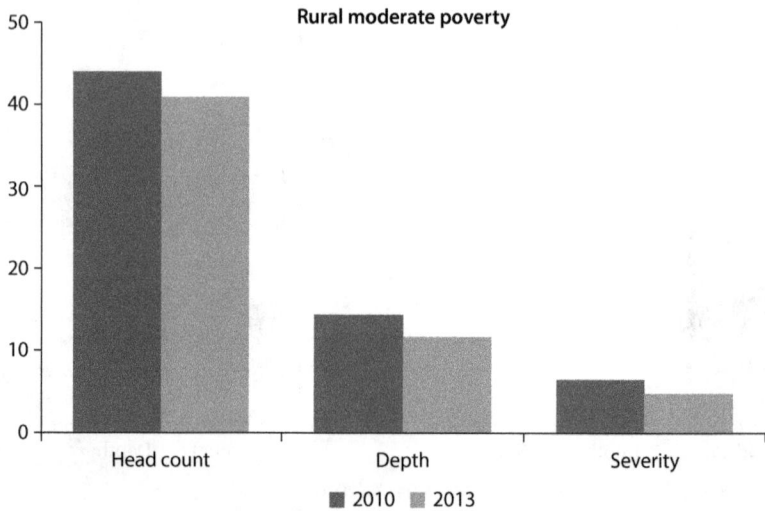

Sources: Estimates are based on IHS3 panel and IHPS data.
Note: IHS3 = Third Integrated Household Survey; IHPS = Integrated Household Panel Survey.

42 percent when expected shocks, particularly rainfall shocks, also were considered (McCarthy, Brubaker, and de la Fuente 2016). Furthermore, poverty increased eight percentage points between 2013 and 2015 in a sample of 558 rural households affected by the floods that struck Southern and Central Malawi in early 2015 (McCarthy and others 2016). And given the ongoing drought, a recent food security assessment by the government of Malawi and development partners concluded that around 6.5 million people will not be able to meet their annual food needs in 2016/17.[b] This could translate into higher poverty levels.

a. The IHS2 and IHS3 samples for 2004 and 2010, respectively, were stratified by month and administered throughout the year (typically starting in March and ending one year after). A subsample of the IHS3 sample was selected for follow-up in the IHPS, thus becoming a panel. However, the IHS3 subsample and IHPS sample were administered only from March through November, that is, during the nonlean season in Malawi. Therefore, the poverty rates in 2010, based on the IHS3 panel, and the poverty rates for 2013 based on the IHPS, are not official and should be understood as the lower bound for actual poverty in Malawi given that the lean months, when poverty increases, are not captured in them.
b. See Malawi Vulnerability Assessment Committee National Food and Nutrition Security Forecast, April 2016 to March 2017. Bulletin No. 12/16, Volume 1.

Food insecurity and chronic poverty were also widespread. In 2013, 84 percent of rural poor households reported experiencing food insecurity for at least one month of the year—a 17 percentage point increase since 2010. Poor households had a hard time meeting their daily consumption of calories per capita, and 81 percent consumed fewer than 2,100 kilocalories per capita per day, considered the benchmark needed to lead a healthy life.

Most of the chronically poor in Malawi live in rural areas. Using panel data from IHS3 and IHPS, it is possible to identify individuals who transitioned in or out of poverty and those who stayed in poverty in both periods over 2010–13 (that is, the chronically poor). Of 2.6 million chronically poor nationally, 2.4 million, or 90 percent, resided in rural areas. Uninsured shocks are a major source of both food insecurity and chronic poverty. Rural households are especially vulnerable to being trapped in poverty due to their high exposure to shocks and low capacity to cope with them.

Inequality is rising. For most of the period through 2004, Malawi was a low-inequality country. However, between 2004 and 2010, the Gini index for consumption in rural areas increased from 34 to 38. Furthermore, the share of consumption claimed by the bottom 40 percent fell from 20 to 18 percent. This drop occurred partly because, during the same period, consumption by the bottom 40 percent of the population fell 5 percent, while consumption by the top 60 percent grew 17 percent. Inequality also grew between urban and rural areas. Consumption in urban areas grew for virtually all consumption percentiles, with the poorest enjoying relatively lower, but still positive, growth rates. However, in rural areas, approximately two-thirds of the population experienced negative real consumption growth, and only the top 5–10 percentiles experienced significant growth (figure ES.2). Thus, Malawi's volatile and tepid growth did little to increase the consumption of the rural poor.

Figure ES.2 Growth of Consumption per Capita in Malawi, 2004–10

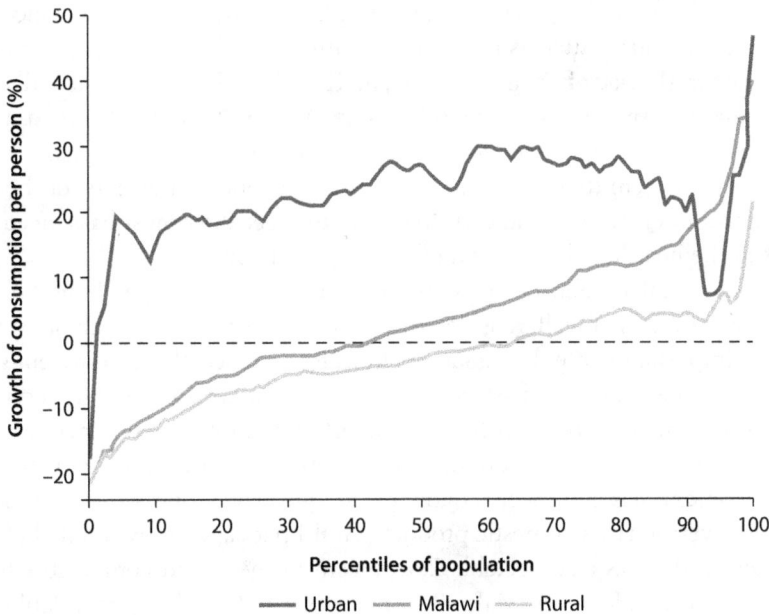

Sources: Calculations are based on IHS2 and IHS3 data.
Note: IHS2 = Second Integrated Household Survey; IHS3 = Third Integrated Household Survey.

Access to essential opportunities and services in rural Malawi is unequal. Although primary school completion rates rose substantially (17 percentage points) between 2004 and 2013 to reach 75 percent (World Bank various years), richer groups experienced greater gains. Wide variations between urban and rural areas still were encountered in the percentage of children with basic skills in reading and numeracy on the basis of scores for standard tests[1] administered to sixth-grade children in 2007. Large gaps in the learning outcomes for sixth graders were also encountered in the numeracy and reading skills between children of high and low socioeconomic status. There were equally large gaps between the nutritional status of children living in wealthier and in poorer households. In 2010, the incidence of stunting was 53 percent for children living in poor households and 45 percent for children living in richer households. Stunting is a major cause of adverse cognitive development, which is associated with delayed school enrollment, lower grade attainment, lower school performance, and, in later life, worse labor market outcomes through lower earnings and productivity. Given the personal and social cost of stunting, prevalence rates are unacceptably high for all income groups. Finally, access to key public services such as electricity, safe water and sanitation, and nonsolid cooking fuels was virtually nonexistent for households in the bottom 40 percent of the consumption distribution.

Reasons for the Persistence of Rural Poverty

To date, rural poverty reduction in Malawi has been elusive. Why? Rural households in Malawi earn income primarily through crop production and employment in the farm labor market (*ganyu*, defined as short-term rural arrangements on household farms, large-scale farms, and plantations). However, reliance on a single income source such as rain-fed agriculture, which is highly prone to price and weather shocks, often is not enough. Therefore, households also diversify into nonfarm activities, especially self-employment in household-owned microenterprises or off-farm wage work in rural or urban areas. Finally, many households rely on remittances, pensions, and other public transfers or benefits (nutritional interventions and cash transfers) to meet their most basic needs and invest in the health and education of future generations.

The potential to transform assets into income that enables households to attain higher levels of welfare is determined by the context in which households operate. Important contextual issues include, for instance, the government's provision of socioeconomic infrastructure, access to markets, and public services; a sound economic environment for investment and employment generation; and the ability to manage risks. From these perspectives, Malawi's broader macroeconomic context has not been conducive to poverty reduction. In particular, Malawi's average gross domestic product (GDP) per capita growth rate between 2004 and 2013 was a respectable 2.4 percent per year and comparable to the regional average. However, Malawi's GDP was significantly more volatile than Sub-Saharan Africa's and, in some instances, was not driven by agriculture, the sector in which most of the rural population is employed.

Between 2004 and 2010, real agricultural GDP grew more slowly than services (wholesale and retail trade, real estate, information and communications, transport and storage, and professional and other services) and industry (mining and quarrying, construction, and manufacturing). Volatility in GDP growth was due partly to macroeconomic instability—exchange rate volatility and high inflation, cost of capital, and fiscal deficits—and partly to large-scale weather shocks, which have struck the country twice in recent years. In addition to this difficult macroeconomic environment, structural impediments to sustained and inclusive growth have created conditions such that agricultural incomes did not grow much, nonfarm opportunities remained limited, and safety nets were largely ineffective.

Weak Growth of Agricultural Productivity

Improving agricultural productivity is necessary to improve the welfare of rural households. Agriculture constitutes the backbone of the Malawian economy, contributing more than 30 percent of GDP and employing 85 percent of the workforce. Most producers are subsistence farmers who cultivate small plots of land with limited opportunities for income diversification. Given the predominantly rural nature of the country and agriculture's importance for rural livelihoods, especially for the poor, agricultural performance has direct implications for economic growth and poverty reduction in Malawi.

Empirical estimates show that, between 2010 and 2013, a 1 percent increase in agricultural productivity would improve consumption expenditure per capita of rural agricultural households by 0.13 percent. Poverty measures such as the poverty gap and severity of poverty would also decline as agricultural productivity rose. Half of the gain from increased agricultural productivity would go to increased food consumption (elasticity of 0.06), measured by caloric intake per capita. Moreover, were maize yields to increase 50 percent, the poverty rate among rural agricultural households would decrease 7 percentage points, lifting approximately 622,015 people out of poverty.

Unfortunately, the growth in agricultural productivity needed to alter the trajectory of rural poverty was not achieved. Maize yields increased between 2010 and 2013, but only 8 percent, and the growth was higher for the nonpoor. Maize yields were 31 percent lower for the poor than for the nonpoor. There also were substantial differences in the productivity of other major crops across poverty status (figure ES.3). Moreover, average maize yields remained relatively low, at 1.4 tons per hectare. Some difference exists between the Malawi Integrated Household Surveys and Food and Agriculture Organization of the United Nations Statistics Division (FAOSTAT) data for maize yield productivity in Malawi in 2013. Despite this fact, the two data sources indicate lower yields compared with yields in other African countries, including Rwanda and Uganda, as well as in countries outside the region.[2] On the basis of its agronomic potential, some recent estimates have suggested that under specific climatic conditions and input application Malawi could achieve an average yield of approximately 4.5 tons per hectare in the longer term (Benson and Edelman 2016).

Figure ES.3 Crop Yields in Malawi, by Poverty Status, 2010 and 2013

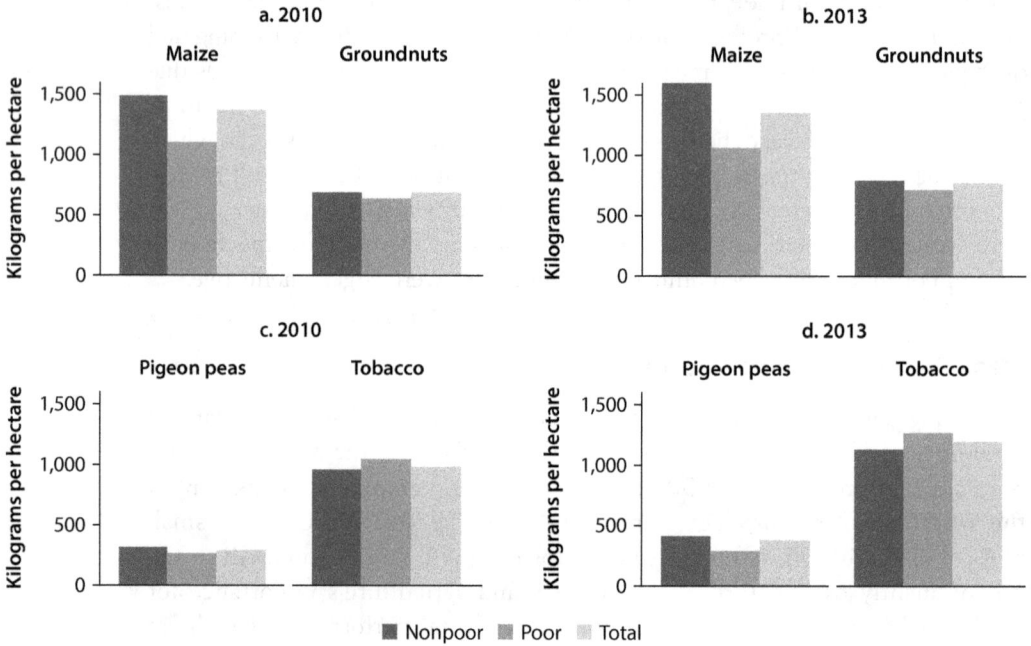

Source: World Bank 2016a.

Agricultural productivity in Malawi remained largely stagnant partly due to the limited adoption of complementary investments in agriculture and access to information. The share of farms with access to complementary inputs (for instance, inorganic fertilizer, improved seeds, and extension services) was low despite suggestive evidence that the joint use of complementary investments raises the productivity of maize more than the use of one input alone. Furthermore, more than half (53 percent) of the maize yield differential between the households that were chronically poor and those that escaped poverty between 2010 and 2013 is explained by changes in the returns to the application of organic fertilizer, use of family labor, access to extension services, and application of the right type of basal fertilizer. Access to and use of adequate information could therefore bring higher yields. As an example, households that stayed in poverty in both periods had lower levels of education and lived in more remote villages than those that escaped poverty. Remoteness and low education are likely to make information for these households harder to obtain and use appropriately and, in the process, to diminish their income-earning capabilities.

Inefficient patterns of public spending on agriculture are at the root of poor agricultural productivity in Malawi. Malawi is one of the largest spenders on agriculture in Sub-Saharan Africa, devoting 4.2 percent of total GDP to agriculture, compared with the regional average of 1.3 percent in 2012. Yet, the composition of spending in agriculture is highly unbalanced. One program, the Farm Input Subsidy Program (FISP), has consistently accounted for more than half of

Figure ES.4 FISP Participation in Malawi, by Consumption Quintile, 2013

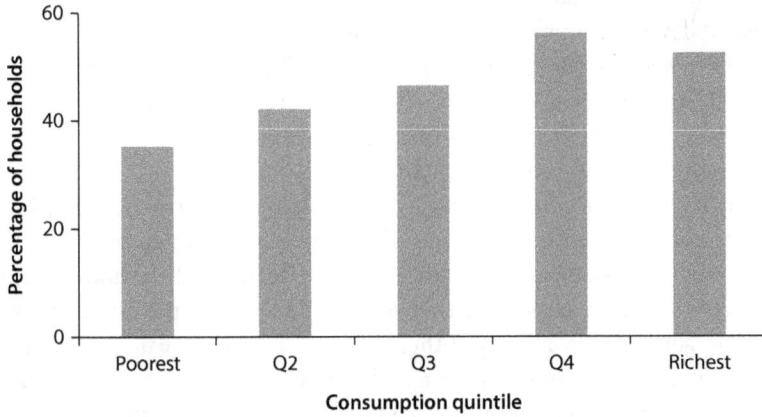

Source: Estimates are based on IHPS data.
Note: FISP = Farm Input Subsidy Program; IHPS = Integrated Household Panel Survey.

total agricultural public expenditures in Malawi. Consequently, the FISP budget crowds out complementary public investments to strengthen markets, develop irrigation, and introduce and diffuse new technologies, all of which are important drivers of robust growth of agricultural productivity.

In the presence of good weather, increased access to inorganic fertilizer, largely subsidized by the government through FISP, is likely to give a modest boost to maize production. However, although the stated aim of FISP is to make inorganic fertilizer available to smallholder, resource-poor farmers, targeting remains unclear. In 2013, approximately one-third of households in the bottom quintile obtained subsidized inorganic fertilizer, compared with half of those in the top two quintiles (figure ES.4). Nearly half of the households in the top three consumption quintiles received FISP assistance, and this incorrect target-ing raises concerns about the program's performance. Is the primary aim to reduce poverty or to boost maize production? Whatever the objectives, the accumulating empirical evidence indicates that FISP has had a small impact on poverty (Ricker-Gilbert 2016) and food security, and yields have not improved much beyond an initial boost when the program was launched. The lack of growth in yield, despite the participation of a large fraction of nonpoor farmers, is a concern. The lack of strong growth in yield also partially explains the modest growth in crop income for the poorest and the otherwise limited effects of the FISP on reducing real maize prices.

Limited Opportunities to Engage in Nonfarm Activities

Many households in primarily agricultural economies such as Malawi are unable to sustain income from a single source such as livestock or crops from rain-fed agriculture. They often need to diversify sources of income to minimize losses from highly risk-prone agricultural activities. They may need to use nonfarm income to overcome thin credit markets and to smooth consumption, finance farm investments, or start businesses. Recent patterns of economic growth suggest that Malawi's economy is very gradually shifting away from agriculture and into nonfarm sectors. More than four-fifths (82.7 percent) of the new jobs created in Malawi between 1998 and 2013 were created in rural areas, but rural agricultural employment declined during that period so that all rural employment growth took place within nonfarm sectors.

Participation in nonfarm sectors, particularly nonfarm self-employment (NFSE), is associated with improved welfare. An exercise to account for changes in poverty by sources of income indicated that, between 2010 and 2013, rising income from nonfarm business activities helped to reduce poverty in rural areas more than income from any other source. Higher participation in self-employment activities (possibly spurred by more access to informal credit) and the profits obtained from them by the poor explain such trends.

Nevertheless, the opportunities for NFSE activities have remained precarious and limited. Although the participation of rural households in NFSE increased from 20 percent in 2010 to 28 percent in 2013, the rates are low relative to other low-income countries in the region. Furthermore, the growth potential of these activities is doubtful. Many rural household enterprises are operated informally from home by young uneducated males. Three in every four business owners have no formal education and no capital services to enhance productivity. Although some enterprises were created between 2010 and 2013, some older ones disappeared, reducing the average age of enterprises. Therefore, household enterprises have a relatively short life span, consistent with the fact that only 8 percent of household enterprises were formally registered in 2013. Perhaps because of the short life span of such enterprises, owners do not invest time and resources in registering their business or, which is more important, in enhancing their productivity.

The productivity of rural nonfarm activities is low. When disaggregating changes in overall productivity into changes within and across economic sectors—or "structural change"—two patterns emerge. Labor productivity within agriculture declined over time, but the shift from low- to higher-productivity sectors was slow. This slow shift suggests that most of the labor leaving the agriculture sector was absorbed into low-productivity activities in other sectors.

Urban areas also outperformed rural areas in off-farm productivity. Revenues from household enterprises and nonfarm wages across all industry groups were considerably higher in urban than in rural areas. The average profit from participation in self-employment was MK 23,400 per month in urban areas in 2010, which is approximately MK 18,000 higher than the average return in rural areas in the same year. Workers in urban areas also consistently earned higher wages than workers in rural areas across all job categories.

Furthermore, the participation of households in NFSE and their associated returns are lower for the poor. Even though nonfarm growth and job creation occurred mainly within rural areas, the poor benefited less from these processes than the nonpoor. Approximately 19 percent of the rural poor in Malawi owned a business in 2013 (compared with 31 percent, on average, nationally). Similarly, in 2013 average returns from those businesses for the rural poor in Malawi were MK 3,200 per month in 2013, less than half, on average, those of the nonpoor (MK 7,300 per month).

Imperfect Safety Nets in a Context of High Economic Insecurity

As argued, low-productivity agriculture and limited opportunities to earn non-farm income constrain household income growth in Malawi. Not surprising, incomes are low. They also are risky because of the constant threat of weather and health shocks. In the current context, financial markets do not provide credit, insurance, or savings products in sufficient scale to enable households to manage risk (that is, to protect themselves from changes in income), start busi-nesses, or buy inputs. Although private transfers—either through remittances from household members or mutual insurance schemes—are useful, they do not necessarily benefit poor households or prove effective against large-scale, com-munity-wide shocks. Therefore, social protection interventions that set a floor for income levels and protect households from income shocks are important tools for controlling extreme poverty and rising inequality. Malawi has two large safety net programs: the Malawi Social Action Fund–Public Works Program (MASAF-PWP) and the Social Cash Transfer Program (SCTP), which are the focus of this book.

The coverage of these programs remains limited, despite recent expan-sions. Public spending on social protection in Malawi is low by international standards. In 2014–15, the annual budget for social protection programs accounted for approximately 0.8 percent of GDP, which was less than two-thirds of average spending on social protection in Sub-Saharan Africa. In 2010, only the School Feeding Program reached more than 10 percent of the population. Even in 2013 when all major SP programs were scaled up in response to a deteriorating economic situation, MASAF-PWP alone covered only 15 percent of the population.

In addition to limited coverage, social assistance programs in Malawi experi-enced high leakage rates. In 2013, around 6 of every 10 beneficiaries of MASAF-PWP or of direct cash transfers from government at the time were not poor. Although existing mechanisms for redistribution within communities could attenuate this leakage, the evidence that they do so is anecdotal.

The MASAF-PWP has the potential to serve as a key safety net for poor households. However, a large-scale randomized controlled trial implemented during the 2012–13 agricultural season found that the program failed to realize its protective role in food security or to increase its beneficiaries' opportunities to exit poverty. In addition to poor targeting and significant rationing,[3] the rela-tively small size (compared with similar programs) of the transfers associated with infrequent projects may have contributed to the lack of impact.

The SCTP, which aims to tackle extreme poverty by providing cash to labor-constrained households, shows promise, but remains small in terms of coverage of the extreme poor. Impact assessments of the pilot SCTP conducted in 2007 found that the transfers increased both consumption and investment in productive assets. Results from another impact evaluation that covered more than 3,300 households from 2013 to 2016 further confirmed the effectiveness of the program in multiple domains, including food security, asset holding, health and education, and psychological well-being. The program keeps improving and expanding its coverage to more districts, which is desirable as a means toward putting in place an effective safety net for the extreme poor.

Achieving Prosperity in Rural Malawi

To summarize, despite progress in some aspects of well-being, rural poverty in Malawi has remained stubbornly high, affecting more than half of the rural population, for more than a decade. The accumulated evidence suggests three proximate causes. First, agricultural productivity is low, especially among the poor and when compared with other low-income countries in Sub-Saharan Africa. Second, opportunities for NFSE are limited, and the returns to such activities are low, especially for the poor. Third, the most prominent safety net programs have low impacts or reduced coverage of the poor population. Therefore, policy actions are needed to remove the obstacles imposed by these three causes. Ultimately, these complementary reforms are intended to lay the foundation for a more dynamic and prosperous rural economy. At their core, they aim to chart a path toward sustainable growth on the basis of increased economic productivity in agriculture, more dynamic structural transformation, better-functioning safety nets, and more inclusive financial markets.

First, to lay the foundation for growth, it is necessary to establish macroeconomic stability. Stability includes bringing inflation, expected to average 23 percent between 2014 and 2016, under control; reducing the cost of capital; and addressing the weak fiscal environment by maintaining upward trends in revenue mobilization and coupling them with expenditure discipline. Stabilizing the macroeconomic environment will encourage investments, growth, and employment generation and bring immediate relief to the poor by controlling inflation. But bringing deficits under control either by reducing spending or increasing revenue could introduce adverse impacts on the poor. Therefore, policy action to correct fiscal challenges should build in safeguards for pro-poor spending.

Second, inclusive growth is unlikely to be achieved or sustained without improving the productivity of agriculture. To date, agricultural growth has been achieved through factor accumulation—primarily by expanding resources such as cultivated land and labor. However, in a country with one of the highest population densities in Africa and shrinking farmlands, the gains from such practices are approaching their limit. In all likelihood, future agricultural growth will have to come from increased agricultural productivity. Four actions are recommended to improve agricultural productivity.

- *Create better balance in the composition of agricultural spending by scaling back FISP.* Scaling back FISP will improve Malawi's fiscal position and free resources for reallocation to complementary investments that have higher returns to agricultural productivity. A study looking at the contribution of specific investments to the value of agricultural revenue on a nationally representative sample of smallholder households interviewed three times between 2004 and 2009 found that the use of improved maize seed has one of the highest returns at national and regional levels (Lunduka and Ricker-Gilbert 2016). The national benefit-to-cost ratio for improved seeds is 2.48, meaning that for every kwacha spent on improved seeds, MK 1.48 are gained in additional benefits. This ratio indicates the potential value of investing in research and development of improved maize varieties that are higher yielding and more resistant to droughts and floods. By contrast, the cost of subsidized fertilizer far exceeds the benefits to farmers, with benefit-cost ratios at 0.42 at the national level. Other interventions, such as irrigation, extension advice, and road investments, have higher returns than subsidized fertilizer in the southern region.

- *Redefine the objectives of the reformed FISP and the target population.* Although the FISP stated goals of increasing agricultural productivity, improving food security, and reducing poverty are admirable, households who should be targeted to increase maize productivity and maize production likely are not the same households who should be targeted to reduce rural poverty. Having multiple goals puts considerable pressure on FISP because, given the program's substantial budget share, the expectation is that it will deliver both increased maize productivity and reduced poverty to rural Malawi. FISP should separate the safety net function (aimed at achieving household food self-sufficiency and reducing poverty) from the increased production function (aimed at achieving national food self-sufficiency). For clarity, it is recommended that the program focus on increasing productivity and crop diversification, while leaving the safety net function to other programs.

- *In the short run, provide e-vouchers that are redeemed at private-sector-supplied input stores and increase the participation of the private fertilizer retailers in the FISP.* These e-vouchers should be flexible, allowing farmers to redeem them for any combination of inputs. Private distributors should be allowed to accept FISP fertilizer coupons.

- *In the medium term, consider transitioning to cash subsidies under FISP, combined with supplementary services such as training and information on new technologies or seeds, because such a bundle is likely to be superior to the current subsidy program.* For example, in 2013, the difference in maize yields between households that were chronically poor and those that escaped poverty was 320 kilograms. Approximately half of that maize yield gap is explained by differences in family labor utilization and extension services obtained as well as the returns to organic fertilizer and applying the right type of basal fertilizer. Training and information are therefore crucial features. Recent work with farmers growing either groundnuts or soy who are members of the National Smallholder Farmers Association of Malawi found that providing transfers and intensive agricultural extension support could alleviate capital and information constraints facing farmers in rural Malawi and boost their productivity (Ambler, de Brauw, and Godlonton 2016). Before switching to cash, policy makers could consider piloting a cash subsidy program.

Third, to sustain agricultural productivity growth and reduce rural poverty, faster structural change is needed. Only about one-third of the persons who are employed (36 percent) in Malawi work outside of agriculture (as of 2013). Industry absorbs about one-fifth (7 percent) of this nonfarm employment, and services employ the rest (29 percent). Despite recent growth, the share of households participating in nonfarm wage and NFSE activities in rural areas is only 14 and 28 percent, respectively. While the participation rates in nonfarm wage employment are similar to those in rural areas in several other African countries, the participation rate in NFSE is below the average of 34 percent in these same countries (Davis, Di Giuseppe, and Zezza 2014). In rural areas, only 8 percent of enterprises are registered—which is an imperfect proxy for formal enterprises—and many of these activities are characterized by low productivity, low pay, and poor prospects for building human capital. Even though most of these jobs are in rural areas, informal nonfarm employment is also high in urban areas. A major constraint on growth in NFSE in rural areas is lack of demand for the products produced by these enterprises. The very low levels of urbanization (16 percent of the population) and the low incomes in rural areas are major reasons for limited opportunities to earn nonfarm incomes. As noted, a productive and dynamic agriculture sector is needed to increase rural incomes, enable workers to move from agriculture to higher-productivity sectors, and support rural nonfarm sector growth. However, a more productive agriculture sector would not be enough or cannot be sustained unless the nonfarm sectors—especially in urban areas—also become productive and dynamic. For rural prosperity to emerge, Malawi needs broad structural transformation, which includes faster and "orderly" urbanization.

Historical and contemporary experience has shown that, when handled properly, urbanization can be a catalyst for inclusive structural transformation. It acts as a major source of demand for agricultural and other rural products. It improves the accumulation of skills, occupational specialization, and labor productivity. It integrates labor markets and fosters creativity and innovation. In short, urbanization builds human capital in the economy, usually in ways that are rarely taught in schools. It is the main locus of formal sector employment. Urban growth has brought immense prosperity to billions around the world, and it could do the same for Malawi. For example, increasing the urban population of Malawi from 16 to 21 percent by 2030 could add 0.7 percentage points to GDP growth per year. Without any growth in population or labor force, Malawi would be 14 percent richer in 2030 by reallocating only 5 percent of rural population to urban areas (World Bank 2016b). Urbanization is also expected to transform food systems to higher-value activities (Tschirley and others 2015). Finally, faster urbanization, combined with higher investment in upgrading urban infrastructure and services—financed by higher government spending funded by imposing higher taxes on richer urban households—would be the best case for structural transformation while reducing rural poverty (World Bank 2016b).

To be sure, urbanization and structural changes to the economy involve complex forces and processes. They call for changes in entrepreneurship and skills, a local context that encourages and provides strong incentives for the private sector to flourish, a trade policy that facilitates technological upgrading, stronger connectivity that lowers the costs of remoteness, trading and mobility, balance between large and secondary towns, and macroeconomic stability that anchors sustainable growth. These factors and more will be necessary to accelerate structural change. Although a full discussion of these forces and processes is beyond the scope of this book, the following actions are feasible and available to policy makers to get the urbanization process under way:

- *Remove policy biases against urbanization.* Malawi's development strategy prioritizes household food self-sufficiency in rural areas, which explains the long tradition of providing input subsidies and export bans for maize. By contrast, existing policy does not enable urban local governments to take more than minimal residual steps. To create smarter and more vibrant urban areas, the capacity of local governments needs to be strengthened and their financial resources expanded. This capacity will include a systematic, focused effort to improve own-source revenue, especially from property taxes, which hold substantial potential to finance urban development.
- *Take more deliberate actions to promote "smarter" urbanization.* Whether the actions involve increasing the size and density of existing cities or creating new cities, policy makers need to take a conscious, planned approach to the efficient management of urban land. Efficient management includes mapping urban land use and improving the quality and reliability of services. Well-managed urban land will encourage mobility and connectivity, clustering of economic activities, protection of the space for public goods (infrastructure, environmental amenities), and efficient provision of services to large, intermediate, and small towns.
- *Promote urban job creation.* In addition to encouraging food self-sufficiency, government policy also needs to prioritize value addition and job creation in urban areas. One of the unintended consequences of keeping households on land (agriculture first policy) is to discourage migration and urbanization. However, for true transformation to occur, it is important to shift what people do and where they do it. Even a small change in the rates of urbanization and urban investment could bring huge welfare gains to Malawi. Therefore, equal or even more weight should be given to urban job creation by revisiting regulatory barriers to the entry of firms, upgrading skills and promoting entrepreneurship, raising the productivity of small and medium enterprises, integrating value chains, and reducing the costs of logistics.

Fourth, credit is a major constraint to both agricultural productivity growth and expansion of nonfarm activities, and digital finance can help to address it. Seasonality of agricultural production and susceptibility to natural disasters (flood and drought) heighten the risks associated with price and yield volatility, which adds to the increasing need for rural financial services. Yet, only 13 percent of rural households in 2010 and 22 percent in 2013 applied for credit. Of these, only 41 percent in 2010 and 31 percent in 2013 were successful in obtaining it. Nonpoor households and male-headed households were more likely to receive credit (and less likely to be turned down) than were poor and female-headed households. Male-headed households received more credit than female-headed households partly because they were, on average, better off and thus deemed more likely to pay back the loan (World Bank 2016a). Enhancing financial inclusion not only would promote access to and use of improved agricultural technologies, build resilience, and thus increase productivity, but also would enable farm households to diversify into nonagricultural production.

Digital finance, combined with other digital technological innovations, has the potential to transform rural Malawi in ways that have never before been possible. Digital payments can reduce transaction costs (cost and time to send and receive payments), increase security and privacy of payments and control over transfers received, especially for women, and help individuals and households to meet emergency expenditures.

Introduction of digital identification (ID) can enhance the reach of mobile banking and deepen financial inclusion. Applying biometric technologies (fingerprinting, for instance) to credit approval can build the history of financial transactions, allow banks to identify good borrowers, and ease the banks' fear of lending, making credit more accessible. The combination of digital finance and digital IDs also can transform public service delivery and create potentially large savings for the government. In short, by increasing overall efficiency in the economy, improving risk management at the household level, and increasing the efficiency of public service delivery, digital finance could create dynamism in Malawi's rural economy. With the right environment and incentives, digital finance could take off rapidly and reach massive scale in a short period of time.

Fifth, Malawi's safety net programs need to be made more efficient and better targeted. Both the MASAF-PWP and SCTP covered approximately 650,000 households per year in 2013–15. In spite of this coverage, the following policy reforms could improve the impact of these programs further:

- *Provide larger transfers to more poor people.* Social protection interventions are much needed in Malawi, but the current system, although recently expanded, has both low expenditure by international standards and limited coverage. Compared with public work programs (PWPs) in other low-income and lower-middle-income countries, the total transfer amount from MASAF-PWP was relatively small. Although the daily wage from MASAF-PWP was similar to wages provided by other programs, the maximum number of working days per year was much lower, yielding a comparatively low total transfer amount. Scaling back FISP subsidies alone, as proposed, would lift some of the fiscal pressures that may have prevented wider coverage. SCTP transfers are more generous and have shown positive impacts, but their coverage among the extreme poor remains minuscule relative to need: The program is aiming to reach its goal of 319,000 households in 2017, covering the 10 percent poorest labor-constrained households in each district. Yet, already in 2010, more than 3 million people in rural areas could not afford the value of a basic food bundle. The ongoing strengthening and expansion of the Social Cash Transfer program as a means toward putting in place an effective safety net for the extreme poor is desirable. In the medium to long term, the MASAF-PWP and SCTP programs should be consolidated with a common registry and common administration. Such a reform is likely to reduce costs and be more effective.

- *Improve targeting for greater impact.* While some redistribution toward the poorest may happen within communities, household survey data suggest that the targeting of existing social protection programs is not exclusively pro-poor. For MASAF-PWP, one way to improve targeting is to verify the existing community-based targeting through proxy means testing. Alternatively, the program could further explore the possibility of rolling out self-targeting starting with a pilot. Self-targeting would require lowering the wage substantially, though this may face political resistance. A lower wage has the potential to attract persons who will have low opportunity cost of time and who could benefit from participation—often the very poor. However, to ensure that total transfers are sufficient to improve household welfare, there should be no limit on the number of days a person can participate in the program. Recent reforms offering more public work during the lean season, providing more days of work (currently 48 days) to a household, and maintaining the same households in each work cycle should be continued and evaluated.

- *Evaluate the value of assets produced under MASAF-PWP.* To date, there has been no evaluation of the assets produced by these programs. A proper and thorough evaluation of assets should be undertaken. If they are found to have no value and the conditions to work are still built into the program design, then the program could focus on a narrower set of assets that create value to communities (for example, conservation of water catchment areas) and reassess them. The alternative is to remove the condition to work and convert MASAF-PWP into a cash program.

Finally, accelerating the demographic transition would boost poverty reduction. Malawi's fertility rate has remained persistently high, particularly among rural poor women (6.1 births per woman). The country's population is expected to double in approximately two decades: from 17.2 million in 2015 to 34.4 million in 2038. For a country that is already one of the most densely populated in

Africa, unchecked population growth will put enormous pressure on limited land resources, service delivery, and poverty reduction. A high fertility rate also lowers productivity because it impairs women's ability to engage in more productive farming or nonfarm work when they spend many of their prime years pregnant, lactating, and otherwise raising children. Moreover, Malawi's young age structure generates an extremely high ratio of dependents to working-age population. Such a ratio is associated with higher poverty levels.

Malawi needs to bend the trajectory of its fertility rate in order to reduce poverty and boost human development. Accelerating and reaping the benefits of a demographic transition will come only if Malawi empowers its women through three interrelated policies:

- *Improve child health and lower family size.* Improving child health will reduce child mortality and the demand for more children, while smaller family size will improve maternal and child health, completing the virtuous circle (Canning, Sangeeta, and Yazbeck 2015).
- *Invest in girls' education.* Curbing early child marriage and early childbearing among adolescents will prolong girls' stay in school, delay childbearing age, and delay fertility. Continued progress in eliminating gender disparity in education, particularly secondary, could help to reduce fertility, since at that level is where education has a significant effect on fertility.
- *Improve access to family planning and contraception.* Especially among the poor, who report higher than desired fertility, and among adolescents, family planning and contraception would curb early child marriage and early childbearing. Reducing the number of pregnancies and encouraging greater child spacing are associated with better maternal health outcomes, and would hasten the transition to smaller family size.

Since fertility is closely linked to poverty, reducing fertility in Malawi could change the population dynamics toward one with a lower ratio of dependents to working adults. In addition, providing better and high-quality education and health services to women and promoting female labor market participation in formal and better-paying jobs will empower women and close the virtuous circle.

Notes

1. The Southern and Eastern Africa Consortium for Monitoring Educational Quality project (SACMEQ 2010) collected test scores for sixth graders in 15 countries in southern and eastern Africa. The latest available data are from 2007.

2. Although national production estimates suggest that maize production and productivity increased substantially from 2005 to 2010, several farm-level studies found relatively modest increases in maize production and yields during the same period (Chibwana, Fisher, and Shively 2012; Holden and Lunduka 2012; Ricker-Gilbert and Jayne 2012; Ricker-Gilbert, Jayne, and Chirwa 2011).

3. Rationing is the controlled distribution of scarce resources, goods, or services, or an artificial restriction of demand.

References

Ambler, K., A. de Brauw, and S. Godlonton. 2016. "Relaxing Constraints for Family Farmers: Providing Capital and Information in Malawi." IFPRI Working Paper, International Food Policy Research Institute, Washington, DC.

Benson, T. and B. Edelman. 2016. "Policies for Accelerating Growth in Agriculture and Agribusiness in Malawi." Background paper for the 2016 Malawi Country Economic Memorandum. International Food Policy Research Institute, Washington, DC.

Canning, D., R. Sangeeta, and A. S. Yazbeck, eds. 2015. *Africa's Demographic Transition: Dividend or Disaster?* Africa Development Forum Series. Gabon: Agence Française de Développement. Washington, DC: World Bank.

Chibwana C., M. Fisher, and G. Shively 2012. Cropland Allocation Effects of Agricultural Input Subsidies in Malawi. *World Development* 40 (1): 124–33.

Davis, B., S. Di Giuseppe, and A. Zezza. 2014. "Income Diversification Patterns in Rural Sub-Saharan Africa: Reassessing the Evidence." Policy Research Working Paper 7108, World Bank, Washington, DC.

Holden, S. T. and R. Lunduka. 2012. "Do Fertilizer Subsidies Crowd Out Organic Manures? The Case of Malawi." *Agricultural Economics* 43 (3): 301–312.

Lunduka, R. and J. Ricker-Gilbert. 2016 "Contribution of Alternative Investments to the Value of Agricultural Revenue for Smallholder Rural Farmers in Malawi." Report prepared for the Poverty and Social Impact Analysis of the Malawi Farm Input Subsidy Program. World Bank, Washington, DC.

McCarthy, N., J. Brubaker, and A. de la Fuente. 2016. "Vulnerability to Poverty in Rural Malawi." Policy Research Working Paper 7769, World Bank, Washington, DC.

McCarthy, N., T. Kilic, A. de la Fuente, and J. Brubaker. 2016. "No Shelter from the Storm? Household-Level Impacts of and Responses to the 2015 Floods in Malawi." Mimeo, World Bank, Washington, DC.

Ricker-Gilbert, J. 2016. "Review of Malawi's Farm Input Subsidy Program in 2016 and Direction for Re-design." Report prepared for the Poverty and Social Impact Analysis of the Malawi Farm Input Subsidy Program. World Bank, Washington, DC.

Ricker-Gilbert, J., and T. S. Jayne. 2012. "Do Fertilizer Subsidies Boost Staple Crop Production and Reduce Poverty across the Distribution of Smallholders in Africa? Quantile Regression Results from Malawi." Paper prepared for the IAAE Triennial Conference, International Association of Agricultural Economists (IAAE), Foz do Iguaçu, Brazil. http://scholar.google.com/citations?view_op=view _citation&hl=en&user=WlE8j48AAAAJ&citation_for_view=WlE8j48 AAAAJ:_FxGoFyzp5QC.

Ricker-Gilbert, J., T. S. Jayne, and E. Chirwa. 2011. "Subsidies and Crowding Out: A Double-Hurdle Model of Fertilizer Demand in Malawi." *American Journal of Agricultural Economics* 93 (1): 26–42.

SACMEQ (Southern and Eastern Africa Consortium for Monitoring Educational Quality). 2010. "SACMEQ III Project Results: Pupil Achievement Levels in Reading and Mathematics." Working Document 1, SACMEQ, Gaborone. http://www.sacmeq .org/sites/default/files/sacmeq/reports/sacmeq-iii/working-documents/wd01 _sacmeq_iii_results_pupil_achievement.pdf.

Tschirley, D., T. Reardon, M. Dolislager, and J. Snyder. 2015. "The Rise of a Middle Class in East and Southern Africa: Implications for Food System Transformation." *Journal of*

International Development Special Issue: The Political Economy of Africa's Emergent Middle Class, 27 (5): 628–646.

World Bank. 2016a. "Malawi Poverty Assessment." World Bank, Washington, DC.

———. 2016b. "Malawi Urbanization Review: Leveraging Urbanization for National Growth and Development." World Bank, Washington, DC.

———. Various years. World Development Indicators. Washington, DC: World Bank.

CHAPTER 1

Recent Trends in Growth, Poverty, and Shared Prosperity in Rural Malawi

Introduction

This chapter looks at trends in growth, poverty, and shared prosperity in rural Malawi between 2004 and 2013. Over most of the past decade, Malawi has maintained positive growth, including in the agriculture sector, in which the majority of the population obtained their livelihood for much of the period. However, growth was volatile. The volatility was due, in large part, to unstable macroeconomic fundamentals, as evidenced in high inflation, fiscal deficits, and the cost of capital (high interest rates). In addition, growth was not shared broadly across population groups. Against this background, this chapter examines the gains and perils faced by poor rural households in Malawi across a broad range of dimensions of well-being. The analysis goes as far back as 2004 and up to the latest year for which survey data are available. Box 1.1 describes the data sources used for this report

This chapter first provides a synopsis of the recent trends in growth in Malawi and the distribution of growth across segments of the population, highlighting the lackluster growth in consumption in the rural areas. This is followed by a description of the progress in nonmonetary dimensions of wellbeing that has been achieved and the ongoing challenges rural populations face in terms of poverty, inequality, food insecurity, and a lack of access to basic opportunities and services. The chapter finally proposes a framework for understanding rural poverty in Malawi.

The chapter finds that rural lives improved only modestly in most dimensions. In 2010, the latest year for which official poverty figures exist, more than half of the rural population stayed poor. Little over one-quarter lived in extreme poverty, defined as the inability to satisfy food needs. More worrisome is that between 2004 and 2010, poverty remained unchanged in rural areas, at around 56 percent, and the share of the extremely poor rose from 24 to 28 percent.

Box 1.1 Data Sources Used in This Book

Most of the findings presented here and in other chapters are drawn from analyses using three data sources, all representative at the national, urban/rural, and regional levels. They are the Second Integrated Household Survey (IHS2) from 2004 to 2005, the Third Integrated Household Survey (IHS3) from 2010 to 2011, and the Integrated Household Panel Survey (IHPS) from 2013. The IHS2 and IHS3 samples were stratified by month and administered throughout the year (typically starting in March and ending one year after). A subsample of the IHS3 sample was selected for follow-up in the IHPS, thus becoming a panel. However, the IHS3 subsample and IHPS sample were administered only from March through November, that is, the nonlean season in Malawi. Findings from IHS2 and IHS3 are comparable because they represent conditions experienced throughout the year. Similarly, findings from the IHS3 panel subsample (but not from the full IHS3 sample) and the IHPS are comparable. To simplify, this book uses 2004 to designate the IHS2 and 2010 to designate the IHS3 cross-section (unless otherwise stated for the panel in 2010).

The rural poor faced significant challenges in consistently securing enough food. In the context of this difficult environment, there have been pockets of progress. There have been steady gains in access to primary education and decreases in child malnutrition and under-five mortality. Unfortunately, many of those indicators are still critically high—in 2015, about 39 percent of children under five were stunted. Furthermore, the recent progress in many of these nonmonetary indicators of well-being has not happened at the same pace for everyone or always reached the rural poor. Between 2004 and 2010, the richer segments of the population experienced greater gains in educational achievements than the bottom 40 percent. There were equally large gaps between the nutritional status of children living in wealthier and in poorer households. The bottom 40 percent experienced little improvement in key nonmonetary dimensions such as access to electricity and running water.

Trends in Growth

Malawi's average annual per capita growth rate for most of the decade from 2004 to 2013 was a respectable 2.4 percent. This rate was comparable to average annual growth in gross domestic product (GDP) per capita of 2.3 percent in Sub-Saharan Africa during the same period (World Bank various years). However, although Malawi's per capita growth was comparable to the regional average, it was significantly more volatile. The coefficient of variation—a measure of deviation from the average—was substantially larger than the regional average.

Malawi's growth has not always been shared equally across population groups. Figure 1.1 shows the growth incidence curves (GICs)[1] for Malawi as a whole and for urban and rural areas between 2004 and 2010—the latest available period for

Figure 1.1 Growth of Consumption per Capita in Malawi, 2004–10

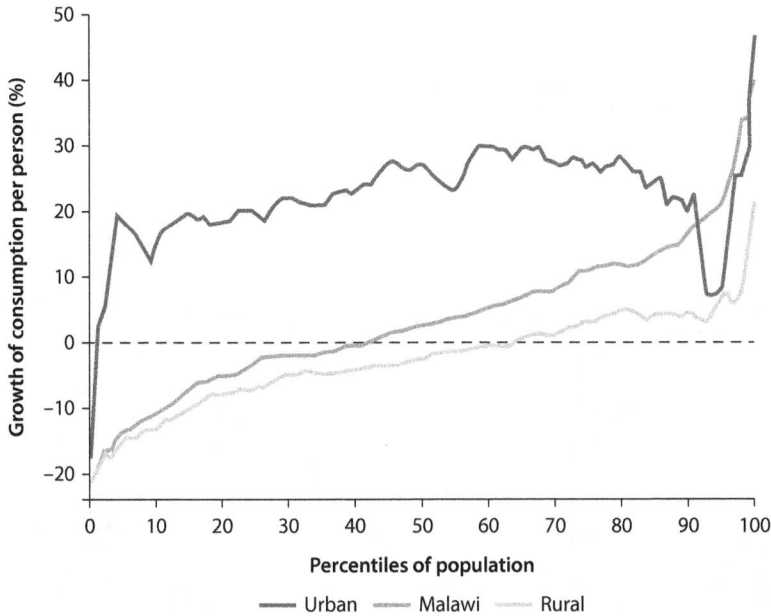

Sources: Calculations are based on IHS2 and IHS3 data.
Note: IHS2 = Second Integrated Household Survey; IHS3 = Third Integrated Household Survey.

which GICs can be drawn. Growth was positive and stronger for people with higher income and relatively weak for people with lower income. Consumption in urban areas grew for virtually all consumption percentiles, with the poorest enjoying relatively lower, but still positive, growth. In contrast, approximately two-thirds of the rural population experienced negative growth in real consumption, and only the top 5–10 percent experienced significant growth. Thus, Malawi's growth did not increase the incomes of the rural poor.

Between 2004 and 2010, prosperity, defined as higher growth of consumption for the bottom 40 percent of the population compared with average growth for the rest of the population, was not shared in rural Malawi. For Malawi as a whole, consumption of the bottom 40 percent fell 5 percent, while consumption of the top 60 percent grew 17 percent. In rural areas, consumption fell for the bottom 40 percent (8 percent), barely grew for the top 60 percent (1 percent), but rose significantly for the top decile (10 percent).

In addition, economic growth was not always driven by agriculture, in which most of the rural population was employed. As panel a in Figure 1.2 shows, between 2004 and 2010, real agricultural GDP grew more slowly than services (wholesale and retail trade, real estate, information and communications, transport and storage, and professional and other services) and industry (mining and quarrying, construction, and manufacturing). Therefore, during the second half of the

Figure 1.2 GDP in Malawi, 2004–10 and 2010–13

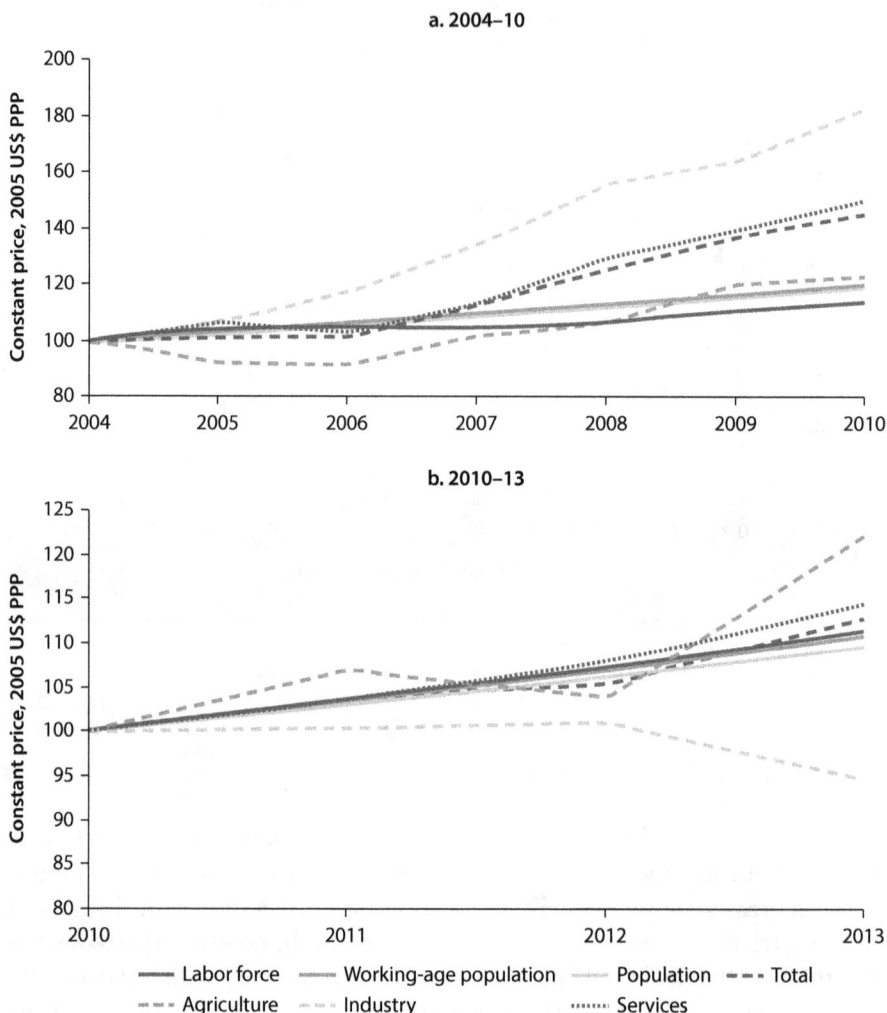

a. 2004–10

b. 2010–13

Source: Jobs Group's macro inputs from World Development Indicators data (World Bank, various years).

2000s urban poverty may have declined due to the superior growth of sectors such as services that usually cluster in urban areas. In contrast, between 2010 and 2013, urban-oriented sectors such as industry lagged and then dipped, whereas agriculture outperformed the economy in two of the three years (figure 1.2, panel b.). Most of this gain may have gone to rural areas.

Macroeconomic instability, characterized by high inflation and volatile exchange rates, has made sustained growth elusive. Between 2000 and 2014, the inflation rate in Malawi (15.4 percent) was 2.5 times higher than the regional average (6.1 percent). Given that household incomes rarely rise as rapidly as inflation, a persistently high inflation rate erodes purchasing power, especially for the poor, and discourages saving. Food price shocks also negatively affect households' perceptions about the reliability of their access to food and, ultimately, food security. Between May 2009 and November 2011, the unit price of maize hovered between MK 40 and MK 50 per kilogram (Malawi's currency is the kwacha). In 2012, the price of maize began to rise slowly and, from November 2012 to March 2013, more than doubled, jumping from about MK 64 to MK 136 per kilogram. Households, especially net buyers, felt worse off as a result of these large surges in food prices. According to the IHPS data, 84 percent of poor rural households interviewed in 2013 reported experiencing food insecurity for at least one month a year—a 17 percent increase from 2010. Furthermore, households who had faced an increase in the inflation rate of maize prices over the 12 months preceding their interview had a greater probability of being food insecure and reported experiencing a higher number of months of food insecurity (see appendix C).

Variations in the exchange rate also had an impact on welfare through the effects on household incomes and the relative prices of tradable and nontradable goods. Between 2000 and 2014, Malawi had to navigate multiple exchange rate regimes. By the end of December 2012, the country suffered a sharp depreciation of the exchange rate, sporadic fuel shortages, and a rise in inflation to almost 35 percent. While these volatilities may have been induced exogenously by factors such as changes in global interest rates and terms of trade shocks or endogenously by deficiencies in domestic policies, these fluctuations all affected price levels and household incomes, with particularly adverse effects on the poor. Being a small, open, and low-income economy with a narrow export base, Malawi is particularly vulnerable to such fluctuations. The coefficient of variation, which captures the volatility in GDP per capita between 2000 and 2014, was three times higher for Malawi (2.6) than for Sub-Saharan Africa (0.85). An overvalued and fixed exchange rate regime prior to May 2012 drove import demand up and discouraged exports. As imports outpaced exports, the incomes of the poor fell as the demand for labor declined. Between 2004 and 2010, poverty fell in urban areas from 25 to 17 percent, but remained unchanged in rural areas, at 56 percent. In contrast, with the floating exchange rate regime that started in 2013, benefits may have accrued mostly to the rural poor, as Malawi's agricultural exports became cheaper, increasing the demand and the incomes of the poor.

In short, Malawi's growth was neither inclusive between 2004 and 2010 nor sustained since 2000. Part of the reason was macroeconomic instability.

Progress in Some Nonmonetary Dimensions of Well-Being

In rural Malawi, the proportion of the rural population suffering from overlapping deprivations in education (not completing primary education or school-aged children not attending school), health (under-five mortality and undernutrition), and living standards (lack of access to electricity, improved sanitation, safe drinking water, as well as lack of ownership of different assets) declined between 2004 and 2013. The indicator used to track multiple deprivations (that is, multidimensional poverty) usually combines the head count of persons deprived in more than one dimension with the average number of deprivations among the deprived (referred as the intensity of deprivation). For rural Malawi, the decline in multidimensional poverty was due mainly to the reduction in the head count of persons deprived in more than one dimension, which fell 8 percentage points between 2004 and 2010—from 75 to 67 percent (figure 1.3). The average intensity of deprivations also declined, but only by a small margin—around 3 percentage points. Judging from panel data, additional improvement may have occurred between 2010 and 2013, with the proportion of people deprived in multiple dimensions falling from 67 to 61 percent between 2010 and 2013.[2]

Gains in education and health outcomes drove the reductions in multidimensional poverty.[3] Rural Malawi experienced noticeable progress in educational access and attainment. The proportion of rural households with school-age children attending school rose 4 percentage points between 2004 and 2010 to reach 57 percent and rose another 4 percentage points between 2010 and 2013. The proportion of households with a member who had completed primary school increased 7 percentage points to 44 percent between 2004 and 2010. Additional progress was made between 2010 and 2013, with that proportion increasing to 48 percent. Malawi reached gender parity with respect to primary school enrollment and narrowed the gender gap disparity at the secondary level to 0.91 in 2014.

Figure 1.3 Proportion of the Population Who Are Multidimensionally Poor in Malawi, 2004–13

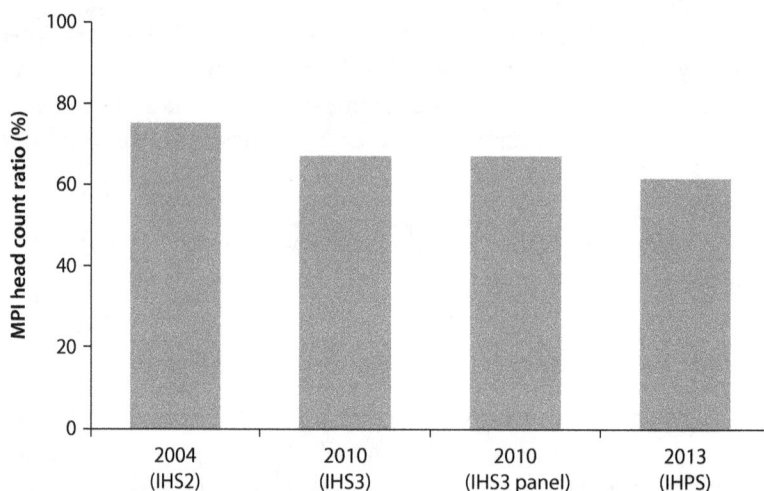

Source: Calculations are based on IHS2, IHS3, IHS3 panel, and IHPS data (World Bank 2016).
Note: MPI head count ratio measures the percentage of people who are poor in three dimensions: health, education, and standard of living. IHS2 = Second Integrated Household Survey; IHS3 = Third Integrated Household Survey; IHPS = Integrated Household Panel Survey.

Progress in health was made by reducing under-five mortality. According to Demographic and Health Survey (DHS) data, between 2004 and 2010, deaths of children under five declined nationally from 133 to 112 deaths per 1,000 live births and declined further between 2010 and 2015 to reach 64 deaths per 1,000 live births (NSO and ICF International 2016). Between 2004 and 2010, the greatest reduction in under-five mortality was in rural areas, in which the number of deaths per 1,000 live births fell from 164 to 130. Although under-five mortality declined nationally for both boys and girls, mortality rates were higher for boys than for girls.

The incidence of child malnutrition has also trended downward. Between 2004 and 2015, the prevalence of stunting among rural children fell 15 percentage points from 54 percent in 2004 to 39 percent in 2015, and the prevalence of underweight fell from 18 to 12 percent (figure 1.4). Marked differences between the Malawi Demographic Health Surveys and the Malawi Integrated Household Surveys are evident in the prevalence of stunting, underweight, and wasting. Despite this fact, the two data sources indicate improvements in the prevalence of stunting and underweight between 2004 and 2010. Gains happened for the rural poor and nonpoor alike, but as discussed later in the chapter, the prevalence of stunting and underweight remains higher among the rural poor.

As a result of the progress accomplished in some health, nutrition, and education aspects, Malawi has partially or fully achieved four of eight of the Millennium Development Goals (MDGs), the set of 2015 targets to address poverty in its many dimensions. These are MDG1c (reducing undernutrition), MDG2a (achieving universal primary education), MDG4 (reducing child mortality), and MDG6 (combating human immunodeficiency virus/acquired immune deficiency syndrome [HIV/AIDS], malaria, and other diseases).

Figure 1.4 Prevalence of Stunting and Underweight in Children under Five Years of Age in Malawi, 2004, 2010, and 2015

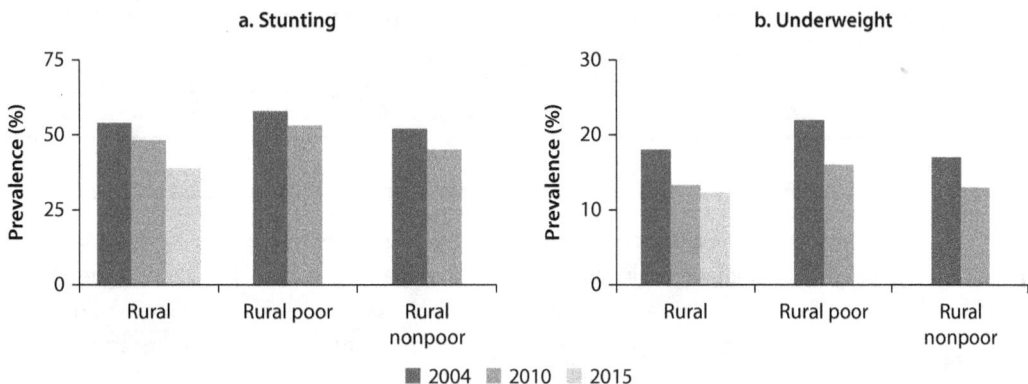

Source: Based on Demographic and Health Survey data.

Ongoing Challenges

Monetary Poverty

Notwithstanding the improvements in nonincome dimensions of poverty, monetary poverty in rural Malawi remains pervasive. In 2010, on the basis of a basket of basic needs that costs MK 37,000 per person per year, more than half of the rural population stayed poor. Little over one-quarter lived in extreme poverty, defined as the inability to satisfy food needs. More worrisome is that the poverty head count in rural areas between 2004 and 2010 remained unchanged, at around 56 percent, and the share of the extremely poor rose from 24 to 28 percent (figure 1.5). During that period, on the basis of projections from the Integrated Household Survey, the rural population increased from 10.8 million to 11.9 million. The combination of an unchanging rural poverty rate and growing rural population resulted in a 700,000 increase in the number of people living in poverty in Malawi. Using the international poverty line of US$1.90 per person per day, Malawi's poverty rate in 2010 remained high—71 percent—and close to stagnant relative to 2004 (box 1.2). The majority of the internationally poor live in rural areas.

Between 2004 and 2010, the depth of poverty, which measures the average consumption shortfall of the poor from the poverty line, and its severity—measured by the poverty gap squared—also went up. The depth of poverty increased from 19.2 to 21.4 percent, and the severity of poverty increased from 8.6 to 10.6 percent.[4] Inequality also increased as the share of total consumption for the bottom 40 percent fell from 19.7 to 17.8 percent. Even though the share of consumption of the top 10 percent remained unchanged at approximately 53.5 percent, the share of the rest of the top 60 percent rose. Income inequality may be even higher. The Gini coefficient in rural areas rose from 0.34 to 0.38, providing further evidence that the disparity between the rich and the poor widened.

While new official poverty estimates in Malawi since the IHS3 for 2010 will only become available with the Fourth Integrated Household Survey (IHS4) from 2016 to 2017, estimates from the most recent household survey—IHPS 2013—which revisited some of the households interviewed in 2010, suggest that rural poverty may have dropped 3 percentage points between 2010 and 2013. The depth and severity of poverty also fell (figure 1.5).

Box 1.2 Poverty Reduction in Malawi and Other Sub-Saharan African Countries

International comparisons of poverty rates show that other countries in Sub-Saharan Africa made significant progress in reducing poverty by the second half of the 2000s (figure B1.2.1). With the exception of Zambia, Malawi's neighboring countries, including Mozambique and Tanzania, achieved faster poverty reduction. Other countries, including Rwanda and Uganda, also sustained larger drops in poverty than Malawi.

box continues next page

Box 1.2 Poverty Reduction in Malawi and Other Sub-Saharan African Countries *(continued)*

Figure B1.2.1 Poverty Head Count Ratio at US$1.90 per Day in Malawi, Neighboring Countries, and World Regions, 2000–11

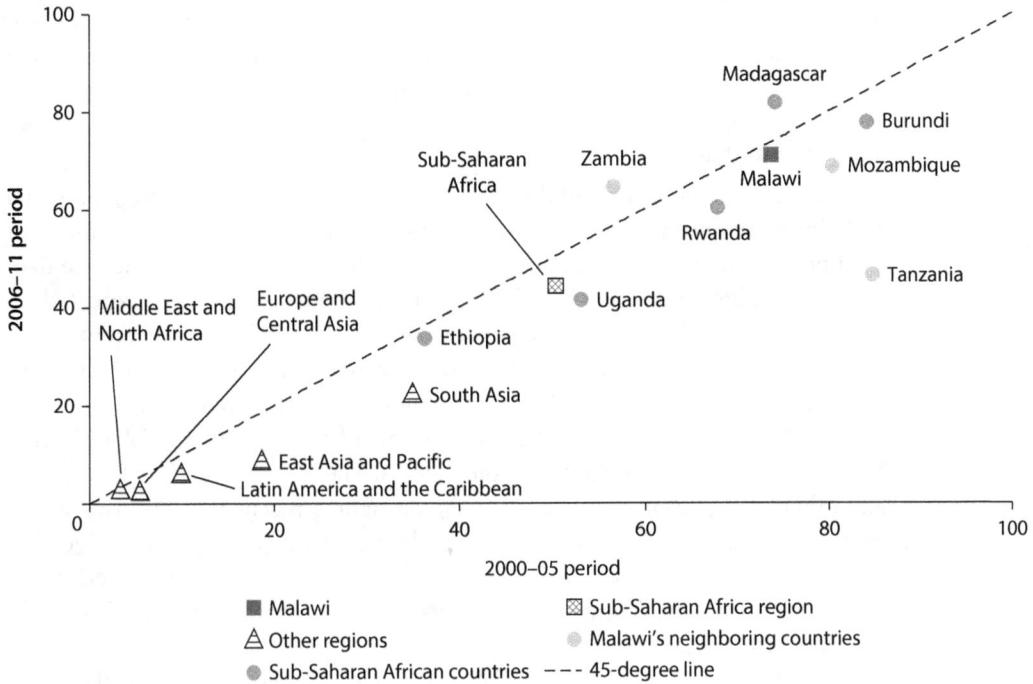

Source: Calculations are based on World Development Indicators data (World Bank, various years).
Note: The poverty rate reported for Burundi during 2000–05 is for 1998.

Figure 1.5 Rural Poverty in Malawi, 2004–13

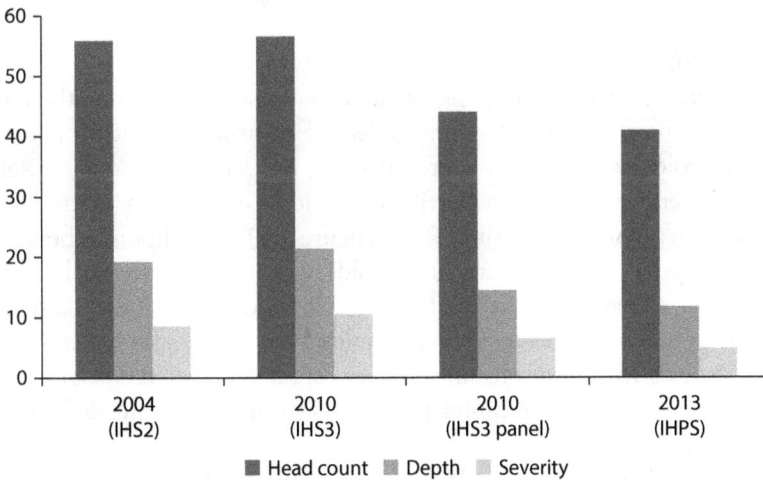

Sources: Calculations are based on IHS2, IHS3, IHS3 panel, and IHPS data.
Note: IHS2 = Second Integrated Household Survey; IHS3 = Third Integrated Household Survey; IHPS = Integrated Household Panel Survey.

However, there are three reasons to be cautious about the rate of rural poverty reduction implied by these data. First, substantial uncertainty surrounds the head count estimates, which, unlike measures of depth and severity, are measured with larger standard errors. Consequently, the rural drop in head count poverty is not statistically significant. Second, the consumption data for households contained in the IHS3 panel and the IHPS were conducted over six months during the nonlean season.[5] Therefore, these data do not account for the lean months when consumption typically drops and poverty increases. Third, any gains probably were short-lived and potentially were reversed given the large-scale floods in 2015 and drought and floods in 2016. Using the IHS3 panel and IHPS surveys, in 2010, when only household characteristics (number of members, location, and sociodemographic profile) were used to predict the likelihood of falling into poverty, 22 percent of households were expected to become poor in 2013. This proportion almost doubled to 42 percent when expected shocks, particularly rainfall shocks, were considered as well (McCarthy, Brubaker, and de la Fuente 2016). Furthermore, poverty increased eight percentage points between 2013 and 2015 in a sample of 558 rural households affected by the floods that struck Southern and Central Malawi in early 2015 (McCarthy and others 2016). And given the ongoing drought, a recent food security assessment by the government of Malawi and development partners concluded that around 6.5 million people will not be able to meet their annual food needs in 2016/17 (Malawi Vulnerability Assessment Committee 2016). This could translate into higher poverty levels.

Most of the chronically poor in Malawi live in rural areas. Using panel data from IHS3 and IHPS, it is possible to identify individuals who transitioned in or out of poverty and those who stayed in poverty in both periods over 2010–13 (that is, the chronically poor). Of the 2.6 million chronically poor nationally, 2.4 million, or 90 percent, resided in rural areas. Chronic poverty, in addition to modest poverty, is skewed toward households headed by women.

Food Insecurity

Food insecurity remains widespread in rural areas, especially among the poor. In 2013, on the basis of subjective and objective measures, about 80 percent of poor households were food insecure. In 2013, 84 percent of poor households reported experiencing food insecurity for at least one month of the year—a 17 percentage point increase since 2010 (figure 1.6). In addition to being more likely to be poor, food-insecure households were more likely to be female-headed, to have relatively worse dietary diversity, and to have lower daily caloric intake per capita than food-secure households. Poor households had a hard time meeting their daily caloric consumption per capita: 81 percent consumed fewer than 2,100 kilocalories per capita per day—the minimium needed to lead a healthy life.

The rural population has a daily caloric consumption per capita close to the threshold of 2,100 kilocalories per person per day. Between 2004 and 2010, the rural population's consumption fell from an average of 2,336 to

Figure 1.6 Food Insecurity among the Rural Poor in Malawi, 2010–13

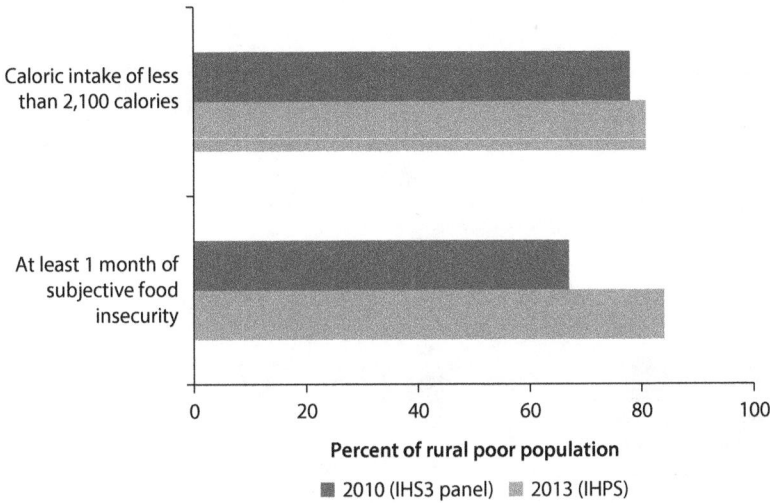

Percent of rural poor population

■ 2010 (IHS3 panel)   ▓ 2013 (IHPS)

Sources: Calculations are based on IHS3 panel and IHPS data.
Note: IHS3 = Third Integrated Household Survey; IHPS = Integrated Household Panel Survey.

2,211 kilocalories per person per day, before rising to 2,289 in 2013.[6] However, rural averages mask the dire situation of the rural poor. From 2004 to 2013, the consumption of poor people was consistently below the 2,100 kilocalories per person threshold. The rural poor were consuming a mere 1,579 kilocalories per person per day in 2010 and 1,534 kilocalories per person per day in 2013, down from 1,733 in 2004.[7]

The primary reasons for food insecurity are inadequate household food stocks and expensive food. In 2013, 81 percent of households in rural areas reported inadequate household food stocks as the primary reason for their food insecurity in the past year (figure 1.7). Such inadequate stocks are driven by inadequate farm inputs, plots of land that are too small to produce enough food, and shocks (such as droughts) leading to crop losses. One in 10 households reported that food in the market was very expensive.[8] The remaining 7 percent of households reported other reasons, including inability to reach markets or to access food in the market. Such a pattern is consistent across regions, poverty status of households, and gender of household heads. To cope with food insecurity, rural households resorted to dietary changes, rationing of food, or both, but such strategies can lead to deteriorating nutrition of household members.[9]

Seasonal patterns of food production and shocks contribute to instability in food availability. Since the agriculture system in Malawi is predominantly rain-fed, crops are grown within a few months of the time that most of the rainfall occurs. This rain-based pattern produces seasonality in food production and, consequently, fluctuations in food availability. The months following planting and prior to harvesting are commonly referred to as the "lean months" because food stocks from the previous year's harvest are low. Once harvesting begins, Malawi

Figure 1.7 Reasons Given for Food Insecurity in Rural Areas in Malawi, 2013

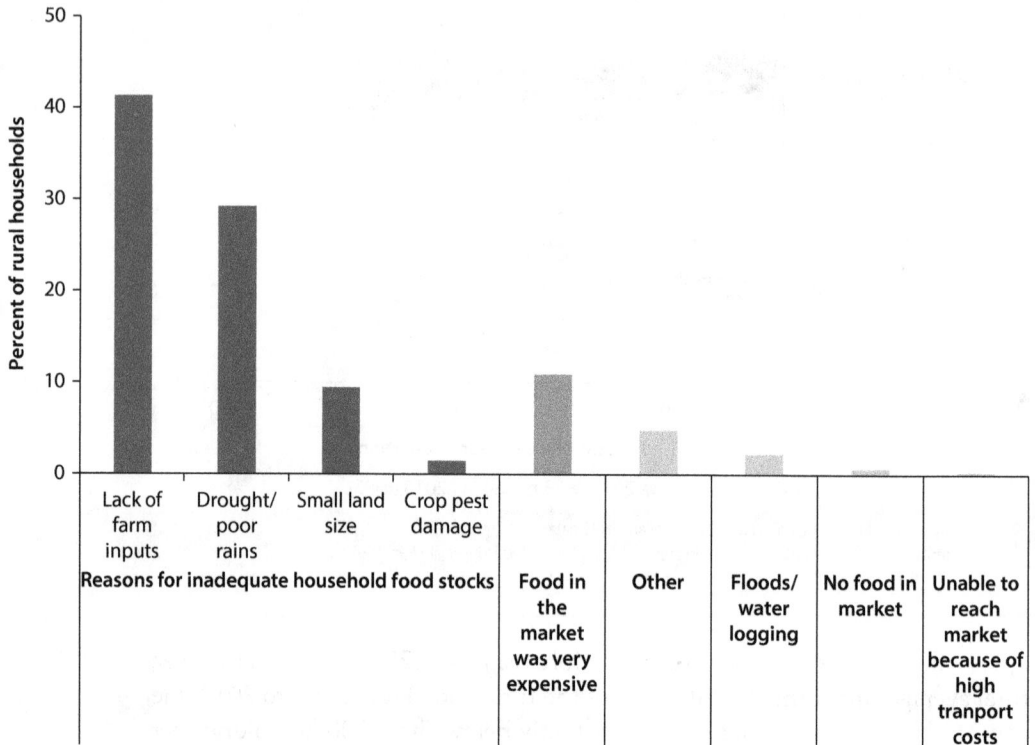

Source: Calculations are based on IHPS data.
Note: IHPS = Integrated Household Panel Survey.

transitions out of the lean season. Food consumption in rural areas follows a seasonal pattern in which caloric intake per capita peaks between April and September and troughs between November and February. When they occur, shocks from droughts and floods exacerbate food availability.

Higher food prices impede access to food for persons who rely on markets and do not have the resources to cope with food price spikes. In Malawi, an increase in the inflation rate of maize prices correlates with food insecurity (see appendix C). A one-unit increase in the inflation rate of maize prices increases the probability of experiencing food insecurity over the last 12 months, or of worrying about food in the last 7 days, by 8 and 5.3 percent, respectively. Individuals who face a one-unit increase in the rate of inflation of maize prices experience an additional 0.37 months of food insecurity, on average (Jolliffe, Seff, and de la Fuente 2016). Compared with prices in other Sub-Saharan African countries, food prices in Malawi are also highly variable, with maize prices being the most variable (see appendix D). The effects of changes in food prices on a population depend on whether they are net buyers or net sellers of food. At least 50 percent of the households in Malawi are net buyers of food. Of these, approximately 54 percent of the poorest households are net buyers and approximately 39 percent are marginal net buyers of food (Palacios-Lopez, Christiaensen, and Pardo 2016). Seasonality in food prices induces seasonality in food consumption for rural net buyers, as shown by the fluctuations in food prices, which inversely track household consumption (Kaminski, Christiaensen, and Gilbert 2014).

Recurrent fluctuations in food availability and access to food give rise to chronic food insecurity. Although predictable, seasonal fluctuations in food production and food prices can contribute to recurring episodes of inadequate food availability and access. The risk of chronic food insecurity, in turn, perpetuates chronic poverty, which is experienced by 25 percent of the rural population.

Limited Access to Basic Opportunities and Services

Despite the improvements across many nonmonetary indicators in the recent past, many of those indicators are still critically high or associated with low quality. Rural areas continue to harbor high rates of under-five mortality and child malnutrition. Malnutrition remains a challenge—in 2015, about 39 percent of rural children under five were stunted, reflecting significant nutritional imbalances in their diets, which lack proteins, vitamins, and other nutrients. This persistence is likely higher among poor children and reflects the continued lack of access to and deprivation in access to health services and living conditions. Stunting is a major cause of adverse cognitive development, which is associated with delayed school enrollment, lower grade attainment, and reduced school performance, and in later life worse labor market outcomes through lower earnings and productivity (Alderman and others 2001; Alderman, Hoddinott, and Kinsey 2006; Glewwe, Jacoby, and King 2001; Mendez and Adair 1999). Stunting can impose additional costs on the education system because additional resources are required to produce one year of learning outcome. Given the personal and social cost of stunting, the existing prevalence rates are unacceptably high, for all income groups.

Although primary school completion rates rose substantially (17 percentage points) between 2004 and 2013 to reach 75 percent (World Bank various years), the primary education sector continues to offer low-quality education and to produce weak performance outcomes. Malawi ranks poorly in student performance in English and mathematics, as indicated by the Southern and Eastern Africa Consortium for Monitoring Education Quality (SACMEQ 2010). At any given time between 2004 and 2013, approximately 20 percent of students in the primary education system were repeaters. Furthermore, the student-to-teacher ratio was very high at 69.

Deprivations in education and health also are costly for the economy. Countries can lose an estimated 4–11 percent of their economic output each year due to malnutrition (Horton and Steckel 2013). In 2012, Malawi's losses due to child malnutrition were equivalent to 10.3 percent of GDP (Government of Malawi 2015). Therefore, reducing child malnutrition and improving the quality of education should be core components of Malawi's long-term commitment to building its human capital.[10]

In addition, progress in access to essential opportunities and services in rural Malawi is unequal and, in some instances, has not reached the poor. While all segments of the population made progress in completion of primary education between 2004 and 2010, the richer segments of the population started from a higher base and experienced greater gains. Among the wealthiest 10 percent of the income distribution, the proportion of households in which at least one member completed primary school is almost than double the proportion of households in the bottom 40 percent (figure 1.8). There were equally large gaps between the nutritional status of children living in wealthier and in poorer households. In 2010, 55 percent of children in the bottom welfare quintile were stunted, compared with 38 percent in the top quintile. Underweight prevalence in the poorest quintile was nearly double that of the top quintile (17 percent versus 9 percent).

Access to electricity and running water is also fairly unequal and virtually nonexistent among the bottom 40 percent. Although telephone ownership increased markedly, rural households still lack access to some critical assets to cook like gas or electric stoves and means of transport beyond bycicles. Nearly everyone in the bottom 40 percent in rural areas relies on organic carbon fuels, which include wood, charcoal, and coal (figure 1.8). These fuels pose substantial health risks due to the air pollution caused by smoke released from their incomplete combustion. Hence, average accomplishments in some health and education outcomes and access to services did not always reach the poor and when they did, those accomplishments happened at a lower pace and from a lower baseline.

Urban areas also exhibit higher rates of school completion and access to safe water and electricity and lower rates of undernutrition, with the exception of stunting. For example, in urban areas, approximately 30 percent of heads of households have completed secondary education, versus 5 percent in rural areas. Wide variations between urban and rural areas still were encountered in the percentage of children with basic skills in reading and numeracy on the basis of scores for standard tests administered to sixth-grade children in 2007.

Rural communities also are located farther from tar or asphalt roads. Acceptable rural access often is defined in relation to an international benchmark: average distance from the nearest paved or all-weather road that does not exceed 2 kilometers. According to a recent incidence analysis investigating the relationship between welfare and distance to roads, even the richest rural communities in Malawi are at a median distance of 5 kilometers from an all-weather road. Urban areas fare much better: the median distance to a paved or all-weather road is 2 kilometers for even the poorest urban communities (World Bank 2016).

The poor also have more limited access to health facilities. More than 50 percent of all communities in Malawi are located more than 3 kilometers

Figure 1.8 Access to Basic Goods and Services in Rural Malawi, by Consumption Deciles, 2004–10

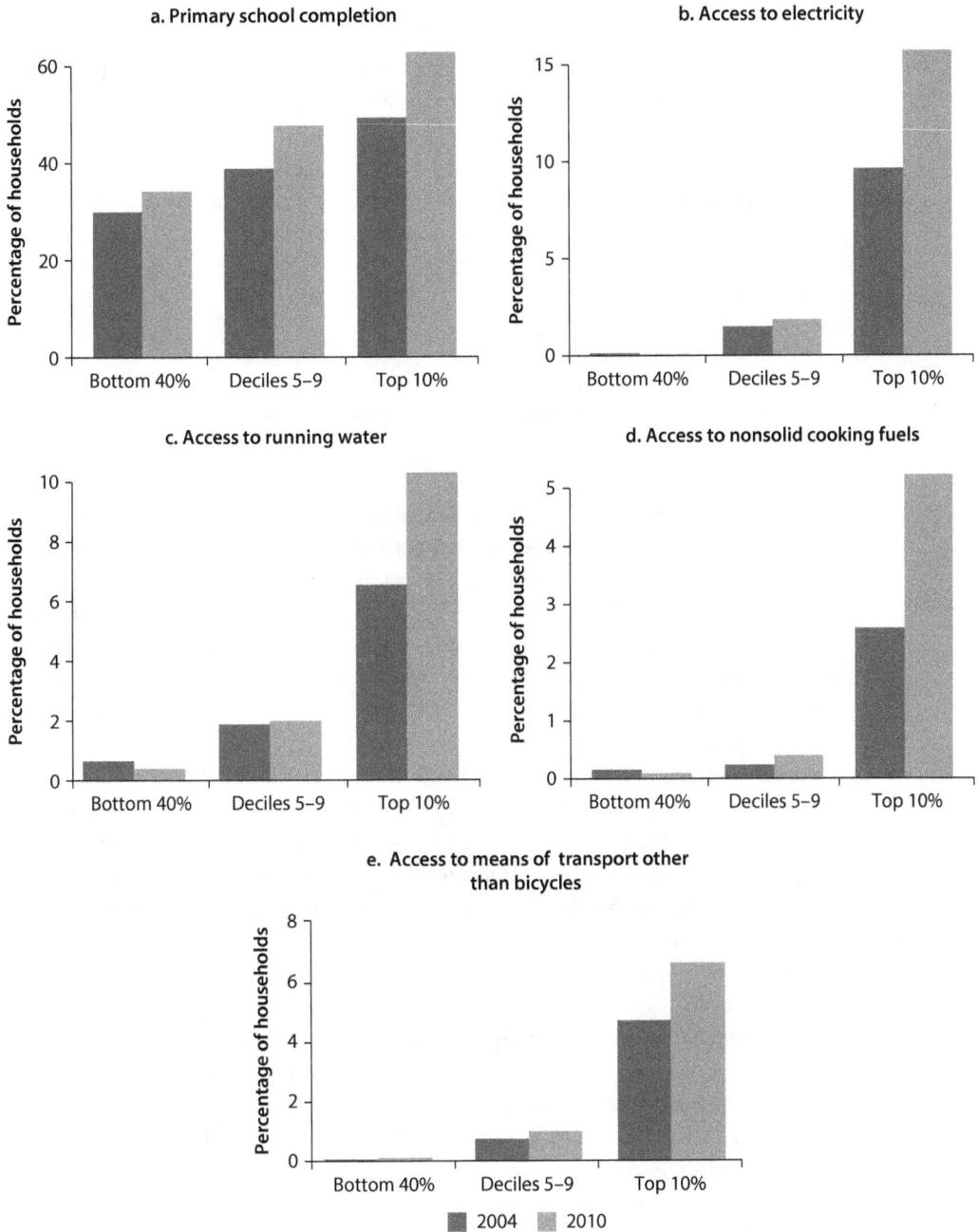

a. Primary school completion

b. Access to electricity

c. Access to running water

d. Access to nonsolid cooking fuels

e. Access to means of transport other than bicycles

■ 2004 ▨ 2010

Source: World Bank 2016, based on IHS2 and IHS3 data.
Note: IHS2 = Second Integrated Household Survey; IHS3 = Third Integrated Household Survey.

from the closest health clinic. A clear inverse relationship is observed between the level of community wealth and distance to the closest health facility—that is, wealthier communities are better served. In addition, persons in better-off households use more private outpatient care than persons in poorer households, who rely more on public outpatient care (World Bank 2016).

The socioeconomic background of rural families may also condition their family planning and fertility decisions, with implications for opportunities later in life. Malawi's fertility rate has remained persistently high, particularly among rural poor women (6.1 births per woman). Box 1.3 tackles this issue in more detail.

Box 1.3 Population Dynamics and Rural Poverty in Malawi

Malawi's population grew from 12.4 million in 2004 to 16.7 million in 2014. During this period, Malawi maintained a growth rate close to 3 percent per year, adding a little under half a million people each year on average. This increase in population is owed largely to a substantial decline in mortality (due to improved nutrition and access to health care) and persistently high rates of fertility, despite increased use of modern contraceptives (from 28 percent in 2004 to 58 percent in 2015 among married women). The country's population is expected to double, from 17.2 million in 2015 to 34.4 million in 2038 (UNDESA 2015).

Fertility remains persistently high, particularly among poor rural women. In 2010, 60 percent of women (the poorest three quintiles) still had rates above 6 births per women, whereas the top 20 percent had half that number. Poor women were 30 percent less likely to use family planning than the wealthiest women. Women in the four bottom wealth quintiles had higher desired fertility (4 children or above) than women in the wealthiest group, but were less likely to meet their ideal fertility (figure B1.3.1). Differences in fertility also indicate inequities in access to family planning, ideal family sizes, and rates of early marriage and childbearing.

Early childbearing and child marriage—important contributors to high fertility—are extremely high. Malawi's adolescent fertility rate continues to be among the highest in the world, with 50 percent of girls marrying before age 18 years and 33 percent bearing children as adolescents (UNDESA 2015). Child marriage and early childbearing negatively affect the health, educational prospects, and employment opportunities of adolescent girls and the health of their children. Married girls also may experience less agency within their household and more intrafamiliar violence. Finally, child marriage lengthens the time a women is exposed to childbearing. Poor adolescents are also more likely to marry young and become mothers. According to the latest DHS data (NSO and ICF International 2016), among young women ages 20–24 years in the bottom two quintiles, 60 percent marry as

box continues next page

Box 1.3 Population Dynamics and Rural Poverty in Malawi *(continued)*

Figure B1.3.1 Observed and Desired Total Fertility Rate in Malawi, by Wealth Quintile, 2010

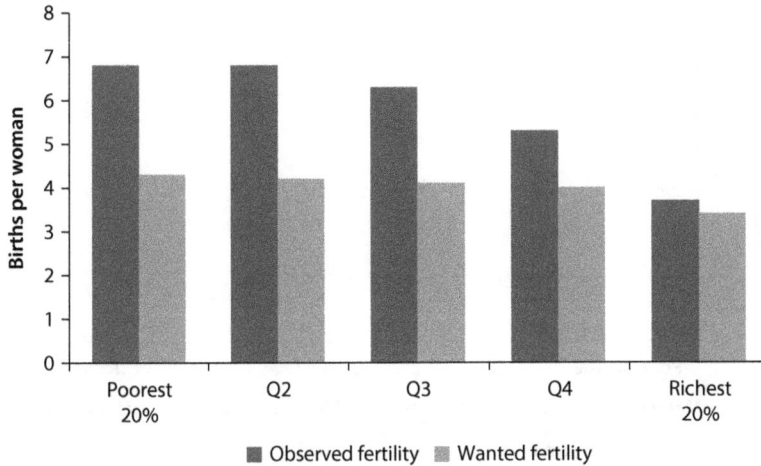

Source: Malawi Poverty Assessment, World Bank 2016.
Note: Q = quintile.

adolescents—approximately 2.3 times more than young girls in the wealthier group (26 percent). Similarly, 40 percent of poor young women are pregnant or already mothers before age 18 years, compared with 22 percent of girls in the richest group (figure B1.3.2). In addition to the poor-wealthy divide, disparities exist between urban and rural areas in early fertility patterns. If Malawi were to eliminate early childbirth, the total fertility rate would decrease by 0.48 births (8 percent).

High birth rates and declining mortality rates are characteristics of a country, such as Malawi, in the early stages of a demographic transition. Such trends result in rapid population growth and an increase in the youth population. Today, 56.2 percent of Malawi's population is less than 19 years old, while only 38.8 percent is working age. In the coming 35 years, these population dynamics will bring important challenges and opportunities.

Poverty. Malawi's young age structure generates a high ratio of dependents to working-age population, which is associated with higher levels of poverty. A new child in the family reduces household income per capita and increases the likelihood that the household will fall into poverty. Malawi's ability to curb poverty will depend on its capacity to accelerate fertility decline, as a one-child reduction in fertility rates could lead to 31 percent higher levels of real GDP per capita by 2050.

Productivity. A high birth rate also lowers productivity because it impairs women's ability to engage in more productive farming or nonfarm work while they spend many of their prime years pregnant, lactating, and otherwise raising children.

box continues next page

Box 1.3 Population Dynamics and Rural Poverty in Malawi *(continued)*

Figure B1.3.2 Trends in Early Marriage and Pregnancies in Women Ages 20–24 Years in Malawi, by Wealth Quintile, 2010

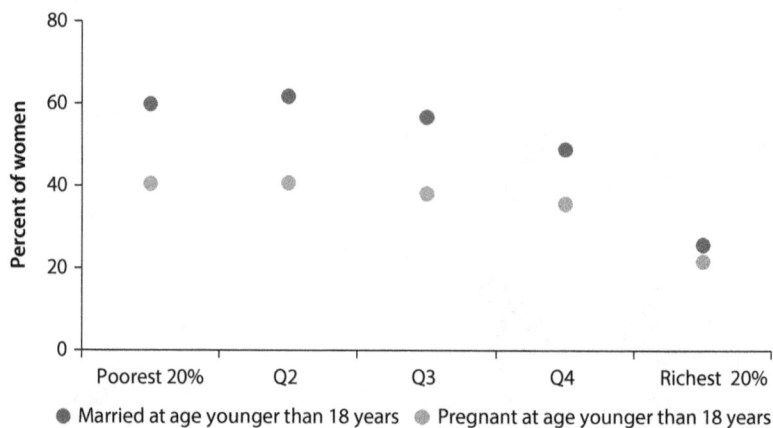

Source: Malawi Poverty Assessment, World Bank 2016.

Land. Malawi's population is exerting pressure on its natural resources, and the situation is likely to worsen. Malawi is one of Sub-Saharan Africa's most densely populated countries, ranking tenth in Sub-Saharan Africa in 2014. Land is the primary source of livelihood for Malawi's largely rural and agricultural population, but rapid population growth and scarcity of cultivable land have contributed to land degradation. Such degradation, as well as the stress brought about by climate change, threatens to worsen food security and nutrition, reduce employment and incomes, and worsen nonmonetary dimensions of well-being for Malawians.

Public services. Malawi will need to meet the growing demand for public services such as education and health, which will require greater revenue generation and investments for public service provision. Provision of basic services to the rural poor will be important.

Despite these challenges, Malawi could benefit from a demographic dividend if it could accelerate fertility declines and create employment for young workers.

Source: World Bank 2016.

Populations residing in female-headed households have benefited from improvements in some nonmonetary indicators of well-being, but their level of access continues to lag behind that of persons residing in male-headed households. Persons residing in female-headed households experienced improvements in educational achievement, access to public services, and ownership of assets. However, their gains happened at a lower pace and/or from a lower baseline than those of persons residing in male-headed households (figure 1.9).

Figure 1.9 Key Nonmonetary Dimensions of Well-Being in Female- and Male-Headed Rural Households in Malawi, 2004–10

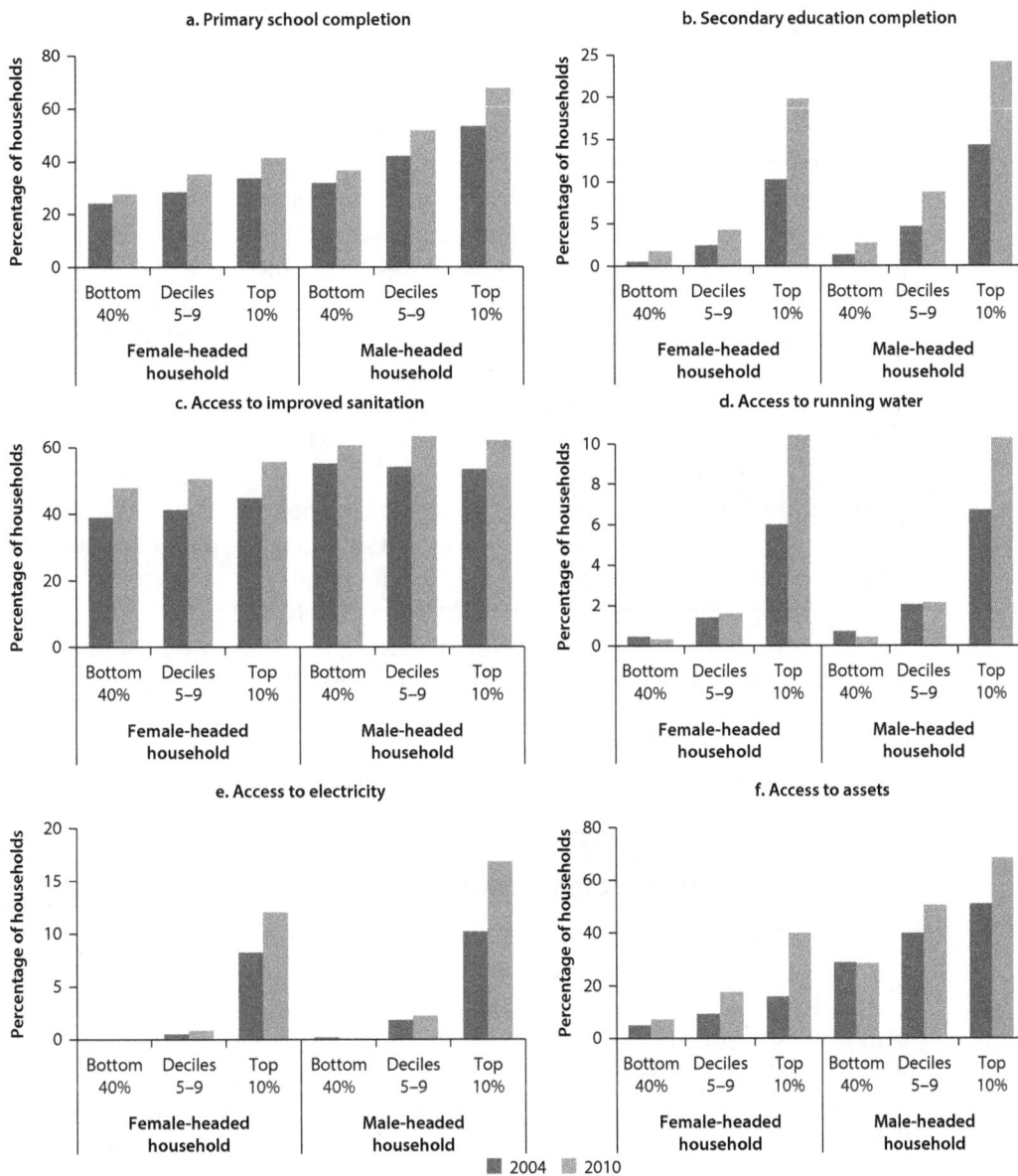

Sources: Estimates are based on cross-sectional IHS2 and IHS3 survey data.
Note: Access to assets comprises the following assets: television, radio, telephone, refrigerator, bicycle, motorbike, or car. IHS2 = Second Integrated Household Survey; IHS3 = Third Integrated Household Survey.

Summary

In the past decade rural Malawi lacked dynamism by most accounts. Malawi achieved economic growth, but that growth was not always shared equally across the population and sectors. Moreover, it was mostly volatile, in large part due to unstable macroeconomic fundamentals evidenced by high inflation, fiscal deficits, and high interest rates. In this difficult environment, there were pockets of progress. Rural lives improved in some nonmonetary dimensions driven primarily by improvements in education and health. In education, access and attainment (completion) improved; in health, child deaths and undernutrition declined. Nevertheless, poverty remained high and its pace of reduction slow compared with better performers in Sub-Saharan Africa such as Ethiopia, Ghana, Rwanda, and Uganda. The rural poor faced significant challenges in securing enough food on a consistent basis. Seasonal variations in production and food prices, as well as sudden drops in food production or price spikes, posed major challenges to food security. And the progress experienced by rural areas in access to essential opportunities and services was unequal and, in some instances, did not reach the poor. The bottom 40 percent of the population continued to be deprived of access to some basic services and experienced little improvement over time, notably in access to electricity and running water. Gaps in access to key assets, services (water, sanitation, and electricity), and opportunities (health, nutrition, and education) not only prevailed across income groups and urban-rural areas, but also between female- and male-headed households.

The next section proposes a framework for understanding why poverty reduction in rural Malawi has been, by and large, elusive to date.

Framework for Understanding Rural Poverty in Malawi

This section outlines a simple framework on the basis of an asset approach (López-Calva and Rodríguez-Castelán 2016) to identify the main elements that contribute to the income generation of households, which can then be related to poverty reduction.

According to this framework, households rely on multiple sources of income from economic activities and transfers to improve their well-being.[11] In rural Malawi, in particular, households are engaged predominantly in crop production and employment in the farm labor market (*ganyu*, defined as short-term and often informal work on household farms, large-scale farms, and plantations). However, it is often difficult to sustain overall income growth when relying on a single source such as rain-fed agriculture, which is highly prone to risks, particularly to price and weather shocks.

For any income-earning strategies to reduce poverty sustainably, it is important for small farmers to diversify their income into nonfarm activities, such as self-employment in household-owned micro or small enterprises, in addition to cropping their own fields or engaging in livestock production.

Finally, many households rely on remittances, pensions, and other public transfers or benefits (nutritional interventions and cash transfers) to meet their most basic needs and improve the income opportunities of future generations through investments in health and education. Targeted public and private transfers also can help to protect households from shocks, avoid costly responses in hard times, and sustain their income over their life cycle.

The capacity of households to generate income depends on (a) the *type of assets owned*, including mainly human capital (education), physical capital (land), and financial capital (access to credit); (b) the *intensity of their use* (participation in labor markets and use of agricultural inputs); and, finally, (c) the *returns to these assets* (price of factors of production such as yields, profits, and wages).

The potential to transform assets into goods and services that entitle households to different dimensions of welfare, including consumption, also is determined by the context in which households operate. Such context includes, for instance, the state's provision of socioeconomic infrastructure, access to markets, and public services and a sound economic environment for employment opportunities. Shocks also can affect the level and value of assets (figure 1.10).

In short, the proposed framework can help researchers and policy makers to understand the components that make up household income as well as to analyze the income generation capacity of different socioeconomic and demographic groups (poor and nonpoor). Households operate conditioned on the availability and use of assets, returns to assets, market prices for inputs, and a context characterized by shocks. Although initial conditions and context matter, success in poverty reduction according to this framework requires a few common elements or pathways for growth to include the poor.

These elements are household and government strategies that aim (a) to raise the labor incomes of the poor through more and better jobs and higher productivity in sectors in which poor people are predominantly engaged as well as to facilitate movement into new, more remunerative activities; (b) to improve the opportunities of the poor through investments in their human capital; and (c) to provide direct transfers to the poor, including safety nets to reduce their vulnerability to shocks through social protection mechanisms.

The following three chapters explore the role that income sources—both agricultural and nonagricultural—and public transfers play in rural

Figure 1.10 Assets Approach to Market Income

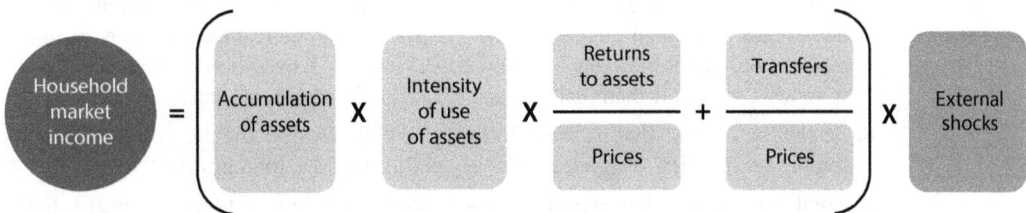

Source: López-Calva and Rodríguez-Castelán 2016.

Malawi. The assessment looks at agriculture (chapter 2), the nonfarm sector (chapter 3), and transfers in the form of social safety nets (chapter 4). Chapter 5 looks at the policy reforms needed in each of these areas to increase incomes in rural areas and make progress on reducing poverty and boosting shared prosperity.

Notes

1. Growth incidence curves plot growth in consumption per capita for each percentile ranked from poorest to highest. Thus, GICs provide a picture of how much growth has favored different population groups.

2. The 2010 and 2013 panel estimates are not fully comparable with the cross-sectional estimates from 2004 and 2010 because the 2010 and 2013 indexes excluded one health indicator that was not available in 2013. The indicator was households who experienced deaths of children under five.

3. Large shares of government expenditures and official development assistance were allocated to health and education (appendix A).

4. Depth of poverty (poverty gap) indicates how far, on average, the population is from the poverty line. In other words, depth of poverty captures the mean consumption shortfall of the population relative to the poverty line. Severity of poverty (poverty gap squared) takes into account the distance separating the poor from the poverty line and inequality among the poor. Conceptually, poverty severity gives greater weight to persons who are farther below the poverty line.

5. The IHS poverty numbers between 2004 and 2010 covered a full calendar year and are not directly comparable to the poverty numbers coming from the IHS3 panel nor the IHPS. The IHS3 panel and the IHPS were conducted over only half of the calendar period typically covered by an IHS and during what happened to be the nonlean months for Malawi. The official monetary poverty estimates for Malawi are derived using the cross-sectional IHS data, so the latest available figures are for 2004 and 2010 (the Fourth Integrated Household Survey [IHS4] from 2016 to 2017 is currently in the field). The poverty rates in 2010, based on the IHS3 panel, and the poverty rates in 2013 based on the IHPS are not official and should be understood as the lower bound for actual poverty in Malawi given that the lean months when poverty increases are not captured in them.

6. To ensure comparability of daily caloric consumption per capita between IHS2, IHS3, and IHPS, samples for IHS2 and IHS3 were restricted to households who were interviewed between March and November.

7. Appendix B shows that, in stark contrast with poor individuals, nonpoor individuals have higher caloric consumption. Although not shown in appendix B, nationally, there appears to be a minimal gender disparity in consumption, as members in female-headed households consumed at most about 110 kilocalories more than members in male-headed households between 2004 and 2013. However, female-headed households were somewhat worse off than male-headed households in terms of dietary diversity.

8. Appendix C shows that increases in the price of maize over the preceding 12 months leading to the IHPS correlates positively with subjective food insecurity.

9. Rural households that reported experiencing food insecurity in the 2013 IHPS resorted to a combination of strategies that are not mutually exclusive: 80 percent of

households consumed less preferred foods or less expensive foods. Others rationed consumption by reducing portion sizes at meal times (69 percent), reducing the number of meals eaten in a day (55 percent), and reducing the consumption of adults so that small children could eat (27 percent). Other households borrowed food from friends and relatives (39 percent).

10. The losses reflect the negative social and economic impacts on health (morbidity and mortality), education (school repetition and dropout rates), and productivity (loss of physical capacity and opportunity cost due to child mortality) for a single year.

11. In terms of *participation by income activities*, households in rural areas are engaged predominantly in crop production and show limited diversification to nonfarm self-employment and nonfarm wage employment. In 2013, approximately 90 percent of rural households drew income from crop production and 48 percent drew income from farm wage income. Among households, 28 percent earned income from nonfarm self-employment and 14 percent earned income from nonfarm wage activities. A third of rural households received transfers. In terms of *shares of total income*, the share of income was approximately 49 percent from cropping, 18 percent from farm wage income, and 7 percent from livestock. The share of nonfarm self-employment in total income was 14 percent, while the share of nonfarm wage income remained relatively low at 7 percent. Transfers accounted for about 4 percent of total rural household income, on average.

References

Alderman, H., J. R. Behrman, V. Lavy, and R. Menon. 2001. "Child Health and School Enrollment: A Longitudinal Analysis." *Journal of Human Resources* 36 (1): 185–205.

Alderman, H., J. Hoddinott, and B. Kinsey. 2006. "Long-Term Consequences of Early Childhood Malnutrition." *Oxford Economic Papers* 58 (3): 450–74.

Glewwe, P., H. G. Jacoby, and E. M. King. 2001. "Early Childhood Nutrition and Academic Achievement: A Longitudinal Analysis." *Journal of Public Economics* 81 (3): 345–68.

Government of Malawi. 2015. *The Cost of Hunger in Malawi: Implications on National Development and Vision 2020: The Social and Economic Impact of Child Undernutrition in Malawi.* Report commissioned by the African Union with support from the United Nations Economic Commission for Africa and the World Food Programme. http://documents.wfp.org/stellent/groups/public/documents/newsroom/wfp274603.pdf.

Horton, S., and R. Steckel. 2013. "Global Economic Losses Attributable to Malnutrition 1900–2000 and Projections to 2050." In *The Economics of Human Challenges*, edited by B. Lomborg. Cambridge, U.K.: Cambridge University Press.

Jolliffe, D., I. Seff, and A. de la Fuente. 2016. "Food Insecurity and Rising Food Prices: What Do We Learn from Experiential Measures?" Mimeo. World Bank, Washington, DC.

Kaminski, J., L. Christiaensen, and C. L. Gilbert. 2014. "The End of Seasonality? New Insights from Sub-Saharan Africa." Policy Research Working Paper 6907, World Bank, Washington, DC.

López-Calva, L. F. and C. Rodríguez-Castelán. 2016. "Pro-Growth Equity. A Policy Framework for the Twin Goals." Policy Research Working Paper 7897, World Bank, Washington, DC.

Malawi Vulnerability Assessment Committee. 2016. "Malawi Vulnerability Assessment Committee National Food and Nutrition Security Forecast, April 2016 to March 2017." Bulletin No. 12/16, Volume 1.

McCarthy, N., J. Brubaker, and A. de la Fuente. 2016. "Vulnerability to Poverty in Rural Malawi." Policy Research Working Paper 7769, World Bank, Washington, DC.

McCarthy, N., T. Kilic, A. de la Fuente, and J. Brubaker. 2016. "No Shelter from the Storm? Household-Level Impacts of and Responses to the 2015 Floods in Malawi." Mimeo. World Bank, Washington, DC.

Mendez, M. A., and L. S. Adair. 1999. "Severity and Timing of Stunting in the First Two Years of Life Affect Performance on Cognitive Tests in Late Childhood." *Journal of Nutrition* 129 (8): 1555–62.

NSO (National Statistical Office) and ICF Macro. 2005. *Malawi Demographic and Health Survey 2004*. Zomba, Malawi, and Calverton, Maryland: NSO and ICF Macro.

———. 2011. *Malawi Demographic and Health Survey 2010*. Zomba, Malawi, and Calverton, Maryland: NSO and ICF Macro. NSO (National Statistical Office) and ICF International.

———. 2016. *Malawi Demographic and Health Survey 2015-16*. Zomba, Malawi, and Calverton, Maryland: NSO and ICF Macro. NSO (National Statistical Office) and ICF International.

Palacios-Lopez, A., L. Christiaensen, and C. G. Pardo. 2016. "Are Most African Households Net Food Buyers?" World Bank, Washington, DC.

SACMEQ (Southern and Eastern Africa Consortium for Monitoring Educational Quality). 2010. "SACMEQ III Project Results: Pupil Achievement Levels in Reading and Mathematics." Working Document 1, SACMEQ, Gaborone. http://www.sacmeq .org/sites/default/files/sacmeq/reports/sacmeq-iii/working-documents/wd01 _sacmeq_iii_results_pupil_achievement.pdf.

UNDESA (United Nations Department of Economic and Social Affairs). 2015. "World Population Prospects: The 2015 Revision. Key Findings and Advance Tables." ESA/P/ WP.241. (Updated 29 July 2015 6:00 PM EDT: see Erratum). Population Division, UNDESA, New York. http://esa.un.org/unpd/wpp/DVD/.

World Bank. 2016. "Malawi Poverty Assessment." World Bank, Washington, DC.

———. Various years. World Development Indicators. Washington, DC: World Bank.

CHAPTER 2

Agriculture and Poverty

Introduction

Agriculture plays a defining role in the Malawian economy, accounting for more than 30 percent of gross domestic product (GDP), employing 85 percent of the population in 2013, and serving as the dominant source of livelihood for rural households. Because it continues to be critical for Malawi's national and household food security, the agriculture sector has drawn significant policy attention in recent years. This chapter examines whether agriculture has lived up to its potential to abate poverty and food security in rural Malawi.

This chapter first provides an overview of the state of agriculture in Malawi. The next section examines the empirical relationship between agriculture productivity growth and poverty reduction using household panel data for 2010–2013, and discusses the recent performance of different crop yields. This section also analyzes the evolution of key factors commonly thought to affect agricultural productivity across poverty categories and gender status. The chapter then highlights the inefficiencies in the Farm Input Subsidy Program as a key constraint to sustainably improving agriculture productivity growth. The chapter finally seeks to ascertain what constrains the rural poor in Malawi from entering and obtaining higher returns in food markets. The factors considered include poor roads, inadequate transportation, and limited information on market opportunities.

The chapter shows that progress in transitioning smallholders from subsistence to commercial production has been limited, and recent improvements in agricultural productivity have also been erratic. Weather variability, declining soil fertility, limited adoption of improved agricultural technologies, inadequate provision of extension services, and restricted access to markets that are already thin and dysfunctional are among the factors that have impeded agricultural growth. The Farm Input Subsidy Program continues to account for more than half of the total agricultural public expenditures in Malawi. Yet, the program has generated limited impact, and crowds out complementary public investments needed to improve productivity. The analysis shows that the path toward sustainably improving agricultural productivity and reducing rural poverty in Malawi requires spending not only on farm subsidies but also on other public goods such as research and development investment, and rural roads.

Status of Agriculture in Malawi

Malawi's agriculture sector is dominated by smallholder farmers, who contribute more than 70 percent of agricultural GDP. The average size of a smallholder farm is approximately 1 hectare. Despite their small size, smallholder farms account for 70 percent of the 2.5 million hectares of arable land under cultivation (Malawi Ministry of Agricultural and Food Security 2011). Smallholder farming is characterized by low rates of diversification into cash crops (except tobacco) and the production of food crops (maize, rice, legumes, and pulses), primarily for subsistence purposes. Maize continues to be the predominant food crop, both in the proportion of farm households cultivating it (approximately 96 percent) and in total area harvested.[1]

Among a variety of economic activities, crop production is the main activity of farm households. In 2010, 83 percent of rural households drew income from crop production, and 62 percent of total household income was generated from crop production. Notwithstanding the importance of off-farm income-generating activities in improving the livelihood of agricultural households, in 2010 only about 2 out of 10 rural agricultural households in Malawi owned or participated in off-farm enterprises, as shown in chapter 3. Furthermore, poor households engage in less diversified economic activities than nonpoor households (World Bank 2016b). Despite the variety of economic activities, the rural population is underemployed for much of the year, except during the peak cropping season, when demand for farm labor is high (Wodon and Beegle 2006).

Weather-related shocks often impose significant losses on rural smallholder farmers, leaving them vulnerable to poverty and hunger. The agriculture sector is prone to drought due to a predominantly rain-fed system and susceptible to the damaging effects of heavy seasonal flooding, particularly in the southern region. These frequent shocks result in losses in production, incomes, and capital for smallholders. Given that smallholder farmers are the largest contributors to agricultural output, such shocks reverberate throughout the economy, affecting the welfare of urban and nonfarm households through price movements. The economic losses associated with droughts and floods are estimated to cost Malawi, on average, 1.7 percent of GDP annually (Pauw, Thurlow, and van Seventer 2010).

Agricultural Productivity Growth and Poverty Reduction

Given agriculture's importance for rural livelihoods, especially for the poor, agricultural performance has direct implications for economic growth and poverty reduction in Malawi.

Improved agricultural productivity is associated with improved welfare of rural agricultural households.[2] Between 2010 and 2013, higher agricultural productivity increased the consumption expenditure per capita of rural agricultural households. A 1 percent increase in agricultural productivity leads to an estimated 0.13 increase in consumption per capita (in logarithms) and an estimated

0.06 increase in food consumption (in logarithms), measured by caloric intake per capita (figure 2.1). Poverty measures such as the poverty gap and severity of poverty also decline with increases in agricultural productivity. Such gains in welfare support the widely held notion that improving agricultural productivity is an effective channel for reducing poverty in Malawi. Simulation results for 2013 indicate that a 50 percent increase in maize yield would reduce the poverty rate among rural agricultural households by about 7 percentage points and lift approximately 622,015 people out of poverty (World Bank 2016b).

Unfortunately, agricultural productivity did not grow enough to alter the trajectory of rural poverty between 2010 and 2013. On the basis of IHS3 panel and IHPS data, although maize yields increased approximately 8 percent between 2010 and 2013 (figure 2.2), average maize yields remained relatively low, at 1.4 tons per hectare. Some difference exists between the Malawi Integrated Household Surveys and FAOSTAT data for maize yield productivity in Malawi in 2013. Despite this fact, the two data sources indicate low yields compared with yields in other African countries, including Rwanda and Uganda, as well as in countries outside the region (figure E.1 in appendix E).[3] On the basis of its agronomic potential, some recent estimates suggest that under specific climatic conditions and input application Malawi could achieve an average yield of around 4.5 tons per hectare in the longer term (Benson and Edelman 2016). The productivity of major crops also differs substantially by poverty

Figure 2.1 Agricultural Productivity and Welfare Improvements in Malawi, 2010–13

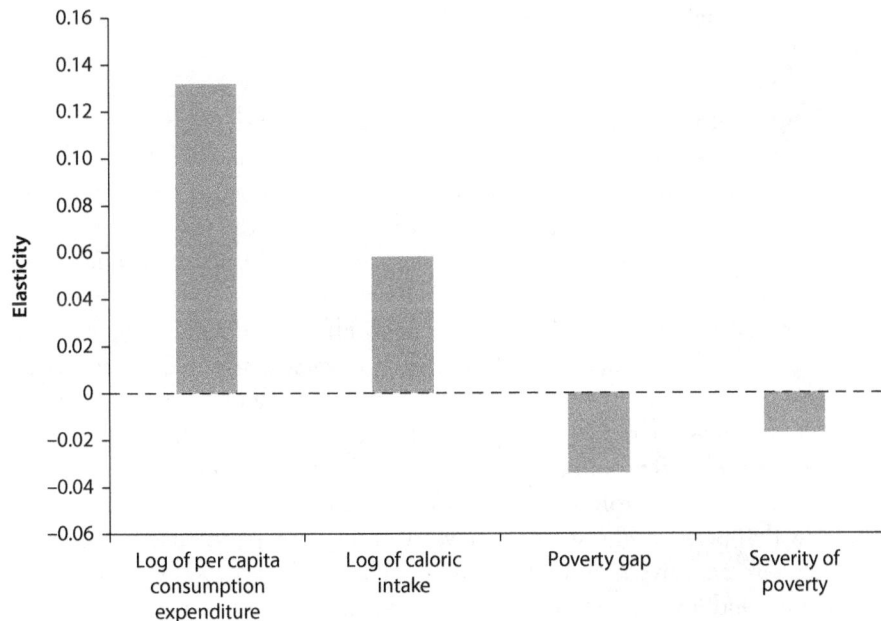

Source: World Bank 2016b, based on IHS3 panel and IHPS data.
Note: IHS3 = Third Integrated Household Survey; IHPS = Integrated Household Panel Survey.

Figure 2.2 Crop Yields in Malawi, by Poverty Status, 2010 and 2013

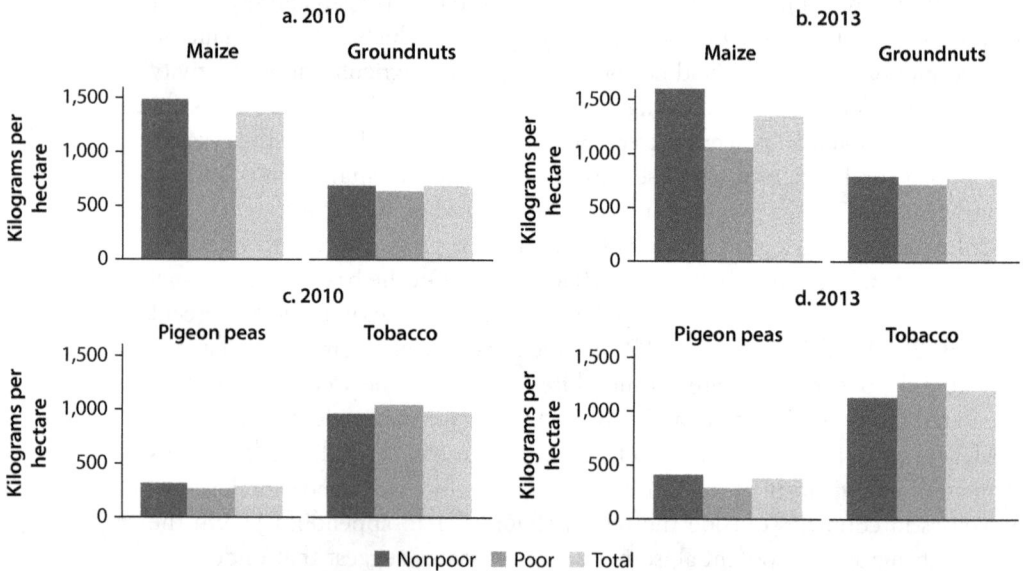

a. 2010 / b. 2013 / c. 2010 / d. 2013 — Maize, Groundnuts, Pigeon peas, Tobacco (Kilograms per hectare)

Nonpoor ■ Poor ■ Total

Source: World Bank 2016b, based on IHS3 panel and IHPS data.
Note: IHS3 = Third Integrated Household Survey; IHPS = Integrated Household Panel Survey.

status and gender. Maize yields were 31 percent lower for the poor than for the nonpoor. Moreover, yields for crops on female-managed plots were significantly lower (17 percent for maize and 16 percent for groundnuts) than yields for the same crops on male-managed plots in 2013 (World Bank 2016b). Details on the determinants of agricultural productivity are presented in appendix F.

Agricultural productivity in Malawi has remained largely stagnant due to limited adoption of modern technologies. This stagnation is exacerbated by heavy dependence on rain-fed agriculture, weak links to markets, and poor research and extension services.[4] Recent analysis suggests that the joint use of complementary investments raises the productivity of maize more than the use of one investment alone (figure 2.3). However, the share of agricultural households with access to these complementary inputs is rather low (figure 2.4). Furthermore, more than half (53 percent) of the maize yield differential between households that are chronically poor and those that escaped poverty between 2010 and 2013 is explained by differences in family labor utilization and extension services obtained as well as the returns to organic fertilizer and applying the right type of basal fertilizer. Access to and use of adequate information could therefore bring higher yields. Findings from empirical models of movements in and out of poverty show that persons who stayed in poverty in the same period had lower levels of education and lived in more remote villages than those who escaped. Remoteness and low education are likely to make information for these households harder to obtain and use appropriately and, in the process, to diminish their income generation capabilities (World Bank 2016b).

Figure 2.3 Use of Complementary Inputs for Farming and Maize Yields in Malawi, by Poverty Status, 2013

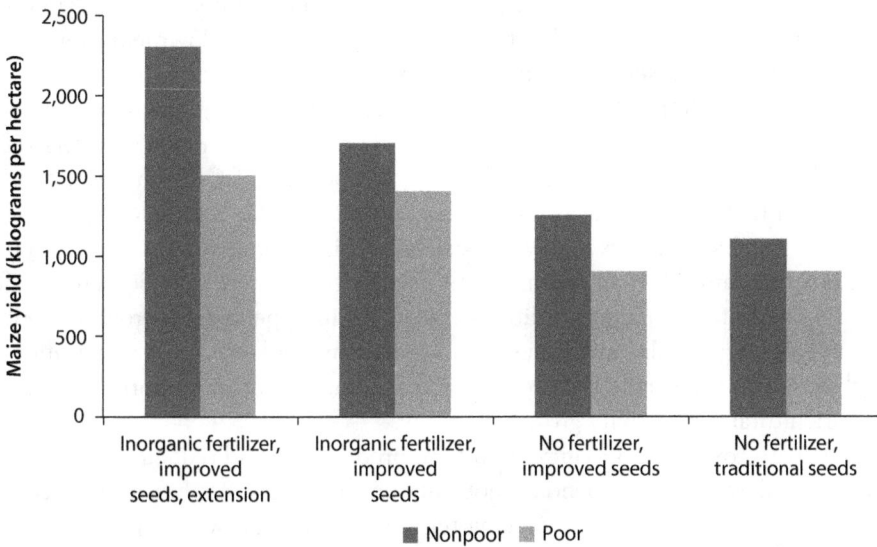

Source: World Bank 2016b, based on IHPS data.
Note: IHPS = Integrated Household Panel Survey.

Figure 2.4 Share of Agricultural Households with Access to a Combination of Inputs for Farming in Malawi, by Poverty Status, 2013

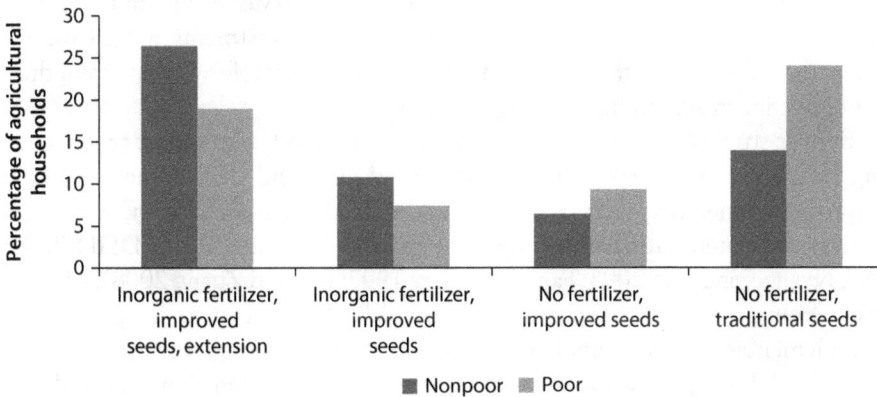

Source: World Bank 2016b, based on IHPS data.
Note: IHPS = Integrated Household Panel Survey.

Furthermore, average yields of major crops differ significantly by gender. The 2010 yields for crops on female-managed plots were significantly lower (26 percent for maize, 30 percent for groundnuts, and 27 percent for pigeon peas and tobacco) than yields for the same crops on male-managed plots (World Bank 2016b). Measuring agricultural productivity by value of output per hectare, Kilic, Palacios-López, and Goldstein (2015) observed that productivity is 25 percent lower on female-managed plots than on male-managed plots. The authors found that 82 percent of the gender differential in agricultural productivity is attributable to gender differences in endowment of assets, use of and access to services, and returns to inorganic fertilizer application.

Inefficient patterns of public spending on agriculture are at the root of poor agricultural productivity in Malawi. Malawi is one of the largest spenders on agriculture in Sub-Saharan Africa, devoting 4.2 percent of GDP to agriculture, compared with the regional average of 1.3 percent in 2012. Yet, the composition of agricultural spending is highly unbalanced. A single program, the Farm Input Subsidy Program (FISP), has consistently accounted for more than 50 percent of total agricultural public expenditures (table E.1 in appendix E), crowding out complementary public investments to strengthen markets, develop irrigation, and introduce and spread the use of new technologies that are important drivers of agricultural productivity growth.

The path toward improving agricultural productivity and reducing rural poverty in Malawi requires spending not only on farm subsidies but also on core public goods that are crucial for long-term, sustainable growth in productivity. A review by Fuglie and Rada (2013) tested the contribution of several aspects to the agricultural growth of a sample of 32 countries in Sub-Saharan Africa over the period 1977–2005. These variables included agricultural research (international and national), economic and trade policy reforms (especially those that changed the terms of trade for agriculture), farmer education (proxied by rates of education in the labor force), irrigation, prevalence of human immunodeficiency virus/acquired immune deficiency virus (HIV/AIDS), and conflict. Improved productivity in Africa is correlated with investments in agricultural research, wider adoption of new technologies, and policy reforms that strengthen economic incentives to farmers (figure 2.5).

Similar studies on China, India, Tanzania, and Uganda also report that spending on public goods, such as agricultural research and development (R&D), improved connectivity of rural areas, a modernized extension system, and irrigation, is associated with high returns (see reviews by Alston 2010; DFID 2005; Fan, Nyange, and Rao 2005; Fan and Pardey 1997; Fan and Zhang 2008). Moving away from an exclusive focus on fertilizer subsidies and toward a package of complementary investments has been shown to deliver huge dividends during periods of high productivity growth in Asia and in Latin America and the Caribbean (Goyal and Nash 2016). In Latin American countries in which a high share of public spending went to subsidize private goods (that is, inputs), the impact on agricultural growth was negative. The reason was that the subsidization tended to crowd out public spending on public goods related to R&D and irrigation, both of which have strong, positive, long-term impacts on growth (López and Galinato 2007). In India, Fan, Gulati, and Thorat (2008) estimated the impacts of different expenditures on agricultural GDP. The findings show that productive investments in marketing systems, research and advisory services, and water management have yielded consistently higher returns than subsidies

Figure 2.5 Impact of Policies to Raise Agricultural Productivity in Sub-Saharan Africa

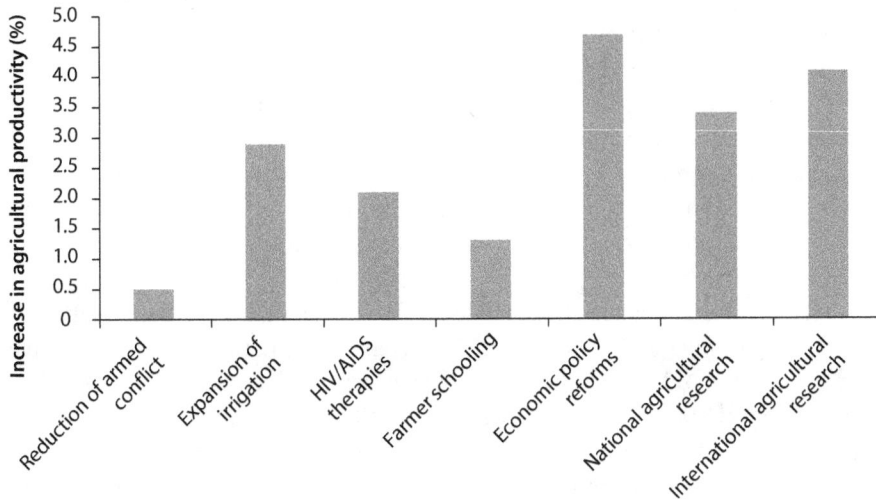

Source: Fuglie and Rada 2013.
Note: HIV/AIDS = human immunodeficiency virus/acquired immune deficiency syndrome.

and been major drivers of productivity growth since the early 1970s (table E.2 in appendix E).

Access to credit exerts a positive effect on agricultural productivity, but has low penetration in rural areas. An empirical analysis of the determinants of agricultural productivity in rural Malawi between 2010 and 2013 found that access to credit, which has been documented to promote access to and use of agricultural equipment, exerts a positive effect on productivity levels (World Bank 2016b). In addition, farmers are usually compelled to sell their produce soon after harvesting for financial reasons, so another way of encouraging them to store and sell during the lean season would be to provide them with credit that they could pay back in the lean season rather than at harvest. Despite these advantages, access to rural credit has stayed very low in Malawi and, as commonly cited in the literature, could be one of the reasons for the country's erratic agricultural productivity.

Seasonality of agricultural production and susceptibility to natural disasters (such as flood, drought) heighten the risks associated with price and yield volatility, adding to the need for rural financial services. Yet, only 13 percent of rural households in 2010 and 22 percent in 2013 applied for credit. Of these, only 41 percent in 2010 and 31 percent in 2013 were successful in obtaining it. Nonpoor and male-headed households were more likely to receive credit (and less likely to be turned down) than poor and female-headed households. Male-headed households received more credit than female-headed households partly because they were, on average, better off and thus deemed to have better prospects of paying back the loan (World Bank 2016b).

Enhancing financial inclusion would not only promote access to and use of improved agricultural technologies and build resilience, but also enable farm households to diversify into nonagricultural activities, as shown in chapter 3.

Effective public spending in agriculture is a vital tool for governments to improve agricultural productivity and accelerate poverty reduction in rural areas. Rebalancing spending priorities across different types of programs is crucial. As mentioned, 50 percent or more of the agriculture budget is dedicated to FISP, which has a high opportunity cost. Approaches that create synergies—and lead to increasing returns—are necessary to address the systemic constraints facing smallholder farmers.

A study by Lunduka and Ricker-Gilbert (2016) calculated the contribution of specific investments to the value of maize revenue on a nationally representative sample of smallholder households in Malawi using three rounds of panel data over the period 2004–09. Table 2.1 shows that the use of improved maize seed has one of the highest returns at the national and regional levels. The national benefit-to-cost ratio for improved seeds is 2.48, meaning that for every kwacha spent on improved seeds, MK 1.48 are gained in additional benefits. R&D investment in improved maize varieties has great potential to create varieties that are higher yielding and more resistant to droughts and floods. Some of the payoff to improved maize seed has come from the FISP, but there is need to continue investing in better seed varieties in the face of climate change.

By contrast, the cost of subsidized fertilizer far exceeds the benefits to farmers across the board, with benefit-cost ratios for subsidized fertilizer of 0.42 at the national level. Other interventions, such as irrigation and road investments, have higher returns in the southern region. Irrigation in maize is very common in the southern districts of Chikwawa and Nsanje. The lower Shire Valley floods during the rainy season but becomes very productive in the

Table 2.1 Benefit-Cost Ratios of Selected Interventions in Agriculture in Malawi, by Region, 2004–09[a]

Intervention	National	North	Central	South
Subsidized fertilizer	0.42	0.20	0.19	0.37
Extension advice[c]	—	—	—	1.35
Irrigation income[b,c]	—	0.96	—	1.45
Road distance from home[c]	4.63	0.28	—	8.66
Use of improved maize seeds	2.48	1.21	6.00	1.27

Source: Lunduka and Ricker-Gilbert 2016, based on data from the Second Integrated Household Survey (2004) and data from the Agricultural Input Support Survey 1 (2007) and 2 (2009).
Note: a. The benefit-cost ratios come from separate regression models for households in the northern, central, and southern regions, along with all households in the national data set. Because the coefficient estimates for the benefits are not calculated from the same households across, there can be different conditional mean estimates.
b. Irrigation was proxied by the amount of income a household earns during the dry season. The only way to earn farm income in the winter is through access to irrigation, given that it typically does not rain during that time of year. The main production modules of the Agricultural Input Support Survey are conducted during the rainy season, so there are no questions regarding irrigation investment.
c. — = intervention did not have a statistically significant effect on production.

dry season, where large amounts of maize both for food and for income are produced using irrigation. By contrast, the low returns to irrigation in the central region could be due to the prevalence of tobacco leading to higher incomes, but whose cultivation is rain-fed. The regional variation in returns to irrigation shows that irrigation has potential to be profitable and add value in places where smallholders can control water use. Extension advice shows only positive returns in the south. The current extension contacts with most farmers have not been to get agronomic advice, but mainly to register farmers into FISP and distribute the fertilizer coupons. This has diluted the impact of extension services and hence the benefits are low. Leaving time for extension officers to do their mandated job by providing agronomic advice could still help farmers to learn about new and better farming practices and technologies that can increase their income.

Inefficiencies in Malawi Farm Input Subsidy Program

Malawi's Farmer Input Subsidy Program is the largest input subsidy scheme relative to GDP in Sub-Saharan Africa. What sets it apart is its vast coverage—more than 50 percent of agricultural households in the country—and high program costs, which have averaged close to 3 percent of GDP annually (Jacoby 2016). Through the program, smallholder farmers receive vouchers to subsidize the cost of fertilizer for maize, modern maize seeds, and legumes. FISP aims to increase maize yields, thereby promoting household and national food security and enhancing rural incomes (appendix L provides a brief history of FISP).

The introduction of FISP in 2005 coincided with a substantial increase in maize production, but after the initial years of success, national maize yields have stagnated. Over time, the program has become increasingly costly and inefficient, without the accompanying improvements in agricultural development or poverty reduction. FISP costs have risen steadily over time, absorbing 8.3 percent of the 2014–15 national budget (figure 2.6). Inefficiencies in FISP implementation have increased costs, resulting in a high fiscal burden to the government and high budget overruns (with substantial carryover of arrears from previous seasons). For example, an inefficient tonnage allocation formula (small quantities provided to many contractors) has raised average purchase costs, and an inefficient fertilizer delivery mechanism has increased logistical costs, compounded by the recent depreciation of Malawi's currency. FISP continues to overrun its budget year after year (figure 2.7). In both FY2014–15 and FY2015–16, the total FISP cost overruns are estimated at approximately MK 45.8 billion (approximately US$61 million)—an average of 30 percent above the budgeted cost. These overruns do not include interest charged on delayed payment. The interest accounted for a sizable proportion of Malawi's budget deficit in the same period.

Moreover, better-off households consistently have been more likely to participate in the program than have poorer households (figure 2.8). Decentralized, community-based targeting systems such as those used by FISP have the benefit of using local knowledge to identify beneficiaries at a relatively

Figure 2.6 Costs of FISP, 2005/06–2013/14

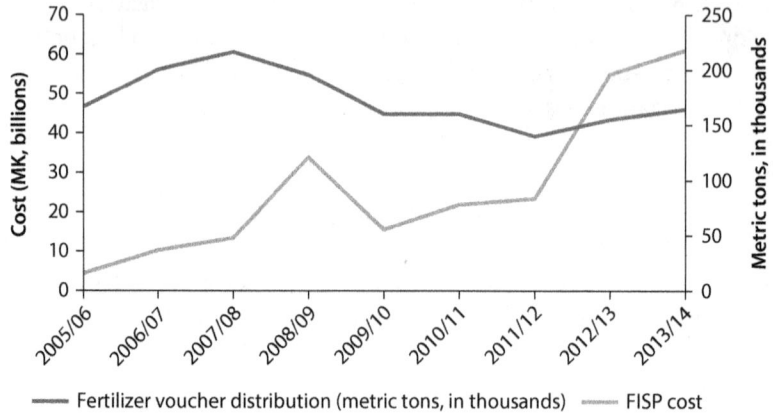

Source: World Bank 2016a.
Note: FISP = Farm Input Subsidy Program.

Figure 2.7 Approved and Actual FISP Budget, 2014/15 and 2015/16

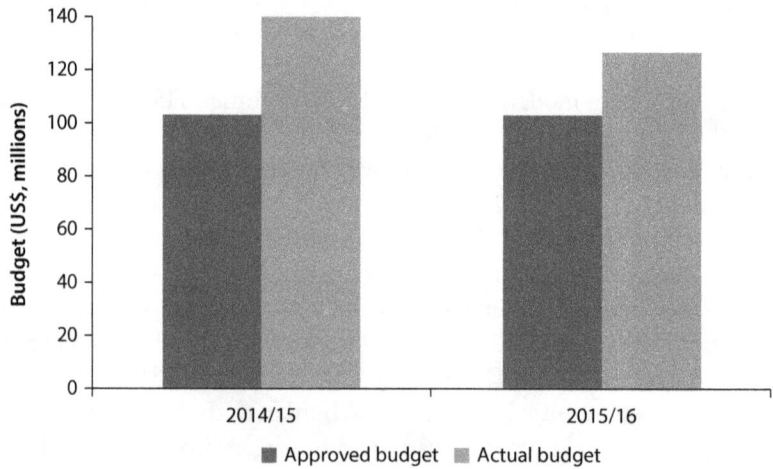

Source: World Bank 2016a.
Note: FISP = Farm Input Subsidy Program.

low cost to the government. However, community-based targeting schemes are more likely to suffer from elite capture, whereby persons with social connections and resources obtain a disproportionate share of the benefits (Pan and Christiaensen 2012). The majority of evidence evaluating Malawi's input subsidy program indicates that, over the program's duration, Malawi's rural poor have not been specifically targeted to receive subsidized fertilizer and seed (Chibwana, Fisher, and Shively 2011; Holden and Lunduka 2012; Lunduka, Ricker-Gilbert, and Fisher 2013). Kilic, Whitney, and Winters (2015) found that, on average, relatively well-off households who are connected to community leadership and

Figure 2.8 FISP Participation in Malawi, by Consumption Quintile, 2013

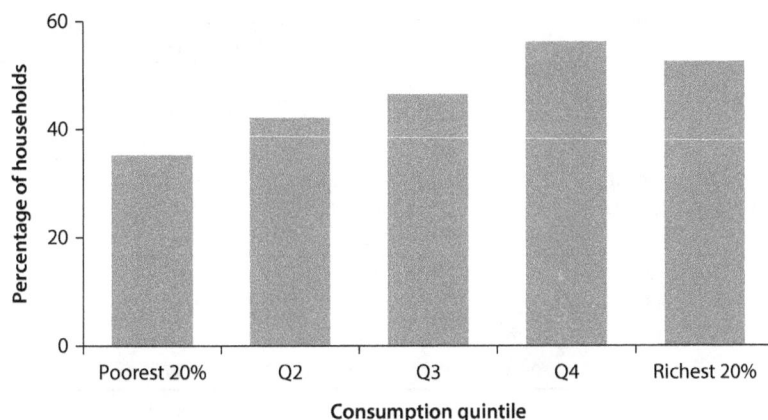

Source: Estimates are based on IHPS data.
Note: FISP = Farm Input Subsidy Program; IHPS = Integrated Household Panel Survey; Q = quintile.

reside in agroecologically favorable locations, are more likely to be FISP benefi-ciaries. Another way to look at targeting is to look at program incidence by quintiles. In 2013, approximately one-third of households in the bottom quintile obtained subsidized inorganic fertilizer compared with half of households in the top two quintiles (figure 2.8). The fact that nearly half of households in the top three consumption quintiles received FISP reflects incorrect targeting and raises concerns about the program's performance.

The benefit-cost estimates of the subsidy program suggest modest returns to fertilizer use at best. Ricker-Gilbert, Jayne, and Chirwa (2011) found that, on average, the maize-fertilizer response rate is 2.7 kilograms of grain per kilogram of subsidized fertilizer acquired by households, which is only 50 percent of the government's expected maize-fertilizer response rate of 5 kilograms. Lunduka, Ricker-Gilbert, and Fisher (2013) found that, using the estimated marginal response to a kilogram of subsidized fertilizer from Ricker-Gilbert, Jayne, and Chirwa (2011), the benefit-cost ratio was below 1.0 in all years from 2005 to 2009, except for 2007, when it was 1.28 (table 2.2).

The vast body of research shows that FISP has had a modest impact on maize yields and overall maize production in Malawi and that much of the increase has been among better-off farmers (for a review, see Ricker-Gilbert 2016). Moreover, FISP has not significantly reduced poverty (Ricker-Gilbert 2016; Harou and oth-ers 2014), and in fact rural extreme poverty rates have risen slightly since FISP began in 2005. Such research findings raise questions about whether, given the enormous fiscal burden imposed by the program and the current implementation strategies, FISP's current objectives can be met.

It often is argued that subsidizing fertilizer is desirable both to boost agricul-tural production and to help poor farmers. However, these two objectives may be in conflict. There is a need to rethink FISP's goals and objectives and perhaps

Table 2.2 Returns to Inorganic Fertilizer Use in Malawi, 2005/06–2008/09
US$ per kilogram

				Benefit-cost ratio		
				Unconditional maize-fertilizer response rate[a]	Conditional mean maize-fertilizer response rate[b]	
Fiscal year	Commercial price of maize (A)	Government cost of fertilizer (B)	Subsidized price of fertilizer (C)	At government cost of fertilizer (D)	At government cost of fertilizer (E)	At subsidized price of fertilizer (F)
2005/06	0.14	0.42	0.15	1.67	0.90	2.53
2006/07	0.13	0.44	0.11	1.50	0.81	3.13
2007/08	0.20	0.43	0.10	2.36	1.28	5.65
2008/09	0.21	1.02	0.05	1.03	0.56	10.84

Sources: Lunduka, Ricker-Gilbert, and Fisher 2013; calculations are based on data from Dorward and Chirwa 2011 and Ricker-Gilbert, Jayne, and Chirwa 2011.
Note: The figures in column D are from an assumed mid-maize grain response rate of 15 kilograms of grain per kilogram of nitrogen in Dorward and Chirwa 2011.
a. Rate of 5 kilograms of maize per 1 kilogram of fertilizer.
b. Rate of 2.71 kilograms of maize per 1 kilogram of fertilizer.

to separate the productivity-enhancing objective from the social safety net objective. Chapter 5 lays out some ideas to reconsider the objectives and target population of FISP.

Stronger Participation in Markets

Most smallholder production is focused on own consumption, with relatively small shares of total production of food crops being sold (table 2.3). Market orientation for most Malawian farmers remains limited. While farmers in Malawi have important agroecological advantages that they can exploit to produce a wide range of crops for own consumption and for commercial use, the range of income-producing crops is considerably more constrained. Agriculture in Malawi is dominated by low-input, low-output, production practices of smallholder farmers. For economic growth to take place, the central role of subsistence agriculture in the livelihood and food security of most Malawian households will have to be reduced.

This orientation toward production of food for own consumption reflects, to a large degree, the existence of thin markets for food crops in Malawi and contributes to the maintenance of these thin markets. Farmers are uncertain whether they will find buyers who will offer them a profitable price for their food crops, so most farmers generate surplus production primarily as a safety margin against the food security risks of a bad cropping season rather than as the result of a commercial decision (Dorward and others 2009). The small transactions that farmers make with their limited surplus maintains this pattern of thin markets for food crops.

Table 2.3 Rural Households Reporting Production and Sale of Selected Crops, 2013
percentage of rural households

Crop	Producing crops	Of those producing, reporting any sales
Maize	94.6	15.7
Local varieties	64.1	12.0
Hybrid or improved open-pollinated varieties	45.7	15.7
Groundnuts	37.0	38.3
Pigeon peas	28.6	26.2
Beans	22.2	50.1
Rice	4.2	38.8
Tobacco	10.5	94.7

Source: World Bank 2016a.

When faced with the decision of whether to market agricultural produce—especially food crops—farmers contend with many factors that increase transaction costs, including poor roads, inadequate transportation, and limited information on market opportunities. These high transaction costs mean that both buyers and sellers face the risk that a transaction will fail altogether, which would drive up risk premiums for those who choose (or are forced) to trade maize and other food crops. These risks depress traded volumes, which result in thin markets and volatile prices (Dorward and Kydd 2004). When faced with uncertain markets, Malawian producers tend to devote more land to low-value food staples for subsistence consumption. Unpredictable prices also hurt Malawi's maize consumers, especially considering intraseasonal price movements. On average, the price of maize in Malawi increases approximately 50 percent from the harvest price in May to the lean-season price in February, when most households have exhausted their own stocks and look to the market for maize (Gilbert, Christiaensen, and Kaminski 2017).

Encouraging entrepreneurship in agricultural markets requires broad support. Investments in building roads and strengthening transportation and communication services need to penetrate even more deeply into rural areas. Remote farmers will not participate if the costs of communication and transport are so high that it makes no sense for them to do so. Equally important are improvements in information available to market participants—especially on crop production and market prices. If both parties to a transaction have dependable information on prevailing commodity prices, in particular, the risk of that transaction failing is minimized. However, as long as domestic agricultural markets remain thin, the economic returns to selling in those markets will be weak.

Summary

While agriculture continues to play a defining role in the Malawian economy, it remains characterized by smallholder production with limited opportunities for income diversification. Most people are locked in low-productivity, subsistence agriculture with inadequate transition toward higher-value commercial production.

The lack of robust growth in agricultural productivity has been a key factor in Malawi's pervasive rural poverty and food insecurity. Revitalizing agricultural productivity by improving farmers' adoption of modern agricultural technologies and practices, enhancing connectivity to markets, and encouraging commercialization will be instrumental to reduce poverty. However, agriculture might not be able to absorb the expanding rural labor force completely, and agricultural advances alone are unlikely to meet the challenge of rural poverty. Higher diversification toward nonfarm activities can play an important role in boosting the local economy, promoting job creation, and alleviating poverty, as discussed in the next chapter.

Notes

1. In contrast with the smallholder farms, estate farms have a minimum size of approximately 10 ha. They produce mainly tobacco, sugar, tea, and other cash crops almost entirely for export. Estate farms usually occupy leasehold or freehold land, whereas the land for smallholder farms is predominantly under customary tenure rights, adding to the insecurity of their food sources.

2. For details on the estimation of agricultural productivity and welfare, see World Bank 2016b, ch. 6.

3. While national production estimates suggest that maize production and productivity increased significantly during 2004–10, several farm-level studies found relatively modest increases in maize production and yields during the same period (Chibwana, Fisher, and Shively 2012; Holden and Lunduka 2012; Ricker-Gilbert and Jayne 2012; Ricker-Gilbert, Jayne, and Chirwa 2011).

4. Among farming households in general and maize-producing households in particular, 42 and 15 percent of households, respectively, participate in markets (IHS3).

References

Alston, J. M. 2010. "The Benefits from Agricultural Research and Development, Innovation, and Productivity Growth." OECD Food, Agriculture and Fisheries Paper 31, OECD Publishing, Paris.

Benson, T., and B. Edelman. 2016. "Policies for Accelerating Growth in Agriculture and Agribusiness in Malawi." Background paper for the 2016 Malawi Country Economic Memorandum. International Food Policy Research Institute, Washington, DC.

Chibwana, C., M. Fisher, and G. Shively. 2012. "Cropland Allocation Effects of Agricultural Input Subsidies in Malawi." *World Development* 40 (1): 124–33.

DfID (Department for International Development). 2005. *Rates of Return to Research: A Literature Review and Critique*. Final Report. Reading, U.K.: Enterplan in association with Overseas Development Group, University of East Anglia, and Cambridge Education Consultants.

Dorward, A., and E. Chirwa. 2011. "The Malawi Agricultural Input Subsidy Programme: 2005–06 to 2008–09." *International Journal of Agricultural Sustainability* 9 (1): 232–247.

Dorward, A., and J. Kydd. 2004. "The Malawi 2002 Food Crisis: The Rural Development Challenge." *Journal of Modern African Studies* 42 (3): 343–61.

Dorward, A., J. Kydd, C. Poulton, and D. Bezemer. 2009. "Coordination Risk and Cost Impacts on Economic Development in Poor Rural Areas." *Journal of Development Studies* 45 (7): 1093–112.

Fan, S., A. Gulati, and S. Thorat. 2008. "Investment, Subsidies, and Pro-Poor Growth in Rural India." *Agricultural Economics* 39 (2): 163–70.

Fan, S., D. Nyange, and N. Rao. 2005. "Public Investment and Poverty Reduction in Tanzania: Evidence from Household Survey Data." Development Strategy and Governance Division Discussion Paper 18, International Food Policy Research Institute, Washington, DC.

Fan, S., and P. Pardey. 1997. "Research, Productivity, and Output Growth in Chinese Agriculture." *Journal of Development Economics* 53 (1): 115–37.

Fan, S., and X. Zhang. 2008. "Public Expenditure, Growth and Poverty Reduction in Rural Uganda." *African Development Review* 20 (3): 466–96.

Fuglie, K. O., and N. E. Rada. 2013. *Resources, Policies, and Agricultural Productivity in Sub-Saharan Africa.* Economic Research Report 145. Washington, DC: U.S. Department of Agriculture, Economic Research Service.

Gilbert, C. L., L. Christiaensen, and J. Kaminski. 2017. "Food Price Seasonality in Africa: Measurement and Extent." *Food Policy* 67: 119–132.

Goyal, A., and J. Nash. 2016. "Reaping Richer Returns: Public Spending Priorities for African Agriculture Productivity Growth." AFR Regional Study Flagship Series, World Bank, Washington, DC.

Harou, A., Y. C. Liu, C. B. Barrett, and L. You. 2014. "Variable Returns to Fertilizer Use and Its Relationship to Poverty: Experimental and Simulation Evidence from Malawi." Discussion Paper 01373, International Food Policy Research Institute, Washington, DC.

Holden, S. T., and R. Lunduka. 2012. "Do Fertilizer Subsidies Crowd Out Organic Manures? The Case of Malawi." *Agricultural Economics* 43 (3): 301–312.

Jacoby, H. 2016. "Smart Subsidy? Welfare and Distributional Implications of Malawi's FISP." Working Paper, World Bank, Washington, DC.

Kilic, T., A. Palacios-López, and M. Goldstein. 2015. "Caught in a Productivity Trap: A Distributional Perspective on Gender Differences in Malawian Agriculture." *World Development* 70 (C): 416–463.

Kilic, T., E. Whitney, and P. Winters. 2015. "Decentralized Beneficiary Targeting in Large-Scale Development Programs: Insights from the Malawi Farm Input Subsidy Program." *Journal of African Economies* 24 (1): 26–56.

López, R., and G. I. Galinato. 2007. "Should Governments Stop Subsidies to Private Goods? Evidence from Rural Latin America." *Journal of Public Economics* 91 (5–6): 1071–94.

Lunduka, R., J. Ricker-Gilbert, and M. Fisher. 2013. "What Are the Farm-Level Impacts of Malawi's Farm Input Subsidy Program? A Critical Review." *Agricultural Economics* 44 (6): 563–79.

Lunduka, R., and J. Ricker-Gilbert. 2016. "Contribution of Alternative Investments to the Value of Agricultural Revenue for Smallholder Rural Farmers in Malawi." Report prepared for the Poverty and Social Impact Analysis of the Malawi Farm Input Subsidy Program. World Bank, Washington, DC.

Malawi Ministry of Agricultural and Food Security. 2011. "Malawi Agricultural Sector-Wide Approach: A Prioritised and Harmonised Agricultural Development Agenda, 2011–2015." Malawi Ministry of Agricultural and Food Security, Lilongwe.

Pan, L., and L. Christiaensen. 2012. "Who Is Vouching for the Input Voucher? Decentralized Targeting and Elite Capture in Tanzania." *World Development* 40 (8): 1619–33.

Pauw, K., J. Thurlow, and D. van Seventer. 2010. "Droughts and Floods in Malawi: Assessing the Economy-Wide Effects." IFPRI Discussion Paper 00962, International Food Policy Research Institute, Washington, DC. http://www.ifpri.org/publication /droughts-and-floods-malawi.

Ricker-Gilbert, J. 2016. "Review of Malawi's Farm Input Subsidy Program in 2016 and Direction for Re-design." Report prepared for the Poverty and Social Impact Analysis of the Malawi Farm Input Subsidy Program. World Bank, Washington, DC.

Ricker-Gilbert, J., and T. S. Jayne. 2012. "Do Fertilizer Subsidies Boost Staple Crop Production and Reduce Poverty across the Distribution of Smallholders in Africa? Quantile Regression Results from Malawi." Paper prepared for the International Association of Agricultural Economists (IAAE) Triennial Conference, Foz do Iguaçu, Brazil. http://scholar.google.com/citations?view_op=view_citation&hl=en&user =WlE8j48AAAAJ&citation_for_view=WlE8j48AAAAJ:_FxGoFyzp5QC.

Ricker-Gilbert, J., T. S. Jayne, and E. Chirwa. 2011. "Subsidies and Crowding Out: A Double-Hurdle Model of Fertilizer Demand in Malawi." *American Journal of Agricultural Economics* 93 (1): 26–42.

Wodon, Q., and K. Beegle. 2006. "Labor Shortages Despite Underemployment? Seasonality in Time Use in Malawi." Working Paper, World Bank, Washington, DC.

World Bank. 2008. *World Development Report 2008: Agriculture for Development.* New York: Oxford University Press.

———. 2016a. "Malawi CEM Background Note on FISP Reform." Mimeo. World Bank, Washington, DC.

———. 2016b. "Malawi Poverty Assessment." World Bank, Washington, DC.

CHAPTER 3

Nonfarm Self-Employment Activities and Poverty

Introduction

Malawi is an agricultural economy, and increasing agricultural productivity and growing farm incomes are critical for reducing poverty, as discussed in chapter 2. However, it often is difficult to sustain income from a single occupation such as rain-fed agriculture, which is highly prone to risk. The expansion of nonfarm activities and diversification of income sources are likely features of the process of economic development. This chapter examines whether both processes are evident in rural Malawi. The analysis goes as far back as 1998 to examine the long-term economic transformation, but the rest of the analysis covers the latest period, 2010–13.

The chapter first examines whether structural transformation has been taking place in Malawi over the past fifteen years since 1998. In other words, were more people employed in services and industry than agriculture in 2013 than 15 years ago? It looks at this transformation by focusing on the prevalence and nature of nonfarm activities in rural areas. Particular emphasis is placed on nonfarm self-employment (NFSE) activities, defined as all business enterprises carried out by household members to earn additional revenue. The chapter provides information on the amount of income these activities generate and for which types of households. The importance of self-employment for consumption growth and poverty is discussed briefly using household panel data for 2010–13. The performance of NFSE across different socioeconomic groups (poor and nonpoor, urban and rural) is then analyzed, also relying on panel data. The chapter finally seeks to ascertain what constrains the rural poor in Malawi from entering and obtaining higher returns from NFSE. Particular attention is drawn to factors such as human capital levels, access to credit, and wealth.

The chapter finds that NFSE activities have risen significantly in recent years. Rising NFSE income has been the driving force behind the reduction in rural poverty. Overall, increased participation of some of the poor in NFSE, along with higher rates of return to these activities, has driven income growth and poverty reduction. Nevertheless, within Malawi, diversification into and returns from NFSE activities have been lower in rural than in urban areas and for the poor than for the nonpoor, so there is scope for improvement.

Structural Transformation in Malawi

Malawi remains an agricultural economy, but a slow process of transformation to nonfarm sectors is taking place. Figure 3.1 helps to visualize Malawi's process of structural change. The vertical axis shows sectoral productivity relative to economywide productivity. A positive value means that a sector generated above-average value added per worker from 1998 to 2013. The horizontal axis shows the percentage point change in employment shares from 1998 to 2013. A negative value means that a sector's share of total employment fell, even though employment in the sector may have grown in absolute terms. Finally, the size of the circles represents a sector's initial contribution to total employment.

Agriculture has the largest circle because 84 percent of Malawian workers identified themselves as farmers in 1998. Agriculture's share of total employment fell almost 20 percent over a 15-year period. Meanwhile, all of the other nonfarm sectors increased their share of employment. The largest expansion in employment between 1998 and 2013 took place within trade services, which includes wholesale and retail trade as well as restaurants, followed by community services, which includes high-productivity services, such as health and education, as well as low-productivity services, such as paid domestic work. Most of the observed increase in employment was within lower-productivity community services.

Figure 3.1 **Structural Transformation of Malawi's Economy, 1998–2013**

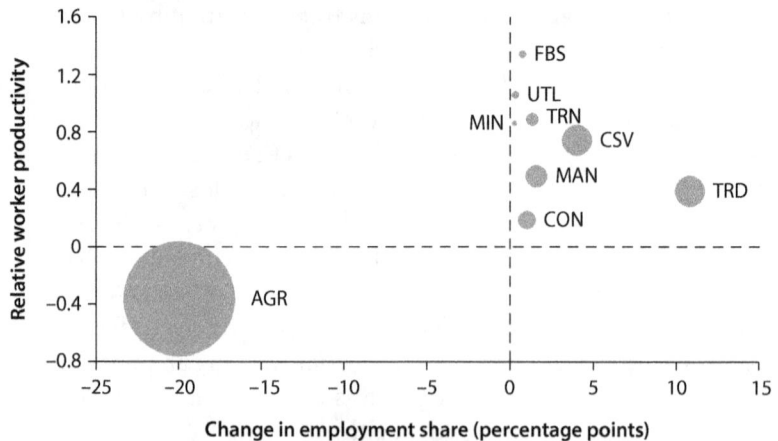

Source: World Bank 2016b.
Note: Size of circle = initial employment share. AGR = agriculture; CON = construction; CSV = public and community services; FBS = financial and business services; MAN = manufacturing; MIN = mining; TRD = trade services; TRN = transport and communication; UTL = utilities (electricity and water).

Table 3.1 Job Creation in Rural and Urban Areas of Malawi, 1998–2013

Sector	Total regional employment, 2013 (%)			Total sector employment, 2013 (%)			Total national change in employment, 1998–2013 (%)		
	National	Urban	Rural	National	Urban	Rural	National	Urban	Rural
All sectors	100.0	100.0	100.0	100.0	11.6	88.4	100.0	17.3	82.7
Agriculture	64.1	16.4	70.4	100.0	3.0	97.0	−16.4	1.6	−18.0
Industry	7.4	16.7	6.2	100.0	26.2	73.8	19.8	2.3	17.5
Mining	0.3	1.1	0.2	100.0	41.9	58.1	1.3	0.6	0.7
Manufacturing	4.1	7.7	3.6	100.0	21.7	78.3	10.4	0.8	9.7
Utilities	0.4	0.8	0.4	100.0	22.3	77.7	1.4	0.0	1.4
Construction	2.6	7.2	2.0	100.0	32.0	68.0	6.7	1.0	5.7
Services	28.5	66.9	23.5	100.0	27.2	72.8	96.6	13.4	83.2
Trade services	16.9	34.8	14.6	100.0	23.2	76.8	62.1	8.8	53.3
Transport, communication	2.0	5.4	1.6	100.0	31.4	68.6	7.4	1.2	6.2
Financial, business services	0.9	3.9	0.5	100.0	49.9	50.1	3.9	1.7	2.2
Community, public services	8.7	22.8	6.8	100.0	31.0	69.0	23.3	1.8	21.5

Source: World Bank 2016b, based on the 1998 and 2008 Population Censuses and 2013 Labor Force Survey.

Most of the expansion in nonfarm employment[1] in Malawi occurred in rural rather than urban areas. Table 3.1 shows the rural and urban share of employment drawn from the 2013 Labor Force Survey and reports the contributions of each sector in urban and rural areas to total job creation between 1998 and 2013. The services sector accounted for more than 25 percent of total national employment as well as for more than 80 percent of nonfarm employment. Most service jobs were in trade services, which accounted for approximately 50 percent of all nonfarm rural jobs.[2]

In contrast, a greater proportion of urban nonfarm jobs are in sectors such as finance, business services, and public administration. Urban employment accounted for 17.3 percent of all new jobs created in Malawi between 1998 and 2013. This share was higher than the 11.6 percent share of national employment in 2013, indicating that urban employment growth over the 15 years was higher than the national average. Thus, the urban economy is an important source of job creation in Malawi. That being said, more than four-fifths (82.7 percent) of new jobs were created in rural areas. Moreover, rural agricultural employment declined over this period, such that all rural employment growth took place within nonfarm sectors. In particular, the involvement of rural households in NFSE activities rose from 20 percent in 2010 to 28 percent in 2013.

Many rural household enterprises are operated informally from home by young uneducated males (table 3.2). In 2010, almost one in two businesses was operated from home. However, between 2010 and 2013, only businesses operating in marketplaces and commercial area shops increased. Household enterprises are relatively young. In 2010, the average business was approximately 12 years old and operated by a 38-year-old owner. In 2013, the average enterprise

Table 3.2 Selected Characteristics of Household Enterprises in Rural Areas of Malawi, 2010 and 2013

Characteristics	2010	2013
Age of enterprises (years)	11.7	9.1
Number of household members per enterprise	1.1	1.3
Outside partner (%)	2.9	3.4
Business operating premises (%)		
Home	49.8	44.0
Marketplace and commercial area shop	29.2	38.0
Roadside and other areas	21.1	18.1
Formal registration (%)	6.2	7.6
Access to electricity (%)	12.8	12.8
Number of enterprises per household (1 to 4)	1.1	1.1
Male owner (%)	57.2	54.6
Owner if household head (%)	69.9	70.4
Age of owner (%)	38.3	39.0
Education of owner (%)		
None	77.1	74.8
Primary School Leaving Certificate	10.3	12.8
Junior Certificate of Education	8.5	7.2
Malawi Middle School Certificate of Education	3.2	4.4
Nonuniversity diploma	0.5	0.4
University diploma	0.4	0.4
Postgraduate degree	0.0	0.0

Source: World Bank 2016a.

Note: Formal registration is with at least one of three institutions: Register of Companies, Malawi Revenue Authority, or Local Assembly.

was 9 years old and operated by a 39-year-old owner. Although some enterprises were created between 2010 and 2013, some older ones disappeared, reducing the average age of enterprises. Therefore, household enterprises have a relatively short life span, consistent with the fact that less than 10 percent of household enterprises were formally registered between 2010 and 2013. Perhaps because of the short life span of such enterprises, owners do not invest time and resources in the registration process. Women run almost as many household enterprises as men. Most business owners have little to no human capital. Three in every four owners have no formal education and lack access to capital services that would enhance productivity.

Commerce and tourism absorb the highest number of the rural self-employed. Wholesale, retail trade, restaurants, and hotels account for half (49 percent) of all household businesses in rural Malawi. This sector is dominated primarily by merchants selling or reselling a wide variety of products, from groceries and food products to clothes, shoes, and more. The food, beverage, and tobacco manufacturing sector comes second and includes mostly street vendors of various food and drinks. The primary sector contains forest-based product enterprises such as bamboo, charcoal, firewood, and timber and represents only 2–3 percent of household enterprises. Men and women operate household enterprises in similar proportions in the commerce and tourism sector. In contrast, the food, beverage, and tobacco manufacturing sector attracts about 46 percent of all women-owned enterprises compared with only 9.5 percent of male-owned enterprises.

All activities, except those in the primary sector, recently experienced increased returns. On average, construction and services generated the highest monthly revenue and experienced more than 40 percent increase in real terms between 2010 and 2013 (MK 8,600 in 2010 and MK 12,200 in 2013; Malawi's currency is the kwacha). However, this sector absorbed only 1 of every 10 household enterprises. Commerce and tourism generated MK 7,000 in revenue per month in 2013. The third most profitable industry—nonfood manufacturing—increased monthly revenue from MK 4,800 in 2010 to MK 5,800 in 2013. The primary sector generates the lowest earnings per month and is the only one in which returns worsened.

NFSE Activities as a Means to Improve Rural Welfare

NFSE activities are an important source of income for many rural households in Malawi. Most of the rural poor in Malawi report agriculture as their primary source of livelihood. Nevertheless, in 2013, up to 10 percent of households in rural areas derived more than 50 percent of their income from NFSE activities alone. The income earned from these activities improved well-being and reduced poverty.

Engagement in NFSE activities is associated with higher growth of consumption. According to the latest available data for Malawi, in 2010–13, participation in NFSE activities correlated with 14 percent higher consumption per capita in rural households.[3] Some poor, uneducated households may have grown their income and escaped poverty by operating nonfarm enterprises. Alternatively, households that were already better off may have invested in and operated high-return nonfarm activities. The Third Integrated Household Survey (IHS3) and Integrated Household Panel Survey (IHPS) panel data enabled us to examine the incomes of households that were poor in 2010, but managed to escape poverty afterward in 2013.

Rising income from NFSE activities was the driving force behind the poverty reduction observed in rural Malawi during 2010–13. The Shapley decomposition in figure 3.2 shows the contributions of different income sources to changes in rural poverty during 2010–13. The downward bars show the size of the poverty reduction that can be attributed to an income source. The total observed drop in the poverty rate would have been 5.5 percentage points had there been no reduction in other income sources, including livestock and nonfarm wages. Income from self-employment accounted for 44 percent of that potential reduction (2.4 of 5.5 percentage points).

Figure 3.2 Contribution of Income Sources to Changes in Rural Poverty in Malawi, 2010–13

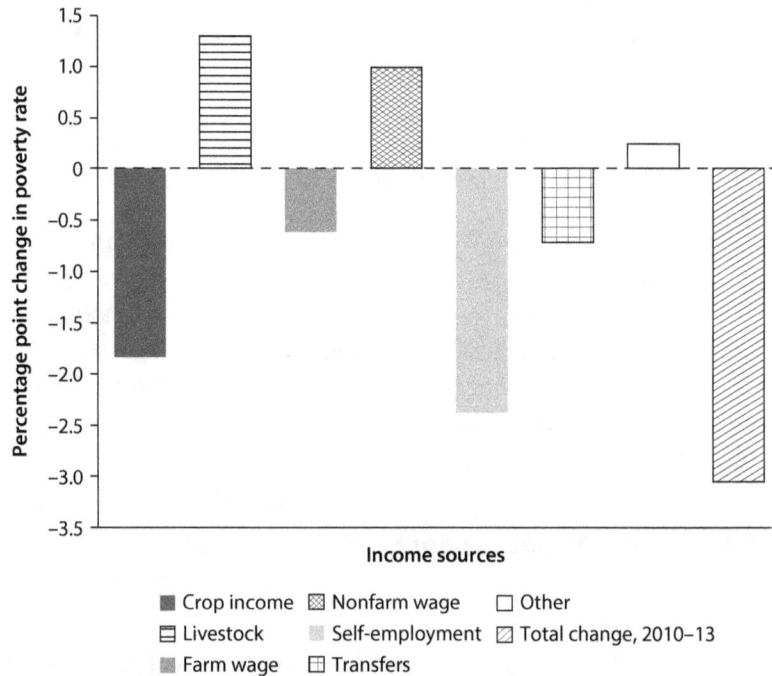

Source: World Bank 2016a.

The prominent role of NFSE income in reducing poverty is consistent with the higher rates of participation and higher returns resulting from these activities for the rural households that moved out of poverty ("climbers"). The proportion of climbers that moved out of poverty and participated in NFSE activities more than doubled between 2010 and 2013 from 14 to 29 percent. The average returns per month obtained from participating in NFSE activities also doubled from MK 2,800 in 2010 to MK 5,500 in 2013. As a result, the contribution of NFSE income to total income in rural areas for self-employed "climbers" doubled from 7 percent in 2010 to 15 percent in 2013, becoming almost as important as agricultural wage income during the same period (figure 3.3).

Taking up self-employment in the nonfarm sector also may help rural households to hedge against shocks inherent to rain-fed agriculture, such as floods and droughts. An analysis of the IHS3-IHPS panel data suggests that droughts and high food prices experienced between 2012 and 2013 increased the chances of falling into poverty for households that were nonpoor in 2010, but having a family enterprise reduced the probability of falling into poverty due to these shocks (figure 3.4).[4] This evidence is only suggestive because household exposure to shocks is endogenous to where the household members live and to the activities they carry out.

Figure 3.3 Participation Rates and Share of Total Income of Rural Households That Moved Out of Poverty, by Income Source, 2010–13

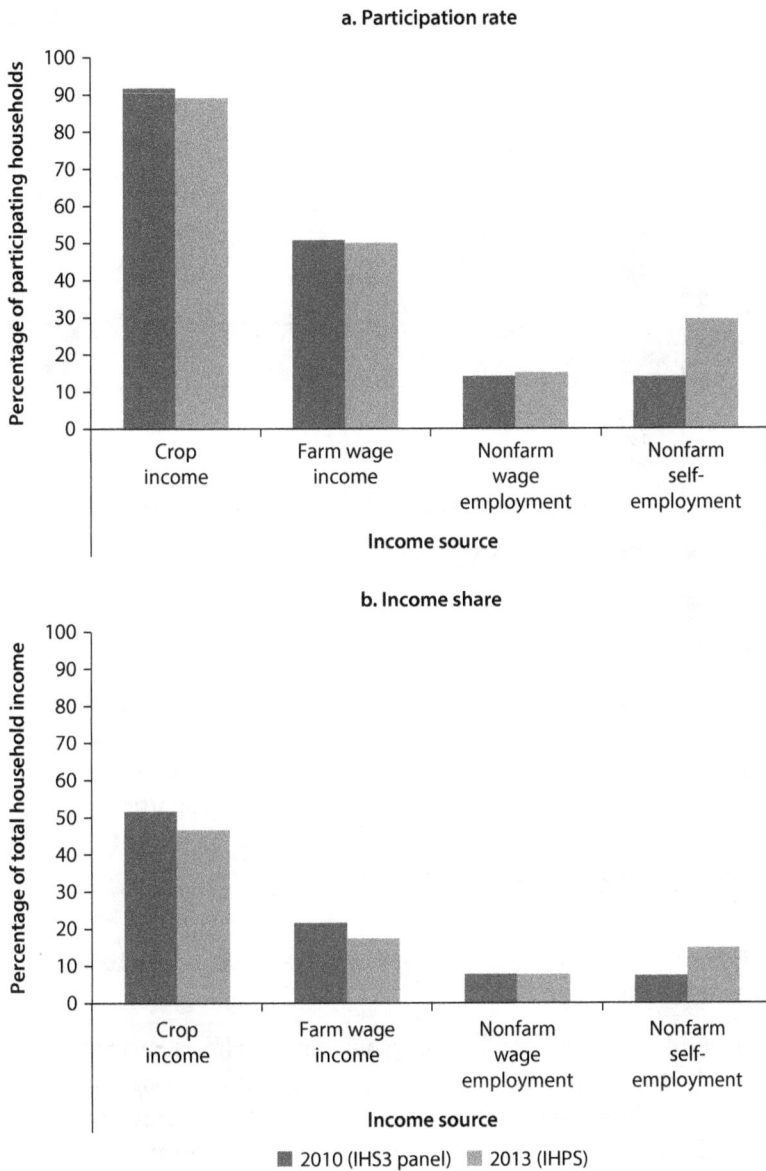

a. Participation rate

b. Income share

■ 2010 (IHS3 panel) ▨ 2013 (IHPS)

Source: World Bank 2016a.
Note: IHS3 = Third Integrated Household Survey; IHPS = Integrated Household Panel Survey.

In sum, nonfarm enterprises are correlated with higher consumption growth and less vulnerability to agricultural production and food price shocks. Poverty decompositions by income sources suggest that rising income from nonfarm business activities helped to reduce poverty in rural areas more than any other source of income between 2010 and 2013. Long-term economic development or positive

**Figure 3.4 Probability of Falling into Poverty as a Result of Shocks among Rural
Households with and without Nonfarm Enterprises in Malawi, 2010–13**

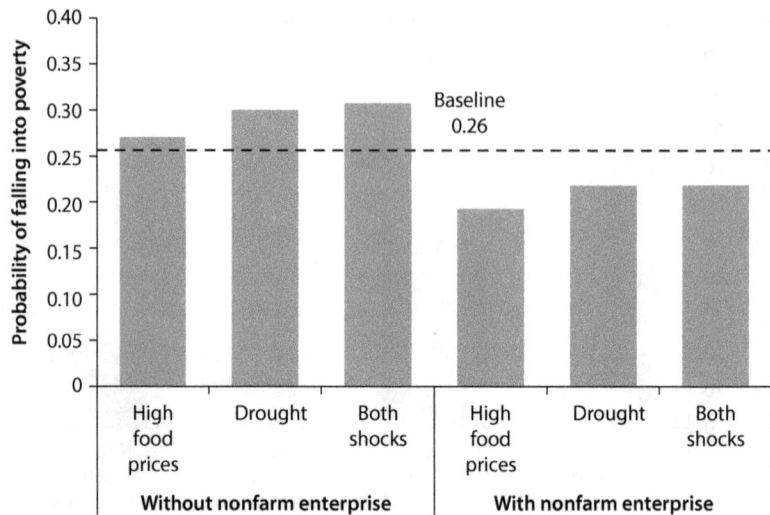

Source: Calculations are based on IHS3 panel and IHPS data.
Note: IHS3 = Third Integrated Household Survey; IHPS = Integrated Household Panel Survey.

structural transformation typically associates with the declining importance of
agriculture as more people move into higher-productivity activities within services
and industry. Thus, even though rural incomes still were not well diversified and
were concentrated in the agriculture sector, the growing proportion of households
doing NFSE activities and their positive effects on welfare suggest that a broader
process of transformation may be under way.

Lower Returns on NFSE Activities in Rural Areas (Relative to Urban Areas) and for the Poor

The leading role that rural nonfarm employment has played in structural change
in Malawi is consistent with the country's small urban population and slow
urbanization process. Figure 3.5 compares Malawi to the rest of Sub-Saharan
Africa. The horizontal axis shows the share of the total population in urban areas,
and the vertical axis shows the percentage point gap between urban and rural
population growth rates in 2014, with a higher value implying more rapid urbanization. Malawi's urbanization rate is half the regional rate. Urbanization in
Malawi is slower than in other agrarian countries with low urban population
shares, such as Ethiopia, Rwanda, and Uganda. Neighboring countries, such as
Tanzania and Zambia, display faster urbanization rates. According to World Bank
(2016b), Malawi's urban population increased 0.11 percent a year during
2010–14. This rate is below the Sub-Saharan African average of 0.48 percent and
is the eighth slowest urbanization rate in the region.

Figure 3.5 Urbanization in Countries in Sub-Saharan Africa, 2000–14

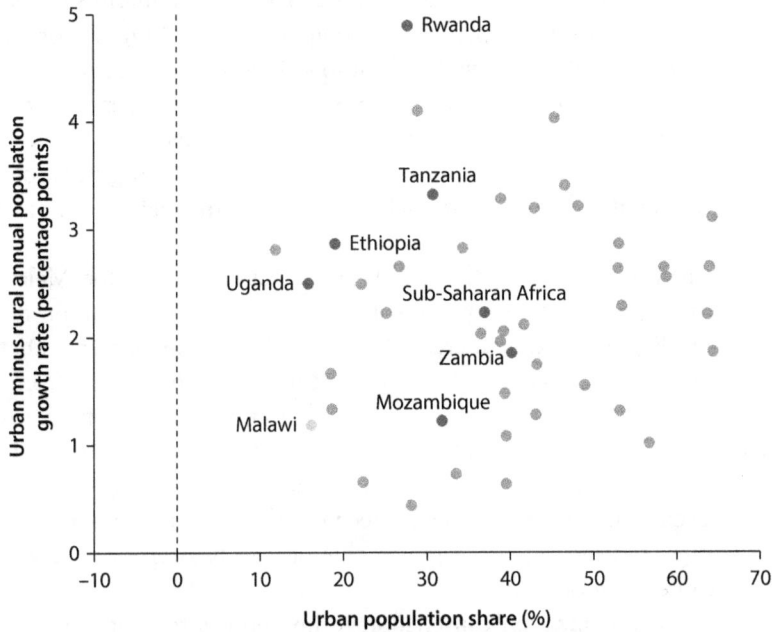

Source: World Bank 2016b.
Note: Orange dots represent other countries in Sub-Saharan Africa.

The low rate of urbanization in Malawi is not surprising at all given that an agriculture-oriented perspective lies at the heart of Malawi's first two Growth and Development Strategies (MGDS), which identified the country's policy priorities for 2006–16 (Government of Malawi 2006, 2011). Given that most poverty is concentrated in rural areas, there has been a general understanding that public investments should be directed toward agriculture to benefit the majority of Malawi's population, who are smallholder farmers living in rural areas. The MGDSs have therefore given particular emphasis to agriculture, food security, and investments in rural villages. A stated goal in both MGDSs is to slow the pace of urbanization, which is viewed as a constraint to future economic development in Malawi.

While most structural change in Malawi has taken place within rural areas, urbanization can contribute to structural change by pulling rural workers into nonfarm activities in primary cities and secondary towns.[5] Revenues from household enterprises and nonfarm wages are considerably higher in urban than in rural areas across all industry groups. The average profit from participation in self-employment was MK 23,400 per month in urban areas in 2010, which was approximately MK 18,000 higher than average returns in rural areas that same year. Workers in urban areas also earned consistently higher wages than workers in rural areas across all job categories. Chapter 5 of this report discusses the impact of increased urbanization on economic growth in Malawi.

Recent rural-urban migration patterns have indeed mirrored the economic prospects in urban areas. Between 2006 and 2010, when nonfarm sectors grew faster and poverty dropped 6 percent in urban areas, 14,000 new working-age migrants (10 years or older) arrived in Malawi's cities and secondary towns each year. Out of the 14,000 migrants, 11,000 moved to major cities, and the remaining 3,000 moved to secondary towns. This inflow of migrants accounted for more than half (that is, 2 percent) of the average annual population growth of cities and secondary towns. Therefore, internal migration was the main driver of urbanization in Malawi.

Nevertheless, according to the latest panel data available for Malawi, in 2010–13, when poverty rose 6 percent in urban areas, the population moving from one locality to another increased from 10.8 to 16.3 percent. Of these migrants, there was an increase of 9.1 percent of those who moved from rural to rural areas and a decrease of 3.9 percent of those who moved from rural to urban areas. This disparity could have been due to the 2012 change in the country's economic situation (NSO 2014).[6] Government clearly should avoid internal and external shocks that can affect the dynamism of urban areas and nonfarm wage returns, and strengthen the prospects of rural migrants for migrating and exiting poverty.

The fact that urbanization can encourage households to engage in NFSE is important because the opportunities for NFSE in poor rural areas remain precarious and limited, even despite the recent contribution of NFSE to lifting households out of poverty. Participation of rural households in NFSE rose from 20 percent in 2010 to 28 percent in 2013, but this level of participation represented a recovery to 2005 levels. Moreover, the rates were low relative to those in other low-income countries. A recent study using panel household survey data to compare NFSE in Malawi with Ethiopia, Niger, Nigeria, Tanzania, and Uganda found that Malawi had the lowest share of rural households operating a nonfarm enterprise (Nagler and Naude 2014).

In addition, the participation of households in NFSE and its associated returns are lower for the poor. Even though nonfarm growth and job creation have occurred mainly within rural areas, the poor have benefited less from this shift than the nonpoor. Between 15 and 19 percent of the rural poor in Malawi owned businesses in 2010 and 2013, respectively (compared with 22 and 31 percent, on average, nationally). Similarly, average returns for the rural poor in Malawi were MK 2,600 per month in 2010 and MK 3,200 per month in 2013. These numbers are significantly lower than the MK 7,000 per month in 2010 and MK 7,300 per month in 2013 observed, on average, among the nonpoor.

The poor are self-employed mainly in low-return activities, such as services and the sale of primary products. The highest returns for the poor in 2013 were in the construction and services sectors (MK 2,800 per month in 2010 and MK 6,500 per month in 2013). Yet again, these returns were significantly lower than the MK 8,600 per month in 2010 and MK 13,800 per month in 2013 observed for the same sectors, on average, across Malawi. More generally, apart from the

Figure 3.6 Participation and Returns from Participation in Self-Employment Activities in Rural Malawi, by Poverty Status, 2013

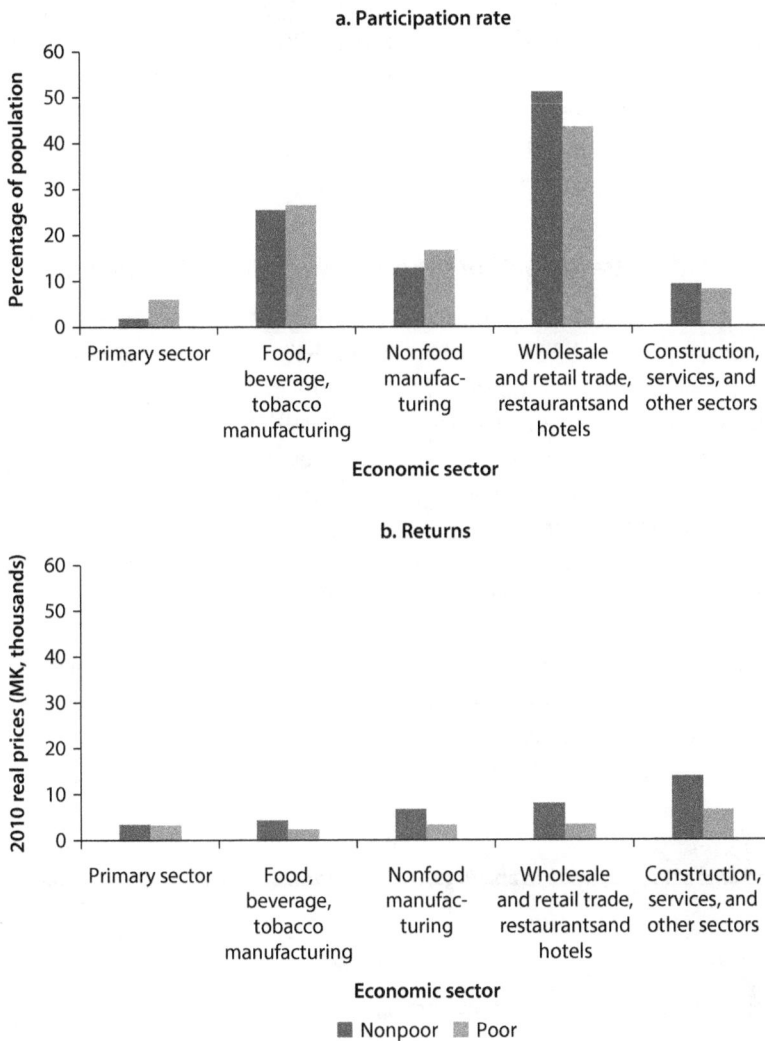

a. Participation rate

b. Returns

■ Nonpoor ▨ Poor

Source: World Bank 2016a.

primary sector, the poor earned significantly lower profits from nonfarm businesses than the nonpoor, irrespective of the sector (figure 3.6).

Women are more marginalized than men in terms of access to the most lucrative enterprise opportunities in rural areas. While the rates of participation in household enteprises are very similar by gender, female-owned household enterprises reported lower returns than male-owned enterprises in almost all industry sectors. The profits generated by male-owned enterprises in the commerce and tourism sector, where most enterprises are concentrated, are almost three times the profits in female-owned enterprises (MK 9,500 versus MK 3,600). The same situation is evident in the food, beverage, and tobacco manufacturing sector, which is the second sector of concentration of female-owned enterprises: male-owned enterprises reported an average profit of MK 9,100, while female-owned enterprises reported an average profit of MK 2,300.

Clearly, there is scope for expanding NFSE activities and improving their returns in rural areas, especially among the poor and women. The factors that increase the opportunities for households to engage in NFSE activities and earn the largest profits are addressed next.

Determinants of Participation in and Returns to NFSE Activities

The IHS3-IHPS panel surveys provided data helpful for understanding the drivers of participation in NFSE and the factors that influenced the returns to participants.[7] The bar chart in figure 3.7 reports the average marginal effects of the main factors (blue) that affect participation in NFSE as well as the factors that influence the returns (orange) to those activities. The direction of the bar indicates whether the variable has a positive (right) or negative (left) effect. The length of the bar represents the magnitude of the effect—that is, how much the probability of participation changes following a unit change in the value taken by the variable. Only variables of interest that have a statistically significant effect are reported.

Wealth and access to credit are key to starting a business or self-employment activity. Many poor households lack liquidity and often lack collateral (appendix G). Loans are sought for different uses. According to the IHPS, half (50.4 percent) of persons with a loan in 2013 borrowed to start a business venture, followed by

Figure 3.7 Key Determinants of Participation in and Returns to Nonfarm Self-Employment in Rural Malawi, 2010–13

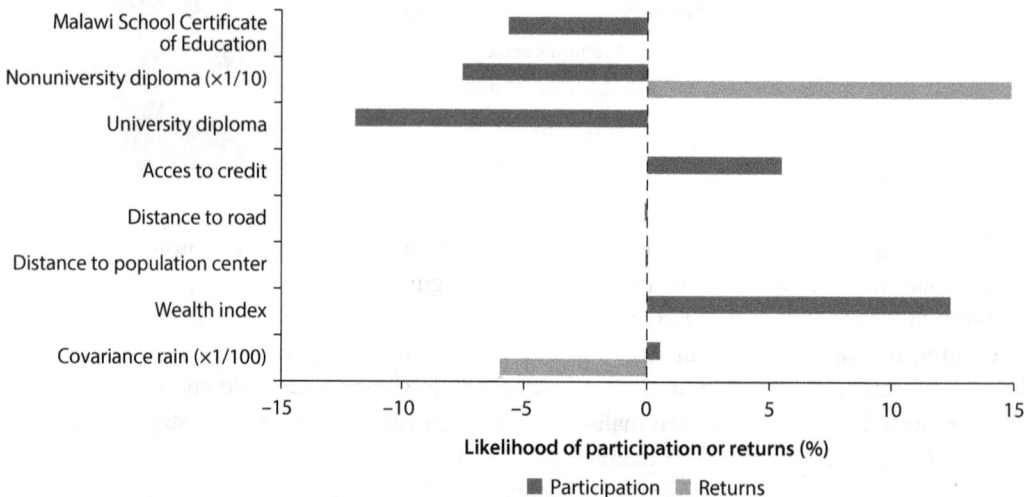

Source: World Bank 2016a.

those who borrowed to purchase agricultural inputs (21.4 percent) (NSO 2014). Having access to credit increased the chances of opening a business in rural areas by 5 percent. In fact, access to credit for the poor increased from 12 percent in 2010 to 19 percent in 2013. This increase may partly explain the increase in participation in self-employment in rural areas between 2010 and 2013.

However, most of this credit came from informal lenders. According to the IHPS, of those who obtained a loan in 2013, only 9 percent borrowed from a commercial bank. Flows from family and friends have merit, but many relatives and neighbors may be cash-strapped and unable to help their poor neighbors during covariate shocks. Thus, while friends and family may help, the formal banking system could massively expand these services, especially among the poor. Despite recent improvements in access to credit, only one in five poor Malawians have access to credit (appendix G).

Access to financial services remains low in Malawi for several reasons. Distance to financial facilities is one of the most critical factors. In order to make financial services more accessible, Opportunity International Bank of Malawi (OIBM) introduced a mobile "bank-on-wheels" service (the banking van) in rural areas where the cost of setting up permanent branches is high. Sharma and Nagarajan (2011) showed that the banking van expanded the outreach of OIBM in rural Malawi within a short period of time, reducing the direct costs of travel for depositors and lowering transaction costs. The government of Malawi could do a lot to ensure that the expansion of banking services continues and would do well to remove the hurdles that affect credit markets in rural areas. Chapter 5 provides concrete recommendations on this matter for rural Malawi.

Remoteness from roads and markets also discourages engaging in self-employment activities. Roads and population centers are located farther from the poor (appendix G), raising the transaction costs of participating in markets. As a consequence, the poor participate less in self-employment activities than the nonpoor, who have easier access to markets for buying inputs and selling their outputs. World Bank (2016a) identified access to credit and the closeness to roads and a population center of 20,000 or more people as pull factors that encourage households to engage in NFSE activities in Malawi. Urbanization—specifically, the formation of towns with a population of 20,000 or more—could create opportunities for households to engage in NFSE activities and earn higher profits.

Households turn to NFSE activities in response to covariate shocks. When climatic disasters affect crops and the conventional sources of livelihood for farmers, an alternative is to pursue activities that generate income outside agriculture. Useful as they are, informal risk-sharing arrangements almost never cover all households nor provide full protection against disasters. Therefore, NFSE may still be needed, and income diversification remains desirable. Figure 3.7 indicates that a 0.1 unit increase in the covariance of rainfall increases the likelihood of participating in NFSE by more than 5 percent in rural areas. At the same time, natural disasters often simultaneously affect many households in the local area from which the demand for services and goods comes, making it difficult to generate higher profits. Providing weather insurance to business owners may improve their chances to engage in nonfarm activities as a choice, not a necessity, and, at the same time, providing insurance to others in the village or town could ensure their continued create demand for goods and services originating from these activities.

When people acquire more education, their likelihood of participating in NFSE declines (because the returns to nonfarm wage activities are higher). The negative effect of educational attainment on participation starts at the Junior Certificate of Education (JCE) level.[8] There is no difference in the expected probability of participating in NFSE between individuals with less than a Malawi School Certificate of Education (MSCE) and individuals with no education. Earning a nonuniversity diploma substantially increases an individual's profits from a household business relative to having no education. Most individuals in rural areas have not earned a university degree or postgraduate degree. At the end of secondary school, students take the MSCE examination. Entry into the University of Malawi is very competitive because space is limited. Only a small percentage of successful candidates are selected for a university education. Some successful candidates who fail to get places at the University of Malawi find places in teacher training, technical, and other colleges for career training courses that provide nonuniversity diplomas. Some of these skills and training could well be applied in self-employment activities.

Summary

Expanded nonfarm activities and income diversification are likely features of economic development in any developing country and could improve welfare. Recent patterns of economic growth suggest that Malawi's economy is very gradually shifting away from agriculture and into nonfarm sectors. Participation in nonfarm activities such as self-employment is associated with higher growth of consumption and, therefore, remains a potential avenue for lifting rural households out of poverty. However, the opportunities for NFSE remain limited and precarious in rural Malawi, where most household enterprises are operated informally from home by young uneducated males. As a result, the returns from nonfarm activities are lower in rural than in urban areas and for the poor than for the nonpoor, so there is scope for improvement.

Wealth and income for investment create opportunities to venture into NFSE. Similarly beneficial is better connecting people to the markets that demand the services offered by these activities. Training and technical skills also can improve the chances of higher returns. Unlocking all of these components can increase the supply of and returns from self-employment activities. On the demand side, nonfarm activities rely heavily on local demand. Access to insurance services for weather-related shocks is limited in Malawi. Rainfall shocks that affect everyone can therefore reduce the demand for goods and services provided by family enterprises. This in turn affects the returns obtained from these activities. During the period covered by this book, no major rains or drought occurred that could have affected profits. Well-functioning safety nets also could protect the welfare of those affected by disasters and help them to avoid joining the ranks of the self-employed out of necessity. For persons already self-employed, effective safety nets could improve the prospects of staying in business. Chapter 4 discusses the performance of safety nets in growing rural incomes.

Notes

1. In this analysis, nonfarm employment comprises both self-employment and wage employment.

2. This is consistent with the Integrated Household Panel Survey (IHPS) data, on which this chapter is largely based, which show that wholesale and retail trade as well as restaurants dominate nonfarm self-employment in Malawi.

3. Using panel regression methods and controlling for other determinants of per capita expenditures such as household characteristics, education, and location, the pooled ordinary least squares regression model, the random-effects model, and the fixed-effects models were estimated, finding consistent results.

4. Figure 3.4 shows the change in probability of falling into poverty between 2010 and 2013, calculated from a probit model. The model results from changing the presence of nonfarm family enterprises in the household and the occurrence of high food prices or a drought vis-à-vis a baseline in which the average household is located in the rural south and has a household head who is male, has no education, and has not changed his labor status between rounds (in both rounds is employed, in both rounds is unemployed, or in both rounds is out of the labor force).

5. Following World Bank (2016b), this book separates urban areas into "primary cities" (for example, Blantyre, Lilongwe, Mzuzu, and Zomba) and "secondary towns" (for example, Balaka, Dedza, Karonga, Kasungu, Liwonde, Luchenza, Mangochi, and Salima). This classification is not based solely on population size, but rather on an urban center's orientation toward nonagricultural activities, population density, and availability of services.

6. Recent internal and external shocks affected nonfarm wage returns and the prospects of exiting poverty in urban areas. Politics and inflation are some of the causes of internal shocks. External, or exogenous, shocks emanate from climate shocks and global economic crisis. The average gap between urban and rural areas in self-employment profits was MK 18,000 and the average wage difference between urban and rural workers was MK 10,800 in 2010. Such urban-rural gaps narrowed during the economic crisis following the depreciation of the kwacha in December 2012, which led to an economic contraction in urban areas and an increase in poverty of 6 percent (reversing the gains achieved in the second half of the 2000s). In 2013, the average gap in profits dropped to MK 5,600 (MK 13,000 in urban versus MK 6,400 in rural areas) and so did the average wage difference between urban and rural workers, which dropped to MK 6,800 per month. Although wages earned in both urban and rural areas fell, wages fell more sharply in urban areas.

7. A Heckman two-stage selection model was used to investigate the determinants of participation in nonfarm self-employment activities and the determinants of returns to participation. The dependent variable to estimate returns is the annual profit

earned from household businesses. Information for 2010 and 2013 is pooled for these regressions. The two-stage model is used to account for the selection issue that arises when exploring the determinants of returns to participation among participants who self-selected.

8. After two years of secondary education, students write the national JCE examination. At the end of secondary school, students write the Malawi School Certificate of Education (MSCE) examination. Students can choose to take examinations in a minimum of six subjects and more if desired, but only the top six are counted toward the final score. MSCE results also are used to select candidates for training courses and employment. Students who do very well in MSCE and pass the University of Malawi entrance examination are selected into university education.

References

Government of Malawi. 2006. "Malawi Growth and Development Strategy. From Poverty to Prosperity. 2006-2011." Malawi.

———. 2012. "Second Malawi Growth and Development Strategy 2011-2016." Malawi.

Nagler, P. and W. Naude. 2014. "Non-Farm Enterprises in Rural Africa: New Empirical Evidence." Policy Research Working Paper 7066, World Bank, Washington, DC.

NSO (National Statistical Office). 2014. "IHPS—Integrated Household Panel Survey 2010–2013." Government of Malawi, Zomba, Malawi.

Sharma, D., and G. Nagarajan. 2011. "Rural Finance Outreach in Central Malawi: Implications for Opportunity International Bank of Malawi." Financial Services Assessment, IRIS Center, University of Maryland, College Park.

World Bank. 2016a. "Malawi Poverty Assessment." World Bank, Washington, DC.

———. 2016b. "Malawi Urbanization Review: Leveraging Urbanization for National Growth and Development." World Bank, Washington, DC.

CHAPTER 4

Social Protection and Poverty

Introduction

Chapters 2 and 3 explored how the labor incomes of the rural poor can be improved by increasing productivity in agriculture, the sector in which most poor people in Malawi are engaged, as well as by facilitating movement into new, more productive activities outside agriculture. Nevertheless, many poor households need basic support to increase their incomes and elevate themselves out of poverty. Nutritional interventions and cash transfers (CTs) can help the poor meet their most basic needs and improve the income opportunities of future generations through investments in health and education. To sustain income over their life cycle, the poor and vulnerable also need to be protected from uninsured risk arising from recurrent shocks, such as natural disasters. Transfers targeted at the poorest and most vulnerable can help them to manage risks and avoid costly responses in hard times.

With more than half of the population living in poverty, the Malawi government has made significant efforts to provide support to poor and vulnerable groups through various social protection (SP) programs. In 2013, the Malawi government adopted the National Social Support Policy (NSSP) to enhance the effectiveness, efficiency, and coordination of all social protection programs. In the same year, the government allowed major SP programs to scale up in response to worsening economic conditions that could have adverse impacts on the poor.

This chapter reviews the current system of social protection (SP) in Malawi, and explores ways to strengthen and expand it. The first section sketches the current SP framework and reviews its budget and performance at reaching the poor; it also assesses whether two of its main programs have managed to protect welfare: the Malawi Social Action Fund–Public Works Program (MASAF-PWP) and the Social Cash Transfer Program (SCTP). The next section points at the main shortcomings of MASAF-PWP. The final section compares MASAF-PWP with similar programs in other low-income and lower-middle-income countries to identify lessons for improving its performance.

The chapter finds that Malawi's SP programs have low overall budgets relative to international standards. SCTP has positive impacts on welfare, but remains small in coverage. MASAF-PWP has a wider reach, but does not improve food security nor increase the use of fertilizer among its beneficiaries. MASAF-PWP has the potential to represent a key safety net for households, but has failed so far to realize its protective role on food security due to a combination of rationing, poor targeting performance, and low transfer amounts. On the basis of a review of other public work programs, there is still a compelling need for a social protection system that provides broader and better coverage to the poor and guarantees a faster and more appropriate response to shocks, by promoting a rapid rollout of programs during the lean season, increased responsiveness of geographical targeting to large weather shocks, and improving access and flexibility of households to take up safety net programs after being affected by shocks.

Malawi's Imperfect Social Protection Programs

Overview of Current Social Protection System

The current SP framework laid out in the NSSP identifies three groups as potential beneficiaries of SP programs: the intrinsically destitute, or ultra-poor, who include households headed by orphans and the abandoned elderly who will need support no matter what; the able-bodied extremely poor households with low productivity or very few assets and small landholdings, who could be helped with supplemental income and complementary capital or agricultural inputs to improve their productivity; and the moderately poor, whose consumption from subsistence agriculture keeps them in a reasonable position, but who often will need a temporary safety net.

At the same time, the government has identified four types of interventions to support these groups: (a) the ultra-poor receive cash transfers in return for providing labor on public works, which build productive community assets; (b) those who are most vulnerable and labor constrained, including the elderly, disabled, and sick, receive unconditional social cash transfers (SCTP); (c) school-age children receive meals through school feeding programs; and (d) poor households receive micro-credit and village savings from public work earnings and loan schemes coupled with livelihood and skills development interventions (Community Savings and Investment Promotion, COMSIP) to enable them to "graduate" from public work.[1] Table 4.1 provides an overview of the main social protection programs in Malawi.

The shift to direct cash transfers targeting ultra-poor people is particularly recent. These programs are primarily donor funded. Many CT programs are small scale and operate in a few districts or during a certain season. The SCTP, currently funded mainly by the European Union, has the biggest CT coverage. SCTP started as a pilot project in 2006 and is expected to scale up to a national program by 2017. As of 2014–15, the SCTP budget was US$18.4 million.

Table 4.1 Major Social Protection Interventions in Malawi

Program	Geographic distribution	Beneficiaries	Target group	Targeting mechanism	Benefits
Malawi Social Action Fund–Public Works Program	All 28 districts	450,131 households (as of November–December 2015)	Poor and credit-constrained households	Pro-poor geographic targeting, followed by a combination of community-based targeting (eligible households) and self-selection (participating households) via a low wage rate	Daily wages (MK 600) for 48 days a year, in two cycles (planting season from October to December and postharvest season from June to July). The cycles are subdivided into two consecutive 12-day waves. Payments are made within one to two weeks of the end of each wave
Social Cash Transfer Program	18 districts	170,114 households or 754,694 people (as of March 2016)	Ultra-poor and labor-constrained households with no able-bodied adult ages 19–64 years or with more than three dependents per working-age adult	Community-based targeting and proxy-means testing	12 monthly cash transfers: 1 member = MK 1,700; 2 members = MK 2,200; 3 members = MK 2,900; 4+ members = MK 3,700; + MK 500 per primary-school-age child; + MK 1,000 per secondary-school-age child
School Feeding Program	13 districts	635,000 students as of 2010	Primary-school-going children	Geographic targeting (food insecurity, enrollment, attendance, and dropout rates)	School meals and monthly take-home rations of 12.5 kilograms of maize

Sources: Beegle, Galasso, and Goldberg 2015; Davis and Handa 2015; UNICEF-UNC Transfer Project website (https://transfer.cpc.unc.edu/); World Bank 2011.

Note: MK = kwacha.

Figure 4.1 Major Programs as a Share of the Social Protection Budget in Malawi, 2014–15

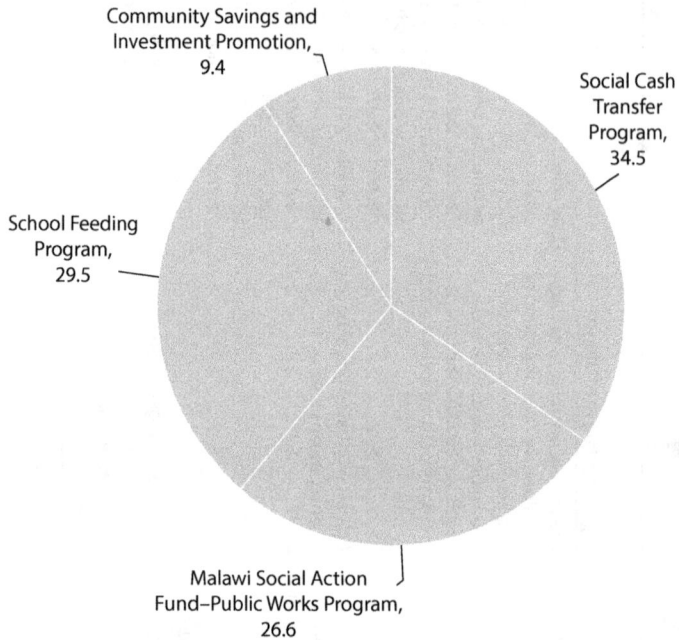

percent

Community Savings and Investment Promotion, 9.4

Social Cash Transfer Program, 34.5

School Feeding Program, 29.5

Malawi Social Action Fund–Public Works Program, 26.6

Source: Local Development Fund 2015 (e-mail communication).

Small Social Protection Budget

The amount of public spending on social protection in Malawi is low by international standards. The government's annual budget for SP programs was US$53.2 million in 2014–15.[2] This spending accounted for only 2.9 percent of total government expenditure and represented approximately 0.8 percent of gross domestic product (GDP). On the basis of international standards, Malawi's social protection budget is less than two-thirds of the average spending on social protection in Sub-Saharan Africa.[3]

As of 2014–15, the two largest social protection programs in terms of budget were the SCTP and MASAF-PWP. Together, these two programs accounted for more than 60 percent of the SP budget. However, they were relatively small in size, at 0.3 and 0.2 percent of GDP, respectively.[4]

The School Feeding Program is another important part of the SP budget. Although several programs operate across Malawi, the biggest ones are funded by the World Food Programme and by Mary's Meals. Figure 4.1 provides the relative sizes of major SP programs as a share of the SP budget.

High Inclusion Rate of the Nonpoor

Social programs have limited coverage in Malawi, but most have expanded recently. In 2010, only the School Feeding Program reached more than

10 percent of the population. In 2013, major SP programs were scaled up in response to a deteriorating economic situation induced by a sharp depreciation of the exchange rate, sporadic fuel shortages, a rise in inflation to almost 35 percent, and a public financial management crisis. MASAF-PWP alone covered nearly 15 percent of the population.

In addition to limited coverage, social assistance programs in Malawi experienced high leakage rates. Table 4.2 presents the leakage rates (or inclusion errors), defined as the percentage of individuals who receive transfers and are not poor; exclusion errors, defined as the percentage of poor individuals who do not receive transfers; and coverage, defined as the percentage of the population who receives the transfer. In 2013, across most social assistance programs, at least 50 percent of the beneficiaries were not poor, on the basis of the national poverty line. That same year, around 6 of every 10 beneficiaries receiving support from the MASAF-PWP or direct cash transfers from the government at the time were nonpoor. The next sections detail the effectiveness of MASAF-PWP and the SCTP.

Table 4.2 Coverage Rates, Exclusion Errors, and Inclusion Errors of Selected Social Safety Net Programs in Malawi, 2013

percent

Program	Coverage of total population	Exclusion error of the extremely poor	Inclusion error of the nonextremely poor	Exclusion error of the poor	Inclusion error of the nonpoor
School Feeding Program	18	86	91	82	62
MASAF-PWP	15	85	89	84	59
Free maize	10	94	93	90	63
Free food (other than maize)	7	95	93	93	62
Other (specify)	3	99	96	97	59
Food or cash-for-work program	2	98	83	99	67
Inputs-for-work program	1	100	95	99	71
Other direct cash transfers	1	100	95	100	87
Scholarships or bursaries for secondary education	1	99	80	99	50
Free distribution of likuni phala to children and mothers[a]	1	98	59	99	36
Direct cash transfers from government	0	99	66	100	59
Scholarships for tertiary education	0	99	77	100	77
Supplementary feeding for malnourished children at a nutritional rehabilitation unit	0	100	81	100	76

Source: World Bank 2016.
Note: MASAF-PWP = Malawi Social Action Fund–Public Works Program.
a. Likuni phala = porridge made of maize.

Welfare Impact of MASAF-PWP

As the second largest SP program in budget spending, MASAF-PWP seeks to improve both food security and the use of agricultural inputs. First, the program aims to provide cash to poor and able-bodied households in exchange for their short-term labor. For a 48-day project, the total payment amounts to US$44—a substantial sum compared with the country's annual per capita gross national income of US$320 (World Bank 2015). In addition, the program intends (at least in past years) to enable poor, credit-constrained households to finance the purchase of subsidized fertilizer and improved maize seeds by implementing the public work program (PWP) in the planting months of the main agricultural season when the Farm Input Subsidy Program (FISP) vouchers are also distributed.

Although other public work programs in Sub-Saharan Africa have shown positive impacts on welfare (box 4.1), MASAF-PWP has not demonstrated similar performance. Indeed, the program has had an insignificant impact on food security. A large-scale randomized controlled trial (RCT) was conducted during the 2012–13 agricultural season in Malawi to estimate the short-run impacts of the program. The surveys found that households offered PWP did not have more lean-season food security than those not offered the program. Across all eight

---

Box 4.1 Evidence of Positive Welfare Impacts of Public Work Programs in Africa

The Productive Safety Nets Program (PSNP) in Ethiopia, which is the second largest social safety net in Africa, has had significant welfare impacts when offered with agricultural support packages. In addition, the program is linked to the Other Food Security Program, which provides credit and agricultural extension services and funds irrigation and water harvesting schemes (World Bank and United Nations 2010). A survey in 2008 revealed that the beneficiaries were more likely to be food secure, to use improved agricultural technologies, and to operate nonfarm businesses.

The Labor Intensive Public Works Program (LIPWP) in Ghana has had positive impacts on employment, food consumption expenditure, and food security for children.

Participants of Cash for Work in Sierra Leone increased their monthly incomes by 26 percent. In addition, participants significantly increased the likelihood of creating enterprises and investing in homes and existing businesses. The program also increased asset accumulation in small livestock.

However, it is not clear which components of these successful programs were effective in yielding positive welfare impacts. Complementary interventions may be a key to the success of PSNP. According to World Bank (2015), PSNP in Ethiopia had various innovative features, such as public work activities to strengthen climate resilience, a risk-financing facility to help households to cope better with transitory shocks, and targeting methods to identify and assist the community members most vulnerable to climate shocks.

Other public work programs share some common features that may explain why MASAF-PWP has not proved successful. These features are discussed in the section "Lessons Learned from Public Work Programs in Low-Income and Lower-Middle-Income Countries".

---

indicators for food security outcomes as well as the principal components analysis index for these eight measures, the effect of PWP on households receiving it compared with households not receiving it was not statistically different from zero (Beegle, Galasso, and Goldberg 2015).

In addition, MASAF-PWP beneficiaries did not display increased application of fertilizer. While households participating in the PWP were more likely to receive fertilizer subsidy coupons, which was in line with the intended link between MASAF-PWP and FISP, there was no evidence that these households used fertilizer more than households not part of the PWP. In fact, there was no statistical difference in the expenditure on fertilizer and the quantity of fertilizer used between households that received PWP and households that did not (Beegle, Galasso, and Goldberg 2015).

Positive Results from SCTP

The main objective of SCTP is to tackle extreme poverty. SCTP aims to target extremely poor and labor-constrained households. To be eligible, households must reside in the bottom expenditure quintile and below the national extreme poverty line. Moreover, they must either have no household member age 19–64 capable of working or have more than three dependents per working-age adult.

Besides its poverty-related objective, the program aims to raise children's school enrollment and attendance. Specifically, by providing an additional transfer for each child in primary school and an even higher transfer for each child in secondary school, the program encourages households to keep their children in school.

Early impact assessments of the pilot SCTP show that it has been effective in increasing households' consumption and investment in productive assets and reducing vulnerability to shocks. Several analyses that are based on data collected for a pilot impact evaluation survey of SCTP in the Mchinji District from 2007 to 2008 have found that households participating in SCTP had higher consumption (Cohn 2012; Miller 2011; Miller, Tsoka, and Reichert 2011; Romeo, Asfaw, and Davis 2013), higher ownership of and investment in productive agricultural assets (Bonne and others 2013; Covarrubias, Davis, and Winters 2012; Miller 2011), and less vulnerability to seasonal shocks (Cohn 2012).

Moreover, the pilot SCTP improved children's health, education, and labor outcomes. Specifically, children in beneficiary households had lower risk of being sick, higher odds of using health care services, higher educational expenditures, fewer absences, and lower labor participation outside the home (Baird and others 2015; Luseno and others 2014; Miller and Tsoka 2012; Romeo, Asfaw, and Davis 2013).

Recent results from a three-year impact evaluation of SCTP further confirm the effectiveness of SCTP in multiple domains, including food security, asset holdings, health and education, and psychological well-being. This extensive impact evaluation covered more than 3,300 households in two districts, Salima and Mangochi, from 2013 to 2016. The results showed that the take-up rate is high: approximately 95–99 percent of eligible beneficiary households were enrolled and received payments from the program. By the endline of the survey, beneficiary households were consuming significantly more food, and also investing more in livestock and productive assets such as agricultural inputs. These households also were less likely to make purchases on credit and more likely to pay their debts. Children in SCTP benefited as well. They had higher school enrollment rates and more regular school attendance. They also were fed better and more frequently. The children were less likely to be sick and, when ill, more likely to seek treatment. The qualitative component of the impact evaluation found that beneficiary households were more optimistic about the future and less distressed overall (Angeles 2016; Angeles and others 2016). Finally, these findings were consistent with results from cash transfer programs being implemented in other developing countries (box 4.2).

Box 4.2 Evidence of Positive Impacts of Cash Transfers in Developing Countries

Studies have reported strong welfare impacts of cash transfers. Gertler, Martinez, and Rubio-Codina (2012) showed how, in Mexico, cash transfers increased investment in agricultural production as well as consumption. CT recipients used 74 percent of the transfers on consumption and invested the rest in productive assets. After 18 months, recipients had increased their agricultural income 10 percent. Angelucci, Attanasio, and Di Maro (2012) found positive effects of CTs on the consumption of nondurable and durable goods and on saving and borrowing in Mexico. Evans and Popova (2014) reviewed 19 studies on the impact of cash transfers on the purchase of temptation goods and found no significant impact.

Cash transfers also support the development of microenterprises. Bianchi and Bobba (2013) found that they also increased entry into entrepreneurship in Mexico and that the CT program promoted entrepreneurship by increasing participants' willingness to take risks. Five years after one-time cash transfers were provided to microenterprise owners, De Mel, McKenzie, and Woodruff (2012) found a 10-percentage-point increase in enterprise survival rates and higher profits for male-owned businesses.

Cash transfers are more effective in smoothing consumption when they are given more frequently and in a more timely manner. Bazzi, Sumarto, and Suryahadi (2015) investigated the importance of timely receipt of CTs to deal with negative income shocks in Indonesia. Haushofer and Shapiro (2013) examined how the frequency of transfers affected food consumption. These authors found that monthly transfers of small amounts were more likely to improve food security, whereas lump-sum transfers were more likely to be spent on durables.

Furthermore, with regular and predictable payments, cash transfers could help households to increase productive investment by reducing credit constraints and managing risk. Rigorous impact evaluations of CT programs in seven countries in Africa carried out by the Food and Agriculture Organization's From Protection to Production Project found that cash transfers had positive impacts on long-term land investment, accumulation of productive assets, value and volume of crop production, and saving (Asfaw and others 2012; Berhane and others 2015; Daidone, Davis, and others 2014; Daidone, Dewbre, and others 2014; Pellerano and others 2014; Sudhanshu and others 2014).

Possible Reasons for Low Impacts of MASAF-PWP

The evaluation of MASAF-PWP point to a lack of impact on key outcomes. This section delves into potential reasons for the failure of MASAF-PWP at the time it was assessed in 2012–2013 to raise welfare and improve food security.

Mis-Targeting

MASAF-PWP is designed to target the poor through a two-stage approach: pro-poor geographic targeting followed by a combination of community-based targeting and self-selection of beneficiaries. First, the amount of funds allocated to each of the 28 districts in the program is based on that district's population, poverty rates, and other measures of vulnerability. Second, once the districtwide budget is set and a subset of extension planning areas is selected, the fund is allocated to villages in which a group of village headmen works with village committees to select eligible households. Finally, the wage is meant to be so low that only the poor would choose to participate in the PWP.

The program is rationed nationally with funding sufficient to cover only 15 percent of eligible households. Therefore, targeting issues are expected to be prominent. For instance, among participating households, many are not poor farmers, as initially targeted by the program. Table 4.2 illustrates this high rate of leakage. Such inclusion errors are likely to contribute to ineffective targeting. The poor targeting performance of MASAF-PWP can be better examined at each stage of targeting—namely, community-based targeting and self-selection.

First, MASAF-PWP's community-based targeting is not efficient. There is little correlation between the food security levels of households and their participation in the program, which may suggest that the village selection process is based on different criteria than those used to measure poverty and food security. The orange line in figure 4.2 presents the participation rate of households chosen by the village across the distribution of baseline food consumption, indicating that villages are as likely to select better-off households as to select poor households to participate in PWP.

Self-selection into the program does not seem to work either. When households were randomly offered to participate in the PWP without being screened through the village selection process, the average take-up rate was uniformly approximately 50 percent across the distribution of baseline food consumption (blue line in figure 4.2). This take-up rate indicates that the wage was high enough to attract richer as well as poor households.

Suboptimal Timing of PWP Implementation

MASAF-PWP is implemented in two cycles. The first cycle takes place during the planting season between October and December to align with the distribution of FISP vouchers. The second cycle is carried out during the postharvest period, June and July, to promote micro-savings and investments. The government offers PWP after the harvest season to encourage households to earn additional income to invest in productive activities or to hedge against shocks.

Figure 4.2 MASAF's Targeting Scheme

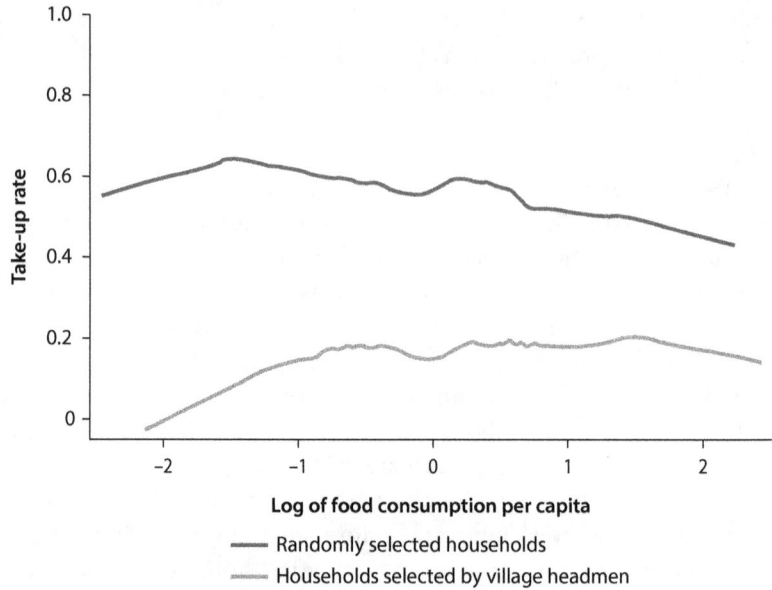

Source: Beegle, Galasso, and Goldberg 2015.
Note: MASAF = Malawi Social Action Fund.

The timing of PWP implementation during the planting season may not be optimal, as it does not promote the use of fertilizer coupons (Beegle, Galasso, and Goldberg 2015). As a result, the program fails to improve agricultural productivity through the use of inputs, which is one of its twin objectives, and, at the same time, diverts resources away from the lean season, when households struggle to meet their needs.

Insufficient Transfer Amount
The fact that wages paid to PWP households do not translate into increased consumption suggests that the transfer amounts may be insufficient to improve food security. With a total transfer amount of US$44 spread over six months, the amount of additional income may not be enough to improve the consumption of households significantly. Compared with similar PWPs implemented in other low-income and lower-middle-income countries, the total transfer amount from MASAF-PWP is in the lower bound (see table H.1 in appendix H).

Lack of Complementary Support
Although MASAF-PWP aims to improve agricultural productivity by encouraging the use of agricultural inputs, the program offers no additional support to boost productivity, such as extension services, except cash. There is no evidence that households participating in PWP use fertilizer differently than households not participating. Although fertilizer use is unchanged in the central and southern

regions, it is higher in both participant and nonparticipant households in the north (Beegle, Galasso, and Goldberg 2015). This lack of difference indicates that farmers may not have the necessary knowledge about the optimal amount of fertilizer to use.

Lessons Learned from Public Work Programs in Low-Income and Lower-Middle-Income Countries

In light of the problems highlighted above within MASAF-PWP, this section now summarizes the lessons learned from public work programs in other low-income and lower-middle-income countries and compares them with MASAF-PWP in Malawi.

PWPs are used as social protection tools in various countries. The impacts of PWPs on reducing poverty depend on how well the poor are covered and whether the benefits are sufficient—that is, they depend on the transfer amounts, targeting, and timing of the programs.

Transfer amounts. Compared with PWPs in other low-income and lower-middle-income countries, the total transfer amount from MASAF-PWP is relatively small. Although the daily wage from MASAF-PWP is similar to the wage provided by other programs, the maximum number of working days per year is much lower, yielding a comparatively low total transfer amount. For comparison, MASAF-PWP offers households a sum of US$0.62 purchasing power parity (PPP) a year, whereas the Mahatma Gandhi National Rural Employment Guarantee Scheme (MGNREGS) in India provides US$12.67 PPP. This amount can be as high as US$15.44 PPP in the PSNP in Ethiopia and US$225.97 PPP in Ghana. A 2015 World Bank assessment of safety nets in 157 countries found that, in most countries, the size of the safety net transfers was inadequate to close the poverty gap (World Bank 2015). Given that Malawi's transfer amount is much lower than that of any of the other countries, it is reasonable to assume that it is not sufficient to close Malawi's poverty gap.

Targeting. There are two principal types of targeting: *poverty-based targeting* and *self-targeting*. For example, the MGNREGS in India is not specifically targeted to the poor. It guarantees a certain number of days of employment to anyone needing a job. In practice, however, many poor individuals self-select into the program given the low wages offered. The PSNP in Ethiopia targets chronically food-insecure households. Proxy means tests are costly to implement and effective for identifying long-term poverty, but not short-term shocks. MASAF-PWP does bring a combination of approaches to target its beneficiaries. However, given that many of the poor are excluded and the program benefits a large share of the nonpoor, there is still need to strengthen its targeting performance. Building registries and management information system platforms is expensive, but critical for successful poverty-based targeting.

Timing. Comparable PWPs elsewhere are less restrictive in the season of the year in which the labor opportunities are offered. For example, in India, households hit by an idiosyncratic shock can join MGNREGS as needed throughout the year, providing more insurance against shocks. In contrast, MASAF-PWP limits the availability of public works to a few months a year.

Additional supports. Other PWPs provide additional support such as employment training and extra cash for unexpected shocks. For example, in Ethiopia, public work is offered mainly during the lean season. However, additional food and cash assistance is provided when unpredicted shocks occur. According to World Bank (2015), when droughts caused food shortages and famine in East Africa in 2011, Ethiopia was the only country in the region in which the poverty rate did not increase. During the droughts, PSNP expanded coverage from 6.5 million to 9.6 million and increased the duration of benefits from six to nine months a year. By contrast, MASAF-PWP is not catered for addressing unexpected shocks and is inflexible. Therefore, households have fewer opportunities to insure against shocks.

Summary

Malawi's social programs mainly comprise cash transfers, school meals, and public works. This social protection system, although recently expanded, is characterized both by low expenditure by international standards and very limited coverage. In addition, the targeting of such programs is not very pro-poor and needs to be revisited. In 2014/15, the annual budget for social protection programs accounted for approximately 0.8 percent of GDP, less than two-thirds of the average spending among countries in Sub-Saharan Africa. Given the low budget, in 2013 for instance, each SP program covered less than 10 percent of the poor population, with the exception of the School Feeding Program and MASAF-PWP. In addition to limited coverage, social assistance programs in Malawi experienced high leakage rates, with about 6 of every 10 beneficiaries being nonpoor in the MASAF-PWP and direct cash transfers from government at the time. Despite their multiple positive impacts, the coverage of social cash transfers targeting the extremely or ultra-poor remains minuscule relative to need. It is desirable the ongoing strengthening and expansion of the Social Cash Transfer program as a means toward putting in place an effective safety net for the extreme poor. Moreover, the MASAF-PWP, the second largest social protection program in Malawi, provides relatively low levels of benefits and has not had a significant impact on welfare when assessed. There is scope for improving the MASAF-PWP program and for designing a new insurance program or enhancing the insurance role of existing ones.

Notes

1. Public works beneficiaries have been organized into savings groups under the MASAF-supported COMSIP.
2. Excluding pension budget.
3. The average SSN spending as percentage of GDP for Sub-Saharan Africa from 2010–2016 is 1.35 based on ASPIRE. (The Atlas of Social Protection Indicators of

Resilience and Equity). The World Bank's ASPIRE online tool is the most up-to-date compilation of global social protection and labor (SPL) estimates, including data from 120 countries—mostly those that are low income and lower middle income. ASPIRE provides open and accessible household-level data on populations' social and economic status; assessments of SPL programs, including weaknesses such as low coverage and poor targeting; SPL program impacts on poverty and inequality; and ways to improve household data collection for SPL programs.

4. A recent report from the International Labour Organization also confirmed that the SCTP and MASAF-PWP are the two biggest social protection programs, although their calculation of the sizes of these two programs as a share of GDP is slightly different from ours (Juergens and Pellerano 2016).

References

Angeles, G. 2016. "Three-Year Impact Results from Malawi's Social Cash Transfer Programme (SCTP)." Presentation at the Transfer Project Workshop, University of North Carolina and University of Malawi Centre for Social Research, Addis Ababa, April 7.

Angeles, G., C. Barrington, S. Handa, P. Mvula, and M. Tsoka. 2016. "Malawi Social Cash Transfer Program. Endline Impact Evaluation Report." University of North Carolina at Chapel Hill and University of Malawi Centre for Social Research.

Angelucci, M., O. Attanasio, and V. Di Maro. 2012. "The Impact of Oportunidades on Consumption, Savings, and Transfers." *Fiscal Studies* 33 (3): 305–34.

Asfaw, S., B. Davis, J. Dewbre, G. Federighi, S. Handa, and P. Winters. 2012. "The Impact of the Kenya CT-OVC Program on Productive Activities and Labor Allocation." FAO (Food and Agriculture Organization of the United Nations), Rome, November.

Baird, S., E.Chirwa, C. McIntosh, and B. Ozler. 2015. *What Happens Once the Intervention Ends? The Medium-Term Impacts of a Cash Transfer Programme in Malawi.* Grantee Final Report. New Delhi: International Initiative for Impact Evaluation.

Bazzi, S., S. Sumarto, and A. Suryahadi. 2015. "It's All in the Timing: Cash Transfers and Consumption Smoothing in a Developing Country." *Journal of Economic Behavior and Organization* 119 (November): 267–88.

Beegle, K., E. Galasso, and J. Goldberg. 2015. "Direct and Indirect Effects of Malawi's Public Works Program on Food Security." Policy Research Working Paper 7505, World Bank, Washington, DC.

Berhane, G., S. Devereux, J. Hoddinott, J. Hoel, K. Roelen, K. Abay, M. Kimmel, N. Ledlie, and T. Woldu. 2015. *Evaluation of the Social Cash Transfer Pilot Programme, Tigray Region, Ethiopia.* Endline Report. Paris: United Nations Children's Fund (UNICEF), June.

Bianchi, M., and M. Bobba. 2013. "Liquidity, Risk, and Occupational Choices." *Review of Economic Studies* 80 (2): 491–511.

Bonne, R., K. Covarrubias, B. Davis, and P. Winters. 2013. "Cash Transfer Programs and Agricultural Production: The Case of Malawi." *Agricultural Economics* 44 (3): 365–78.

Cohn, R. M. 2012. "Impact Evaluation of Malawi Social Cash Transfer: Assessing Heterogeneity of Results According to Gender of Household Head." Master's thesis. Lund University, School of Economics and Management.

Covarrubias, K., B. Davis, and P. Winters. 2012. "From Protection to Production: Productive Impacts of the Malawi Social Cash Transfer Scheme." *Journal of Development Effectiveness* 4 (1): 50–77.

Daidone, X., B. Davis, J. Dewbre, and G. Tembo. 2014. "Zambia's Child Grant Program: 24-Month Impact Report on Productive Activities and Labor Allocation." FAO, Rome.

Daidone, X., J. Dewbre, K. Covarrubias, and B. Davis. 2014. "Lesotho Child Grants Program: 24-Month Impact Report on Productive Activities and Labor Allocation." FAO, Rome.

Davis, B., and S. Handa. 2015. "How Much Do Programmes Pay? Transfer Size in Selected National Cash Transfer Programmes in Sub-Saharan Africa." Transfer Project Research Brief 2015-09, University of North Carolina Carolina Population Center, Chapel Hill, NC; UNICEF, Florence.

De Mel, S., D. McKenzie, and C. Woodruff. 2012. "One-Time Transfers of Cash or Capital Have Long-Lasting Effects on Microenterprises in Sri Lanka." *Science* 335 (6071): 962–66.

Evans, D. K., and A. Popova. 2014. "Cash Transfers and Temptation Goods: A Review of Global Evidence." Policy Research Working Paper 6886, World Bank, Washington, DC. http://www.gsdrc.org/document-library/cash-transfers-and-temptation-goods -a-review-of-global-evidence/.

Gertler, P. J., S. W. Martinez, and M. Rubio-Codina. 2012. "Investing Cash Transfers to Raise Long-Term Living Standards." *American Economic Journal: Applied Economics* 4 (1): 164–92.

Haushofer, J., and J. Shapiro. 2013. "Household Response to Income Changes: Evidence from an Unconditional Cash Transfer Program in Kenya." Princeton University, Princeton, NJ.

Juergens, F., and L. Pellerano. 2016. "Social Protection in Malawi: Summary of the Assessment-Based National Dialogue Report." International Labour Organization, Geneva.

Luseno, W. K., K. Singh, S. Handa, and C. Suchindran. 2014. "A Multilevel Analysis of the Effect of Malawi's Social Cash Transfer Pilot Scheme on School-Age Children's Health." *Health Policy and Planning* 29 (4): 421–32.

Miller, C. M. 2011. "Cash Transfers and Economic Growth: A Mixed Methods Analysis of Transfer Recipients and Business Owners in Malawi." *Poverty and Public Policy* 3 (3): 1–36.

Miller, C. M., and M. Tsoka. 2012. "Cash Transfers and Children's Education and Labour among Malawi's Poor." *Development Policy Review* 30 (4): 499–522.

Miller, C. M., M. Tsoka, and K. Reichert. 2011. "The Impact of the Social Cash Transfer Scheme on Food Security in Malawi." *Food Policy* 36 (2): 230–38.

Pellerano, X., M. Moratti, M. Jakobsen, M. Bajgar, and V. Barca. 2014. "Child Grants Program Impact Evaluation: Follow-Up Report." Oxford Policy Management, Oxford, U.K.

Romeo, A., S. Asfaw, and B. Davis. 2013. "Cash Transfers, Agriculture, and Child Nutritional Status: Evidence from Malawi." Draft report prepared for the From Protection to Production Project, FAO, Rome.

Sudhanshu, X., M. Park, R. Darko, I. Osei-Akoto, B. Davis, and S. Daidone. 2014. "Livelihood Empowerment against Poverty (LEAP) Program: Impact Evaluation Report." University of North Carolina, Carolina Population Center, Chapel Hill.

World Bank. 2011. *Effective and Inclusive Targeting of Social Support Programs in Africa: Malawi Country Case Study; Synthesis Report.* Washington, DC: World Bank.

———. 2015. "The State of the Social Safety Nets 2015." World Development Indicators database, World Bank, Washington, DC. http://data.worldbank.org/data-catalog/world-development-indicators.

———. 2016. "Malawi Poverty Assessment." World Bank, Washington, DC.

World Bank and United Nations. 2010. *Natural Hazards, Unnatural Disasters: The Economics of Effective Prevention.* World Bank, Washington, DC.

CHAPTER 5

Toward a Dynamic Rural Economy

Introduction

The preponderance of evidence suggests that, in the past decade, rural Malawi lacked dynamism. As preceding chapters document, consumption growth was sluggish, and food security and poverty were elevated. Between 2004 and 2010, a majority of rural households—the bottom seven deciles—saw no consumption growth. In contrast, almost every income group in urban areas experienced a boost in consumption above 10 percent. Given its current trajectory, Malawi is unlikely to meet the Sustainable Development Goal of eliminating extreme poverty. This chapter proposes a set of policy options to improve the living conditions of Malawi's rural population. The proposal calls for policies that create the foundations for sustainable and inclusive growth, increase productivity and efficiency in the economy, and protect the vulnerable.

Create Conditions for Macroeconomic Stability and Structural Transformation

Although Malawi's growth rate in 2016 is estimated to be 2.5 percent, per capita growth is forecast to remain unchanged through 2020. To improve the prospects for greater prosperity and inclusion, Malawi needs to minimize the immediate downside risks to growth and lay the foundation for long-term growth.

To lay the foundation for growth, it is necessary to establish macroeconomic stability. In the Malawian context, three actions are needed to achieve stability: bring inflation, expected to average 23 percent between 2014 and 2016, under control; reduce the cost of capital, which is too high, as evident from interest rates above 40 percent; and address the weak fiscal environment by maintaining the upward trends in revenue mobilization and coupling them with expenditure discipline. Immediate actions to stabilize the macroeconomic environment are good not only for growth but also for the poor, especially if growth comes from diversified sources. Macroeconomic stability also could bring immediate relief to the budgets of the poor because lower inflation would increase the purchasing power of the kwacha, Malawi's currency. A reduction in the cost of capital would increase access to finance for a larger share of the population. Consumers would be able to afford purchases, entrepreneurs would improve profit margins, and welfare would improve.

Increase Agricultural Productivity

Inclusive growth is unlikely to be achieved or be sustainable without improving the productivity of agriculture. With 84 percent of the population living in rural areas and approximately 64 percent working in agriculture, substantial and sustained agricultural growth is necessary to improve the welfare of the rural population. To date, agricultural growth has been achieved through factor accumulation, primarily through expanding resources such as cultivated land and labor. However, given that Malawi has one of the highest population densities in Africa and shrinking farm sizes, the gains from continuing such practices are approaching their limit. In all likelihood, future agricultural growth will have to come from higher agricultural productivity. But how?

Reform FISP

One key reform is to achieve better balance in the composition of agricultural spending. Malawi was the second largest spender on agriculture in Sub-Saharan Africa, devoting 12.73 percent as a share of overall public spending compared with the regional average of 5.18 percent between 2000 and 2014. In 2014, Malawi was the largest spender out of 47 countries with close to 25 percent of its public budget going into agriculture. Yet, the composition of Malawi's agricultural spending is highly unbalanced. When administrative costs are included, the Farm Input Subsidy Program (FISP) alone accounts for 75 percent of the total agricultural budget. Nevertheless, the body of research (reviewed by Ricker-Gilbert 2016) shows that FISP has had only a modest impact on agricultural productivity and poverty. Moreover, much of the increase in productivity has occurred among better-off farmers. Especially considering the enormous fiscal burden imposed by the program, such research findings raise questions about FISP's overall effectiveness and sustainability. In particular, such a skewed allocation to a single program crowds out spending on other productive investments that have achieved substantially higher returns (Goyal and Nash 2016). Thus, scaling back and reforming FISP are recommended both to enhance its impact and to free up resources for reallocation to complementary investments that would have higher returns. This reform would have several payoffs.

First, scaling down the cost of the program would improve Malawi's fiscal position. Despite an increase in domestic revenue mobilization, the 2014 fiscal deficit, estimated at 8 percent of the gross domestic product (GDP), was due partially to the ongoing suspension of official aid and the weak export earnings caused by the global slowdown. Excluding the costs of procurement and retail distribution, FISP subsidies alone make up 2 percent of GDP—equivalent to 25 percent of the fiscal deficit. Clearly, reducing FISP subsidies would lift some of the fiscal pressures. Second, the reform would free up resources that could be spent on complementary investments that have yielded high agricultural returns (chapter 2).

Redefine the Target Population and Improve Targeting

FISP's stated objective is to provide subsidies to resource-poor smallholder farmers. To meet this objective, coupons are distributed to districts and then to extension planning areas within each district. However, once the coupons reach the districts, there has been significant variation over time and across villages in how traditional authorities, local governments, and the Ministry of Agriculture and Food Security have allocated these coupons to beneficiaries. As a result, it is difficult to infer the criteria for identifying participants. Figure 5.1 shows that the 1.5 million recipients of FISP were distributed uniformly across almost the entire consumption continuum in 2013, which is the latest year for which a household survey is available to make this computation (figure 5.1), and also across the size range of landholdings (see figures I.1–I.3 in appendix I). These realities cast doubt on whether FISP is achieving its objective of reaching poor farmers.

For future reform, to maximize returns, it is important to consider carefully the objectives and the target population of a scaled-down program. A more modest subsidy program, which is part of agricultural spending activities, could be targeted to farm households—"productive farmers"—who are poor, risk averse, credit constrained, and therefore less likely to purchase fertilizer and high-yielding seeds. These criteria are proposed in recognition that, at this stage in Malawi's development, its rural financial markets are thin, incomplete, and

Figure 5.1 FISP Recipients in Malawi, by Consumption Decile, 2013

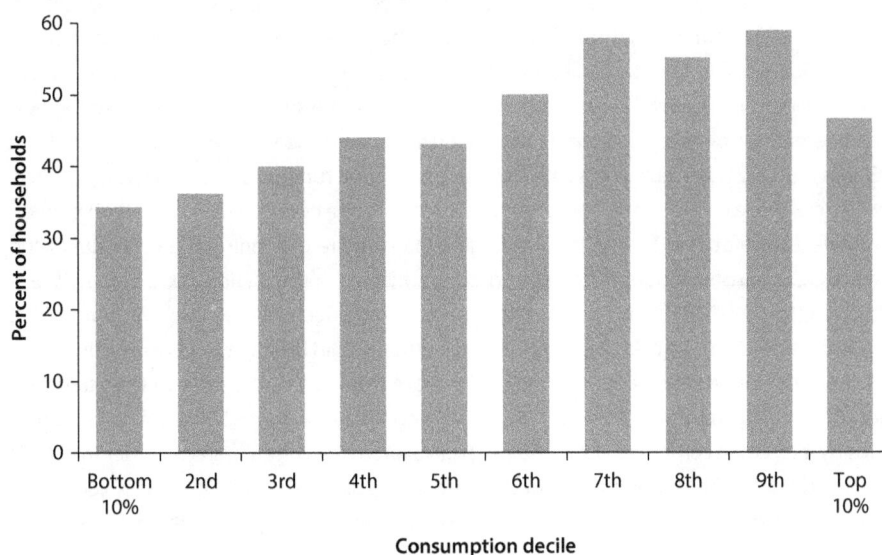

Source: Estimates are based on Integrated Household Panel Survey data.

unable to provide adequate insurance or credit so that farmers can meet their need for production inputs.

One target could be rural farm households in high-potential agricultural areas, as identified by a combination of geographic targeting, proxy means testing, and community targeting that considers a mix of poverty status, labor endowment, and landholding. Reorienting FISP in this way would sharpen the focus on raising productivity and encouraging commercialization. Some poor households would be left out of FISP as a result of the shift in its focus and target populations and would need to be compensated (box 5.1).

Offer In-Kind or Cash Transfers?

In addition to defining the target population, an important question is how best to deliver the subsidy. One option is to continue the current practice of distributing in-kind fertilizer subsidies but to reform the administration of the program. Ideally the subsidy program should be designed to build strong input markets. These markets could be achieved by providing input vouchers redeemed

---

Box 5.1 Safety Nets as a Possibility for Poor Farmers Left Behind in a FISP Reform

A change in the focus of FISP objectives and scope inevitably would lead to questions about what to do with the poorest, most food-insecure, and most vulnerable farm households that are participating in the current FISP but that may end up not participating in the more modest program. Such farm households should be enrolled and supported through safety net programs. In the 2016/17 agricultural season, the caseload of FISP beneficiaries was reduced from 1.5 million to 900,000 households. According to some conservative estimates using the IHPS 2013 data, such reduction in the number of beneficiaries would remove benefits to around 115,000 poor rural households. In addition, the FISP reduced the fertilizer price subsidy from 97 to 65 percent accompanied by a full shift to the private sector for its transportation. These changes increased the cost paid by consumers for the subsidized fertilizer, so the percentage of poor beneficiaries that receive and still redeem the voucher would reduce from 23 percent to 21 percent—or about 16,000 fewer poor rural households (Jacoby 2016a). Because of these distributional consequences, there will be a need to put in place an expanded and effective safety net for the poor. Doing so may require expanding the coverage of the Social Cash Transfer Program (SCTP) and/or the Malawi Social Action Fund–Public Works Program (MASAF-PWP). Provided these programs reach effectively the poor left out of FISP, the welfare gains for the poor from such a policy action would be larger than the status quo, as the poorest households benefit substantially more from cash than from in-kind transfers. Recent estimations suggest that even after reducing the number of FISP beneficiaries and its subsidy rate, when combined with a rebate (equivalent to the current transfer under the SCTP) to the number of households envisaged for expansion under the SCTP (about 144,000 extra households), there would be an important drop in extreme poverty and in the poverty gap.

---

through private input dealers. An example would be a flexible input voucher program to enable beneficiaries to redeem their subsidies for the input mix that best meets their needs instead of for a predefined package of inputs (Ricker-Gilbert 2016). Another variant of the in-kind transfer would be an e-voucher, which would provide all the benefits of an in-kind voucher, but without the logistical and administrative costs of a paper form.

There are good reasons to maintain an in-kind subsidy, whether delivered through an e-voucher or in-kind paper. For a country such as Malawi, whose input markets are yet to be well developed, an in-kind voucher system (or, equivalently, an e-voucher) could provide private input suppliers with predictable demand every year. Predictability, in turn, would enable suppliers to invest in improving the diversity of inputs they offer, building relationships with farmers, and gaining market share over the medium to long term.

However, although the rationale for keeping in-kind coupons for some time is understandable, over time, it is desirable to transition to cash subsidies. The gains from replacing the in-kind fertilizer subsidy with a modest cash subsidy program are potentially large.[1]

Providing subsidies in the form of cash brings flexibility to household decision making. With cash, a household is likely to allocate spending optimally. Part of the cash is likely to be used to meet immediate needs such as food, health care, or school. Some of the cash may be saved for future needs such as farm input purchases at the time of planting or harvest. Alternatively, the cash may be used to start a business. In other words, cash empowers farm households to make decisions that maximize their welfare. As discussed later, cash transfers increase agricultural production more than in-kind transfers (Ambler, de Brauw, and Godlonton 2016). Two thought experiments[2] showed that the welfare gains for the rural poor would be larger if the subsidy were distributed in cash rather than in kind (boxes 5.2 and 5.3).

Box 5.2 Potential of Cash versus In-Kind Transfers to Reduce Poverty

In the first thought experiment, household data from the Third Integrated Household Survey (IHS3), conducted in 2010, were used to simulate the household welfare effects of receiving the FISP subsidy in cash. Most beneficiaries of the subsidy received benefits through increased production. These benefits could be monetized by valuing the net increase in maize production using prevailing maize prices. For this simulation, FISP beneficiary households were identified, and their household welfare (as measured by consumption) in the absence of FISP was estimated by subtracting from their total consumption the monetized value of the net increase in maize production from receiving two bags of maize fertilizer. In this case, the head count poverty rate in rural areas, initially measured at 56.6 percent in 2010, would have increased 3.0 percentage points.

box continues next page

Box 5.2 Potential of Cash versus In-Kind Transfers to Reduce Poverty *(continued)*

Figure B5.2.1 Effects of a Cash (Instead of an In-Kind) Transfer on Poverty in Malawi, 2010

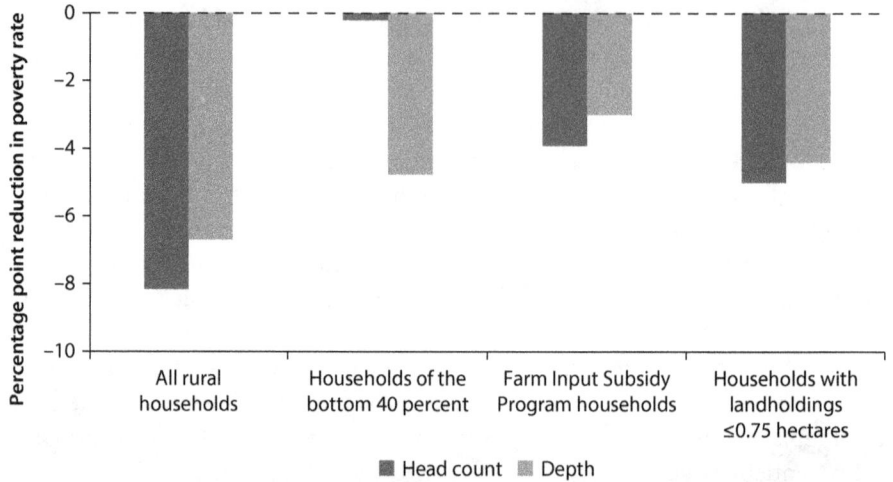

Source: Estimates are based on IHS3 data.
Note: IHS3 = Third Integrated Household Survey.

Then the cash equivalent of the subsidy was added back to consumption by monetizing the intended bundle of inputs, consisting of two bags of fertilizer, one bag of improved maize seed, and one bag of legumes. The result was that, had FISP been distributed in cash and all benefits reflected in the beneficiaries' consumption, the poverty head count would have declined 4.0 percentage points for current FISP recipients. This outcome suggested that the monetized benefits from production using inputs, which are lower than the intended bundle for some households, were smaller than the face value of the FISP subsidy received in cash (figure B5.2.1). Additional results simulating the effect on poverty of a transfer of 75 percent or 65 percent of the value of the FISP package are presented in figure J.1 in appendix J.

Box 5.3 Benefits of Cash Transfers for Poor Farmers

In the second thought experiment, Jacoby (2016b) used household data from the 2013 Integrated Household Panel Survey (IHPS), described in chapter 1, to estimate consumer surplus, or benefits, for each household on the basis of its predicted demand for subsidized fertilizer relative to the counterfactual of commercial purchase. Jacoby then measured (a) the benefit of FISP as the sum of all consumer surplus and (b) the cost of FISP as the difference between the effective price and the subsidized price (times the number of vouchers redeemed).

A key result was that the cost of the subsidy currently exceeds the benefits to farmers. The national benefit-to-cost ratio is 0.91, but varies greatly by percentiles, with greater

box continues next page

Box 5.3 Benefits of Cash Transfers for Poor Farmers *(continued)*

Figure B5.3.1 Benefits of a Cash Payout

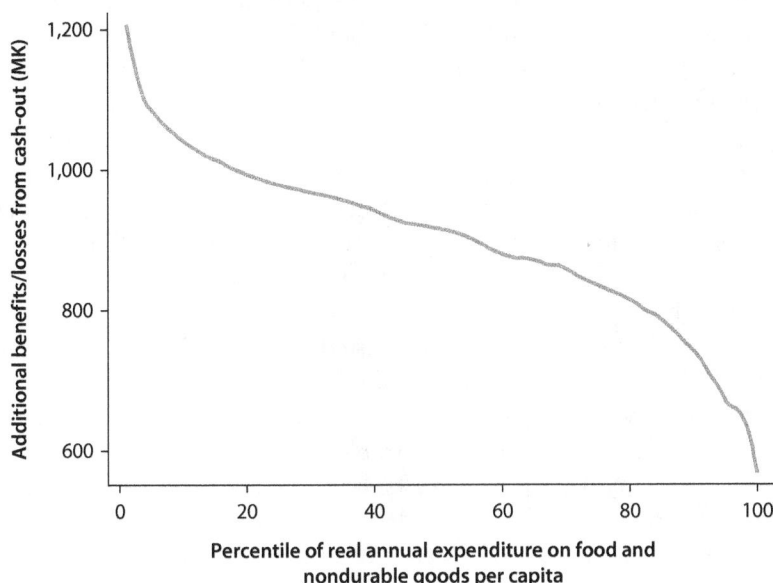

Percentile of real annual expenditure on food and
nondurable goods per capita

Source: Jacoby 2016b.

distortion transferring fertilizer to the poor. As a result, when plotting the benefit incidence curves for FISP, Jacoby finds that demand for fertilizer was low among the poor. Thus, poor farmers would benefit more from the same amount of subsidy given in cash rather than in the form of fertilizers.

Figure B5.3.1 shows that a cash program would be progressive because the benefits would be higher for poorer farmers and would decline with greater income. Moreover, a cash program would not necessarily reduce the demand for fertilizer because the cash likely would reduce the credit constraint that poorer farmers are likely to face. However, this demand could be boosted and sustained through the development of an extension system that provides farmers with information, proper production techniques, and prices, and encourages them to save for inputs.

Empirical evidence also supports the strong welfare effects of cash transfers. Recipients of cash transfers have been shown to increase consumption of durable and nondurable goods, increase savings, reduce borrowing, and take risks by investing part of the cash in productive investments such as microenterprises and agricultural production (Angelucci, Attanasio, and Di Maro 2012; Bianchi and Bobba 2013; De Mel, McKenzie, and Woodruff 2012; Gertler, Martinez, and Rubio-Codina 2012). There also is adequate evidence that cash transfers are not wasted on the purchase of temptation goods (see the review of 19 studies by Evans and Popova 2014).

Provide Both Cash and Information Rather Than Cash Alone

Limited access to information is attributed to lower productivity of the rural poor. Recent work decomposing the maize yield differential in rural Malawi between the chronically poor and households that escaped poverty between 2010 and 2013 found that more than half (53 percent) of the yield gap is explained by changes in the returns to application of organic fertilizer, use of family labor, access to extension services, and application of the right type of basal fertilizer. Access to and use of adequate information could have increased these returns. However, households that stayed in poverty during both periods lived in more remote villages and had lower levels of education than those that escaped from poverty, making it harder for them to obtain information and use it appropriately.

A recent randomized controlled trial tested precisely whether a combination of cash or in-kind (input packages) transfers and intensive agricultural extension support could alleviate capital and information constraints facing farmers in rural Malawi and boost their productivity (Ambler, de Brauw, and Godlonton 2016). The pilot program, lasting two years, was implemented by the National Smallholder Farmers Association of Malawi (NASFAM) in collaboration with the International Food Policy Research Institute and Innovations for Poverty Action in Ntchisi and Dowa Districts with 1,200 NASFAM members growing either groundnuts or soy. The pilot compared outcomes in terms of agricultural productivity, crop adoption, and land allocation. In the capital treatment, farmer groups were randomly allocated to a control group, a cash group that received framed cash transfers at planting (US$36), mid-season (US$22), and harvest (US$26), or an input group that received transfers of equivalent value, with 50 percent given in-kind (for example, seed, hoes, inoculants, storage sacks). In the information treatment, farmers received standard NASFAM extension services run by lead farmers or intensive extension services, including at least three one-on-one visits from professional extension workers in addition to group trainings. Transfers were only given in the first year, and extension services were randomized again in the second year.

Results demonstrate that both transfer treatments led to increased production, especially cash transfers. For the cash group, the gross value of agricultural output increased 21 percent. The transfers led farmers to shift from tobacco to groundnuts and soy, with groundnut yields for the cash group increasing approximately 30 percent. After one year, the intensive extension services did not change production or input use. Production increases appeared to be driven by increased investments in farming, as total input expenditures rose approximately 30 percent. The cash transfer group increased the use of both pesticides (57 percent increase) and *ganyu* (defined as short-term work on household farms, large-scale farms, and plantations) (67 percent increase). Transfers did not change fertilizer use. Lastly, complementarities were found between the intensive extension and transfer interventions in input use.

Another promising feature of the NASFAM pilot was that transfers were "labeled (or framed)," without imposing conditions on beneficiaries. Policy makers often use conditional transfer programs to ensure that subsidies are spent as intended by the program. Drawbacks of conditional transfer programs are targeting and conditionality, which make them expensive to administer. Targeting and conditionality have been estimated to account for 60 percent of the administrative costs of Progresa in Mexico, 49 percent of the costs of the Programa de Asignación Familiar in Honduras, and 31 percent for the Red de Protección Social in Nicaragua (Caldés, Coady, and Maluccio 2006). Despite the numerous empirical results supporting the inherent benefits of cash transfers, concerns remain that farm households may not spend the extra cash as intended. Therefore, "labeled (or framed) cash transfer" programs, which do not impose conditions but explicitly label transfers for specific purposes, have reduced the costs associated with conditionality and encouraged beneficiaries to use transfers for the intended purposes.

Provide Cash and Training Skills to Also Boost Self-Employment Activities

Giving people cash that relieves credit constraints, sometimes in combination with business plans, short business or skills training, supervision, and mentoring can stimulate self-employment and help people to raise their incomes. Generally speaking, there are two types of interventions. *Supply-side interventions* provide some key input or service, such as capital or skills training, to individuals or very small enterprises. *Demand-side programs* increase the demand for the labor of unskilled workers through, for example, public work programs (PWPs) that create infrastructure. The influx of cash from the current public work program in Malawi could also relieve some of the supply-side constraints noted.

On the *supply side*, there is evidence from a few countries. In northern Uganda, through the Youth Opportunities Program, the government invited men and women ages 18–35 years to form groups of about 20 and to prepare proposals to get vocational training and start individual enterprises. The groups received grants of nearly US$8,000 (nearly US$400 per person). Four years later, a randomized evaluation showed that cash grants helped to increase hours of work by 20 percent and earnings by 40 percent. Some studies looked at cash and in-kind transfers to existing business owners, especially in Ghana and Sri Lanka, finding that male business owners realized relatively high returns, increasing both the size and profitability of their business (Blattman and Ralston 2015).

The *demand-side* approach seems feasible for Malawi in principle. The Community Savings and Investment Promotion (COMSIP) groups are the largest savings group program in Malawi and emerged out of the MASAF cash transfers for public works.[3] Supported by MASAF, its membership consists of MASAF public works beneficiaries. Through the mobilization efforts of the community development extension workers of the Ministry of Gender, COMSIP has facilitated the organization of 99,153 public work participants (33,712 male, 65,441 female) into 4,457 savings groups. Average savings amount to MK 6,727 (US$20) per member. The groups have mobilized MK 434.6 million (US$1.3 million) in savings and invested in various income-generating activities. The groups have formed 135 cooperatives. These groups have the potential to be powerful vehicles for providing messaging and training on health, nutrition, and literacy, and for improving livelihoods and assets. The 2012 Tracking Study found that 79 percent of group members reportedly had generated income equal to more than 50 percent of the initial cash transfer received.

Under MASAF IV, it is expected that these dynamics will continue and that the interventions will allow more households to improve their livelihoods through the savings generated by income from the SCTP and PWP and investments resulting from support received through COMSIP. While self-assessments indicate that about half of the members in these groups no longer feel food insecure due to their improved financial status, a more robust evaluation is needed.

Achieve a Diversified Crop Mix

These reforms are likely to alter the crop mix in Malawi. FISP targets maize production. Naturally, farmers will have an incentive to shift land, labor, and other inputs to maximize maize production. This shift carries substantial risks to the farmers and to the country. A shock that leads to the failure of maize production is likely to entail large individual and aggregate losses, worsen food security, and diminish poverty reduction. However, decoupling the subsidy from maize would enable households, including poor ones, to diversify to other crops that are not heavy on FISP-supported inputs (Nsengiyumva and others 2015).

Create Functional Food Markets and Value Chains

Farmers often are unattractive credit candidates for financial institutions because of the unpredictable nature of agricultural production. The Warehouse Receipts System (WRS) seeks to lessen this unpredictability. WRS financing is a lending technique that enables farmers, producers, and traders of agricultural commodities to access bank loans by pledging their warehouse receipts against commodities deposited in a warehouse. After harvesting, a farmer can deposit his or her crop in a certified warehouse and receive a document of title called a warehouse receipt. The farmer then can use the warehouse receipt as security for a loan from a participating bank.

WRS reduces the pressure on the farmer to sell immediately after harvest, when prices normally are low. While the commodity is in the warehouse, the depositor can monitor prices and sell when the price is favorable. In addition, the system reduces postharvest losses because the commodity is transferred to a certified warehouse equipped with appropriate facilities to ensure quality and quantity. WRS can provide the credibility and predictability that financial institutions require if they are to increase their lending to farmers. The World Bank Group is working on WRS in several African countries, including Ethiopia, Kenya, and Malawi (box 5.4).

Box 5.4 Warehouse Receipts System Reform Initiatives in Ethiopia, Kenya, and Malawi

In Ethiopia, since 2009 the International Finance Corporation's Warehouse Receipts Financing Initiative has been helping to expand access to financing for farmers, traders, and cooperatives and to develop agricultural commodities markets.

In Kenya, agriculture accounts for nearly 30 percent of GDP and employs close to 75 percent of the population, but only 5 percent of bank lending goes to agribusiness. Banks in Kenya have started to finance farmers through WRS. For example, Chase Bank committed more than US$10 million to WRS financing for 2015. The Eastern Africa Grain Council (EAGC) has certified more than 50,000 metric tons of warehouse storage capacity in Kenya. The institution also has supported the training of more than 13,000 farmers and 200 farmer-based organizations on proper postharvest handling, quality specifications, group marketing and grain consolidation, and access to and use of market information. Soon the system will be able to use information and communication technologies to automate warehouse receipts and link to a market information system that monitors commodities and provides pricing information.

The EAGC participated in a workshop in Malawi to share its successful experiences and lessons learned. Results have been dramatic: six banks have started to finance warehouse receipts for a total of US$9 million of financing, 1,000 farmers and 500 traders are using WRS in Malawi, and 30,000 metric tons of maize are stored.

Seek a More Dynamic and Inclusive Structural Transformation

Beyond its role as the dominant source of income for the rural population, agricultural income is also a major driver of rural nonfarm income. The second major source of income for rural households, rural nonfarm employment includes wage income or profits from family businesses, discussed in chapter 3. Very few employment opportunities exist outside the farm. A major constraint to the growth of nonfarm enterprises is the lack of demand for their products, which in turn limits their growth and employment generation.

While increasing agricultural productivity is essential, it is not enough. A more dynamic structural transformation is needed to sustain rural poverty reduction. Structural transformation occurs when resources, primarily labor, shift across sectors—say, from agriculture to nonagricultural sectors. This shift could happen, for instance, if a rise in agricultural productivity leads to the "release" of labor from agriculture to other sectors, such as manufacturing, services, or both. In general, productivity can grow through the accumulation of capital (land, machines), technological change, or even managerial innovation in existing economic activities in specific sectors—"within" productivity growth—or through a movement of factors of production such as labor from low-productivity to high-productivity sectors. Since the latter kind of change often involves a change in the structure of the economy—that is, labor and other factors of production are reallocated across sectors—it is often associated with "structural" transformation.

Between 2000 and 2010, many African countries, including Malawi, witnessed a movement of labor from agriculture to other sectors (McMillan and Harttgen 2014; table K.1 in appendix K). However, while the share of employment in agriculture declined a little faster in Malawi than the African average (figure 5.2), overall labor productivity also fell (figure 5.3). Disaggregating changes in overall productivity into changes within the sector and across sectors—so-called structural change—reveals two patterns: productivity within the sector (agriculture) declined over time, and the shift from low- to higher-productivity sectors was slow. This suggests that most of the labor leaving the agriculture sector was absorbed into low-productivity activities in other sectors.[4]

Figure 5.2 Change in Share of Employment in the Agriculture Sector in Sub-Saharan African Countries, 2000–10

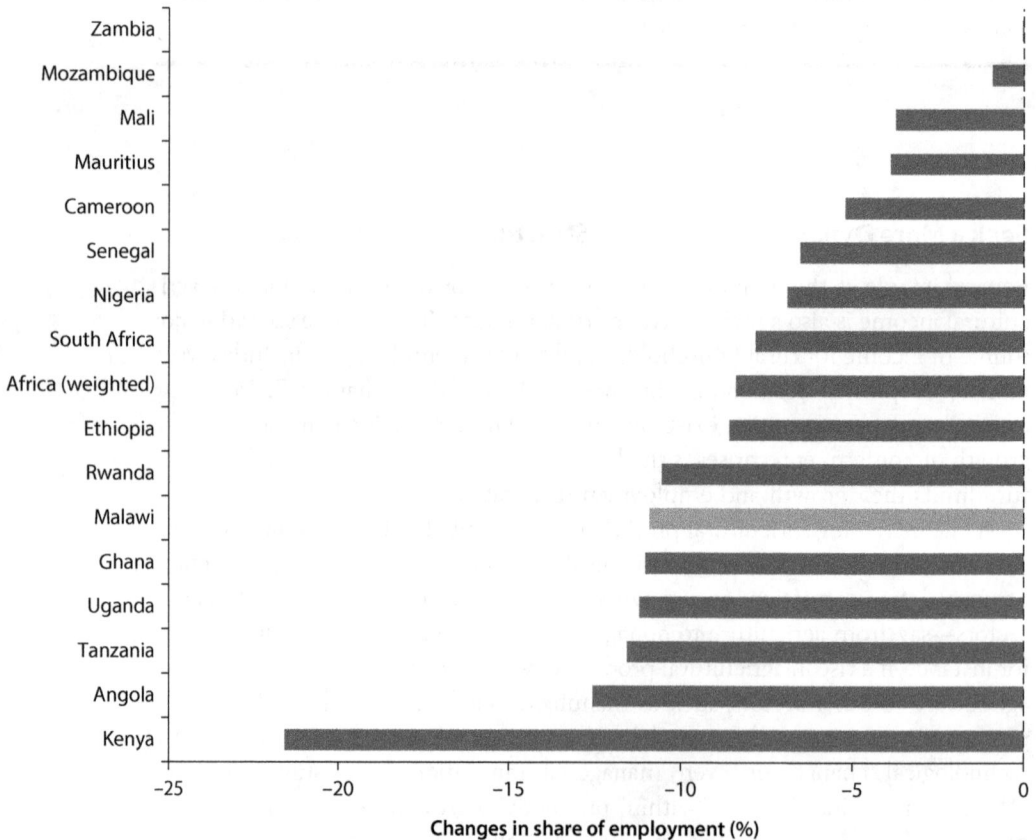

Source: McMillan and Harttgen 2014.

Figure 5.3 Growth in Labor Productivity within Sectors and from Low- to Higher-Productivity Sectors in Sub-Saharan African Countries, Multiple Years Post-2000

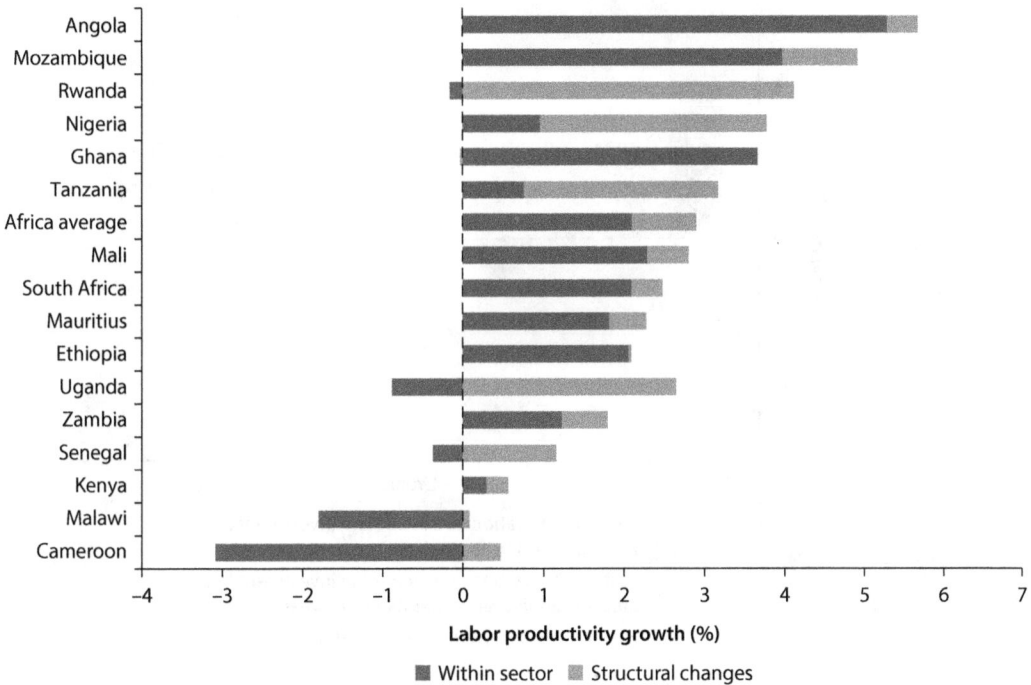

Labor productivity growth (%)

■ Within sector ■ Structural changes

Source: McMillan and Harttgen 2014.

To sustain agricultural productivity growth and reduce rural poverty, faster structural change is needed, which entails faster and "orderly" urbanization. Catch-up growth is the emerging consensus in the vast literature on growth. Catch-up growth means that urbanization is the key to achieving long-term prosperity in Malawi. It would encourage the clustering of activities; easy flow of ideas, especially preexisting nonrival ideas; sharing of skilled labor; and better delivery of services.

Urbanization scenarios projected for 2010–30 indicate that even slightly faster urbanization would go a long way toward accelerating growth in Malawi.[5] The bars in figure 5.4 indicate the extent to which poor households' real consumption under three alternative scenarios deviates from a baseline scenario where the future urbanization rate for 2010–30 is assumed to be the same as the current level. Scenario 1—faster urbanization as a result of migration—envisions a 5 percentage point increase in urbanization in Malawi, where the urbanization rate increases from 16 to 21 percent by 2030. Scenario 2—faster urbanization with urban investment, but rural disinvestment— imagines an increase in urbanization to 21 percent and an increase in investment in urban areas without raising government spending, which implies a

Figure 5.4 Deviation in Poor Households' Real Consumption from Baseline in 2030

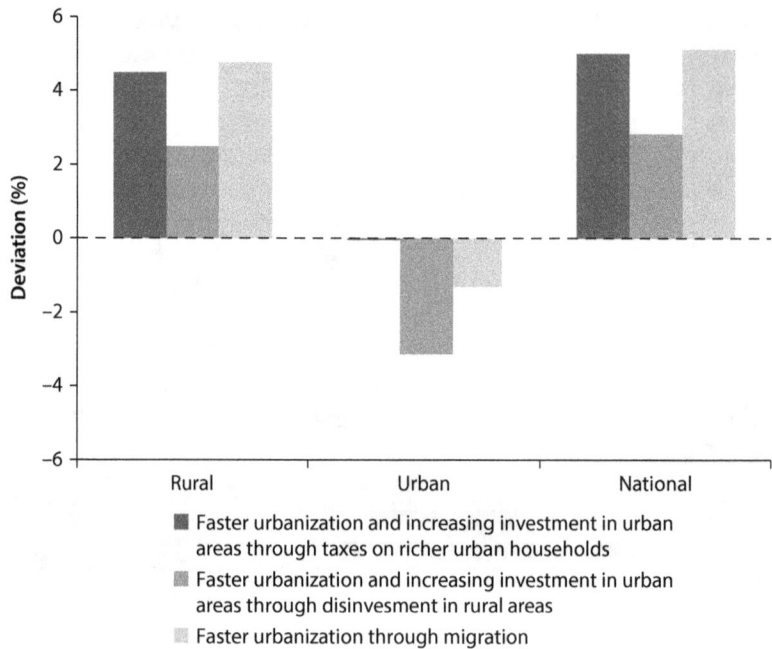

Source: World Bank 2016c.

reduction in rural investment. Scenario 3—faster urbanization with increased urban investment—assumes faster urbanization (21 percent) and increased urban investment that is financed through increased government spending. The additional spending is assumed to come from higher taxes on richer urban households. Under this scenario, urban investment increases, but not at the expense of rural spending.

Four conclusions emerge. First, even slightly faster urbanization will lead to an improvement in rural welfare as measured by households' real consumption (all scenarios). Second, faster migration will bring more meaningful structural change, but may come at the cost of increased urban poverty, if the growing demand for infrastructure and services in urban areas is not met with increased investment (scenario 1). Third, with a fixed amount of public resources, more investment in urban areas will mean less investment in rural areas, which will lower agricultural productivity and hurt the rural poor, who are mostly small-holder farmers (scenario 2). And fourth, a combination of faster urbanization and increased investment in urban areas self-financed by higher taxes on richer urban households, which will allow the level of public investment in rural areas to remain intact, is appealing for both rural and urban areas: it is the best case for structural transformation (scenario 3).

Faster and inclusive urbanization that confers greater benefits in the form of higher productivity and lower poverty can come about through the following:

Remove policy biases against urbanization

Malawi's development strategy prioritizes household food self-sufficiency in rural areas. This explains the long tradition of providing input subsidies and export bans for maize. By contrast, existing policy does not enable urban local governments to take more than minimal residual steps. To create smarter and more vibrant urban areas, the capacity of urban local governments needs to be strengthened and their financial resources expanded. Growing the capacity of cities will include a systematic, focused effort to improve own-source revenue, especially from property taxes, which hold substantial potential to finance urban development.

Take more deliberate actions to promote "smarter" urbanization

Whether the actions involve increasing the size and density of existing cities or creating new cities, policy makers need to take a conscious, planned approach to managing urban land efficiently. This includes explicit mapping of urban land use and provision of better quality and more reliable services. Well managed urban land will encourage mobility and connectivity; clustering of economic activities; protection of the space for public goods (infrastructure, environmental amenities); and efficient provision of services to large, intermediate, and small towns.

Promote urban job creation

In addition to encouraging food self sufficiency, government policy also needs to prioritize value addition and job creation in rural areas. However, for true transformation to occur, it is important to shift what people do and where they do it. One of the unintended consequences of keeping households on land (agriculture first policy) is to discourage migration and urbanization. As noted, even a small change in rates of urbanization and urban investment can bring huge welfare gains to Malawi. Therefore, equal or even more weight should be given to urban job creation by revisiting regulatory barriers to the entry of firms, upgrading skills and promoting entrepreneurship, raising productivity of small and medium enterprises, integrating value chains, and reducing the costs of logistics.

In summary, faster urbanization should be a high priority for public policy because historical and contemporary experience has shown that, when handled properly, urbanization has been a catalyst for inclusive structural transformation. Urbanization creates a major source of demand for agricultural and other rural products. It improves the accumulation of skills, occupational specialization, and labor productivity. Urbanization integrates labor markets that are more creative. It is the main locus of formal sector employment. In short, urban growth has brought immense prosperity to billions around the world and could do so for Malawi as well.

Expand Financial Inclusion to the Rural Population through Digital Finance

Financial inclusion is a critical channel for reducing poverty and boosting productivity (box 5.5). Access to savings, payment, loans, and credit help households to smooth consumption, insure against risk, and encourage investment in agricultural as well as nonagricultural sectors. Past studies have found a positive correlation between financial inclusion and poverty alleviation in low-income and lower-middle-income countries (Beck, Demirgüç-Kunt, and Levine 2007; Bruhn and Love 2014).

Access to formal financial services remains low in Malawi. Only 15.4 percent of Malawians older than 15 have a bank account in a financial institution, and the holding of savings and current accounts declined between 2008 and 2013 (Chirwa and Mvula 2014). Although 76 percent of adults reported that they had some money left after paying for food and basic necessities, only 18 percent saved on a regular basis, and a mere 7 percent had savings in, or had borrowed from, a formal institution. Without access to formal financial services, the poor relied on informal mechanisms such as friends and families, rotating credit societies, and informal money lenders. Although these arrangements can be helpful, they often are insufficient, unreliable, and expensive.

The Making Access Possible Initiative in Malawi identified several barriers to expanding financial services. Proximity and affordability are two major obstacles to introducing a payment system with formal financial institutions. On average, it takes 87 minutes to travel to a bank branch in rural areas (versus 27 minutes in urban areas). In addition, it costs MK 801, on average, to pay for public

---

Box 5.5   Financial Inclusion and Improved Welfare

Evaluations in Malawi have shown that interventions to increase financial inclusion have reduced poverty when they increase access to loans and credit at the district level (Dunga 2014). They increase interhousehold transfers during lean seasons, especially toward the poorest households, and improve food consumption (Flory 2012; Ksoll and Forskningsenhed 2013). They help to diversify agricultural production by encouraging farmers to shift to cash crops (Shaw and Nagarajan 2011). In addition, they help households to cope with health-related shocks and to smooth consumption (Shimamura and Lastarria-Cornhiel 2015). Finally, when commitment savings are combined with value-chain financing of agricultural production, access to financial services yields significant impacts on agricultural production and household expenditure. When some farmers were offered the opportunity to have payments for their harvest of cash crops deposited directly into bank accounts and some were also offered commitment savings accounts, saving and the use of agricultural inputs were both higher. The evaluations also found positive effects on crop sale and household expenditures (Brune and others 2015).

---

transportation to the bank. The cost of opening a bank account is 2 percent of average monthly income. Eligibility and affordability are major barriers to accessing credit, while affordability is the biggest obstacle to getting insurance.

To overcome these hurdles and other constraints to financial inclusion, Malawi should consider scaling up digital finance. Digital finance has the potential to transform rural Malawi and to grease the wheels of dynamism in the rural economy (box 5.6).

Combined with other innovations, digital finance can transform rural economies in ways that have not yet been possible. The introduction of digital identification (ID) can enhance the reach of mobile banking and deepen financial inclusion. In countries such as Malawi that lack a unique ID system, identity fraud is rather common. Lenders tell anecdotes of past borrowers purposefully defaulting and trying to obtain a fresh loan from the same

---

Box 5.6 What Can Digital Finance Bring to Development?

Digital finance can do the following:

- Increase efficiency by enabling people who have no formal accounts, but do have a phone, to make or receive payments; increasing the speed and reducing the cost of transactions; increasing incentives to save through automatic deposits or text reminders; empowering specific groups such as women; and reducing information asymmetry by helping people to estimate their credit score from digital transactions (World Bank 2016d)
- Improve risk management by accelerating the delivery of support, especially in an emergency, to persons hit by a shock
- Improve public service delivery and budget savings through bypassing sources of leakage and enabling automation of public transfers

Under the right environment and incentives, digital finance can take off rapidly and reach massive scale in a short period of time. In rural Malawi in 2013, only 29 percent of survey respondents owned a mobile phone, while another 21 percent had access to a mobile phone (Chirwa and Mvula 2014). Nevertheless, 77 percent of respondents knew how to use a mobile phone to receive money, 80 percent knew how to use one to transfer money, and 72 percent knew how to use one to pay bills.

The attempt of Opportunity International Bank of Malawi (OIBM) to make financial services more accessible illustrates the unmet demand for digital finance and its huge potential. When OIBM introduced a mobile "bank-on-wheels" service (the banking van) in rural areas, where the cost of setting up permanent branches was high, outreach and take-up rose sharply. The "bank-on-wheels" lowered the direct costs of travel and transaction costs (Sharma and Nagarajan 2011). In addition, 97 percent of survey respondents reported that they would like to use financial services with large agro-input dealers. Mobile banking has great potential to expand financial inclusion in rural Malawi.

---

or another institution. In response, lenders have restricted the supply of such services.

Applying biometric technologies (fingerprinting, for instance)[6] to approve credit may ease banks' fear of lending and make credit more accessible. Fingerprinting can make the threat of future credit denial credible by making it easier for financial institutions to withhold new loans from past defaulters and to reward responsible past borrowers with increased credit. As a result, people who have defaulted in the past may take out smaller loans or avoid borrowing altogether. Other borrowers may have greater incentives to ensure that production is successful, either by exerting more effort or by choosing less risky projects. In addition, when production could cover repayment of the loan, those borrowers could be less likely to default intentionally or opportunistically. Tests of fingerprinting technology in Malawi have shown potentially large gains in access to finance and efficiency (box 5.7). For example, paprika production rose among farmers offered agricultural loans, partly because fingerprinted farmers had more incentives for production to be successful to repay the loans. Fingerprinting also led to higher repayment rates of approximately 40 percent among farmers who had had higher ex ante default risks. A rough cost-benefit analysis of the pilot experiment suggests that the benefits from improved repayment greatly outweighed the costs of equipment and fingerprint collection.

The combination of digital finance and digital IDs also can transform public service delivery and potentially save large amounts for the government. In countries where digital IDs have been introduced, they have led to the removal of ghost employees from government payrolls, reduced leakage of public transfers, improved the management of transfers and social programs, and improved electoral integrity.

Box 5.7 Digital IDs Can Be Scaled Up in Malawi

Starting in 2015, loans with fingerprinting verification have been offered in Malawi on a larger scale through the Malawi Microfinance Network. At the moment, two microfinance institutions (MFIs) are using fingerprinting, but the hope is that other MFIs will see the benefit and want to use fingerprinting as well. Such scale-up will be piloted to test whether fingerprinting leads borrowers to produce more farm output and thus raises household welfare and to establish whether the introduction of fingerprinting improves lender responses. A Web service, accessible from anywhere with an Internet connection, will allow MFIs and credit reference bureaus to search for and recall registered information on a particular borrower. While immediately useful for sharing information within an institution (to identify multiple borrowers), the end goal is to tie the unique ID to one credit-sharing institution that encompasses all MFIs.

Meanwhile, NovaTeqni Corporation, a biometrics and secure payment technology firm, has just announced plans to develop an advanced biometric-enabled system—Farmers Registration and Administration System—for the tobacco farming industry. The system will issue smart cards with biometric data for instant identification and will start with a six-month pilot, which could be scaled up to all farmers.

Box 5.8 Digital Finance and Agricultural Productivity in Nigeria

By some accounts, Nigeria has been able to reverse declining agricultural productivity by combining smart subsidization and digital finance. In 2012, Nigeria introduced an innovative mobile wallet, which transferred fertilizer subsidies directly to farmers. The farmers then redeemed the transfers at stores run by private distributors and suppliers. This structure took the government out of the costly business of procuring and distributing fertilizer. The scheme doubled the number of farmers supported by the scheme at a sixth of the cost. The expansion of the scheme is in the works. Expansion is being aided by a digital identification system and biometric signatures, making it easier to roll out broader financial services to a larger and otherwise excluded rural population (Grossman and Tarazi 2014).

Mobile phones also can help farmers to improve their access to fertilizer subsidies (box 5.8), obtain market information and strengthen their links to agricultural markets. For instance, participation in an information and communication technology–based market information system in Malawi has been shown to increase agricultural income and reduce transaction costs among smallholder farmers (Katengeza and others 2014).

Improve the Efficiency of Safety Net Programs

The most well-known safety net program in Malawi—the Malawi Social Action Fund–Public Works Program—aims to provide cash to poor and able-bodied households in exchange for their short-term labor. In recent years, another program, the Social Cash Transfer Program, has been added to the list of major safety net programs. SCTP is designed to reach the extremely poor and labor-constrained households.

Between 2013 and 2015, these two programs covered approximately 650,000 households per year. The empirical evidence presented in chapter 4 indicates that MASAF-PWP has the potential to represent a key safety net for households, but when assessed has had little impact on food security or poverty reduction due to a combination of rationing, poor targeting performance and low transfer amounts. Although SCTP has shown some positive impacts on welfare, it has limited coverage of the poor population. The following policy reforms are intended to improve the impacts of both MASAF-PWP and SCTP:

Provide larger transfers to more poor people

Social protection interventions are much needed in Malawi, but the current system, although recently expanded, has both low expenditure by international standards and limited coverage. Compared with public work programs (PWPs) in other low-income and lower-middle-income countries, the total transfer amount from MASAF-PWP was relatively small. Although the daily wage from MASAF-PWP was similar to wages provided by other programs, the maximum number of working days per year was much lower, yielding a comparatively low total transfer amount. Scaling back FISP subsidies alone, as proposed, would lift some of the fiscal pressures that may have prevented wider coverage. SCT transfers are more generous and have shown positive impacts, but their coverage among the extreme poor remains minuscule relative to need: The program is aiming to reach its goal of 319,000 households in 2017, covering the 10 percent poorest labor-constrained households in each district. Yet, already in 2010 more than 3 million people in rural areas could not afford the value of a basic food bundle.

Improve targeting

Approximately 59 percent of MASAF-PWP participants do not meet the eligibility criteria. Therefore, achieving better targeting of beneficiaries should be a top priority if this and other programs are to have better outcomes. For MASAF-PWP, one way to improve targeting would be to explore the possibility of self-targeting further. This would require lowering the wage substantially. Self-targeting has the potential to attract persons who have low opportunity cost of time and who could benefit from participation—often the very poor. However, to ensure a sufficient number of total transfers to improve household welfare, there should be no limit on the number of days an individual participates in the program. In other words, although the daily wage rate will be lower, the poor can still accumulate as much paid wage as needed. For MASAF-PWP, recent reforms that offer public work during the lean season provide 48 days of work to a household; the same households should be maintained in each work cycle and evaluated. An improved and more flexible targeting design will also have to be introduced if MASAF-PWP wants to protect households from shocks (box 5.9).

Box 5.9 Can MASAF-PWP Cater for Shocks?

Given the recurrent onset of shocks in the country (food price spikes, late onset of rains, excess or deficit rainfall) and the fact that Malawi suffers from high food price seasonality relative to other countries in Sub-Saharan Africa (including the highest gap in maize prices between the lean and postharvest season), public insurance-type programs likely are needed. Cash-for-work transfers can stabilize consumption. At a minimum, they can make poverty more bearable by transferring income to the poorest, partly because an effective social protection floor enables the poor to manage weather shocks better. At best, these transfers can enable households to make choices about livelihoods that yield higher earnings. In addition, providing cash wages for public work to rehabilitate the environment, reverse severe land degradation, and build irrigation and water-harvesting schemes can reduce the base risk to which these communities are subject.

At the time of the random controlled trial implemented during the 2012–13 agricultural season the program was not flexible enough to enable households to participate as a response to shocks. PWP beneficiaries were not more likely to tap into the program when experiencing production or weather shocks. The take-up of PWP was not responsive to the overall number

box continues next page

Box 5.9 Can MASAF-PWP Cater for Shocks? *(continued)*

of shocks (weather, production, food price, or household idiosyncratic) experienced by households during the preplanting and lean seasons. The only exception was that households that were randomly offered the program were marginally more likely to respond to contemporaneous food price hikes during the lean season, confirming the extent of unmet demand for insurance during the season with the highest need. The inability to cope with shocks limits the potential of the program to serve its key consumption-smoothing function as safety net. The lack of responsiveness is likely to ensue from an inflexible assignment of projects to households at a given time of the year (with beneficiaries identified through a village selection process during the preplanting season).

There is scope for improving the MASAF-PWP program and enhancing its insurance role or for designing a new insurance program. Rapid rollout of projects during the lean season, responsiveness of geographic targeting to large weather shocks, improved access of households and flexibility to scale up could go a long way toward smoothing consumption in the aftermath of a shock.

Source: World Bank 2016b.

Evaluate the value of assets produced under MASAF-PWP

A major objective of safety net programs requiring beneficiaries to work is the claim that, in working, beneficiaries create assets that are valuable to the community and the broader society. Yet, to date, the value of assets produced by these programs has yet to be evaluated. Therefore, we propose undertaking a proper and thorough evaluation of the assets. If they are found to have no value, and conditions requiring work remain built into the program design, then the program can focus on a narrower set of assets that create value for communities (such as conservation of water catchment areas) and reassess them. The alternative is to remove the condition to work and convert MASAF-PWP into a cash program.

Address Rapid Population Growth and the Expanding Youth Population

To harness the eventual gains in poverty reduction achieved through these recommendations, Malawi will have to address its rapid population growth and the unprecedented increase in its young population (box 5.10). Malawi's fertility rate has remained persistently high, particularly among rural poor women (6.1 births per woman). The country's population is expected to double in approximately two decades, reaching 34.4 million in 2038. For a country with high population density and limited land resources, population growth will make it difficult for the government to provide or improve public health, schooling, and other services. The high birth rate also lowers productivity because it impairs women's ability to engage in more productive farming or nonfarm work when they spend many of their prime years pregnant, lactating, and otherwise raising children. Moreover, Malawi's young age structure generates an extremely high proportion of dependents as a share of the working-age population. Such a ratio is associated with higher poverty levels. Reducing fertility in Malawi can change the population dynamics to achieve a lower ratio of dependents to working adults. While the link between fertility and poverty runs in both directions, lowering the dependency ratios across households can reduce poverty levels in Malawi.

Box 5.10 Accelerating the Demographic Transition to Boost Economic Growth and Poverty Reduction in Malawi

When high-fertility countries begin the fertility transition, the resulting shifts in age structure can boost economic development. After fertility rates begin falling, the share of children in the population eventually begins declining. At the same time, the share of people of working age (commonly recognized as ages 15–64 years) begins rising. Rising shares of people of working age suggest that the labor supply can grow faster than the total population—even if employment rates remain constant—and thus lead to an increase in workers per capita. There would be an automatic increase in growth in real gross domestic product (GDP) per capita. If the higher numbers of workers are saving at least at the same rate as previous generations, there also would be an increase in aggregate savings. If these savings could be converted into productive investment, they would speed up capital formation and improvements in capital-to-worker ratios—all leading to even faster growth in real GDP per capita. An increase of 1 percentage point in the share of the working-age population is estimated to boost GDP per capita 1.1–2.0 percentage points. The rapid growth of East Asia in past decades has been attributed to its realization of the demographic dividend.[a] As child dependency ratios fall and the share of working-age people increases, per capita income is likely to rise and poverty to fall. Families who have fewer children will have more resources per capita for consumption as well as for investment. Cross-country estimates suggest that a 1 percentage point reduction in the child dependency ratio is associated with a 0.38 percentage point reduction in the poverty head count rate (World Bank 2016b).[b]

Malawi is a high-fertility country, so a modest acceleration in its fertility decline could lead to substantial changes in its projected age structure. The country currently has a total fertility rate of 5.25. Under the United Nations median-fertility scenario, the total fertility rate is projected to fall to only 3.96 children by 2030 and to 3.16 children by 2050 (figure B5.10.1, panel a). If fertility declines are slower, as under the high-fertility scenario, then the future population's share of children will be even higher. In contrast, if fertility declines more rapidly in the future, as under the low-fertility scenario, there will be more potential workers by 2050 due to the higher share of people ages 15–64 years. Scenario analysis suggests that a one-child difference in Malawi's fertility rates by 2050 could lead to differences of 31 percent in real GDP per capita (figure B5.10.1, panel b). Under the medium-fertility scenario, simulations of Malawi's economic growth using the LINKAGE economic model suggest that real GDP per capita could grow from US$314 (constant U.S. dollars) in 2015 to US$446 by 2030 and to US$1,024 by 2050.[c] However, under the high-fertility scenario, growth would be more modest, reaching US$892 by 2050. Under the low-fertility scenario, per capita income in 2050 would be US$1,163.

---

box continues next page

Box 5.10 Accelerating the Demographic Transition to Boost Economic Growth and Poverty Reduction in Malawi *(continued)*

Figure B5.10.1 Simulated Declines in Total Fertility Rate and Rise in Real GDP per Capita in Malawi, 2015–50

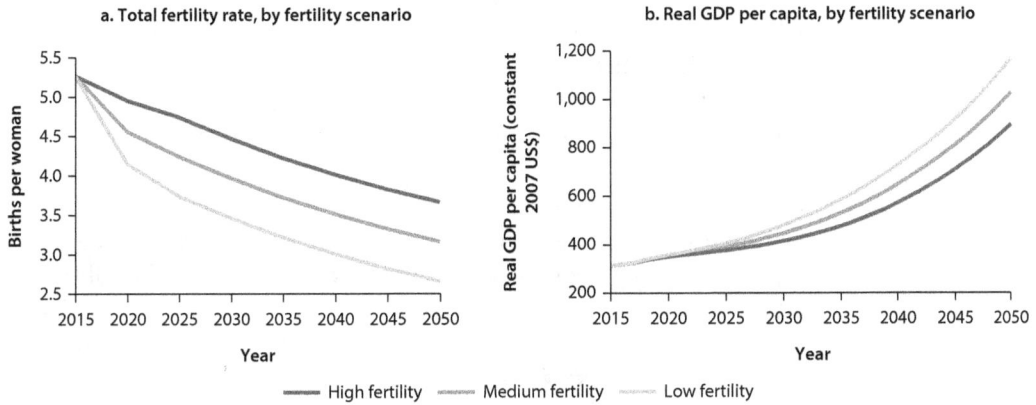

a. Total fertility rate, by fertility scenario

b. Real GDP per capita, by fertility scenario

High fertility   Medium fertility   Low fertility

Source: Simulation results are from LINKAGE, prepared for World Bank 2016b.
Note: The scenarios consider changes in the age structure projected in the United Nations medium-, high-, and low-fertility scenarios.

a. World Bank (2015) provides empirical estimates of the impact of changes in the age structure on growth and poverty reduction, in addition to an extensive review of the demographic dividend literature.
b. The child dependency ratio is the ratio of the under-15 population to the population ages 15–64 years. The aged dependency ratio is the ratio of the over-64 population to the population ages 15–64 years.
c. The LINKAGE model has been used to analyze the growth and poverty impacts of changes in age structure. The model is based on neoclassical growth theory in which aggregate growth depends on labor force, capital stock, and productivity. The growth of the labor supply is determined by the growth of the working-age population in each scenario. Saving is determined endogenously as a function of past saving, GDP growth, the child dependency ratio, and the aged dependency ratio. Past saving and GDP growth affect saving positively; the two dependency ratios affect saving negatively. The reason for the latter is that, as dependency rises, households' propensity to consume increases. The scenario analysis does not account for any possible discrete structural changes in Malawi's economy, such as unanticipated infrastructure investments. Therefore, the simulation results should be considered illustrative and as highlighting the marginal impacts of demographic change rather than as forecasts. For additional details on the methodology, see World Bank (2016b, chapter 9).

Policies in three key interrelated areas would reduce fertility and increase the demographic dividend. First, improve child health and lower family size. Improving child health will reduce child mortality and the demand for more children, while smaller family size will improve maternal and child health, completing the virtuous circle (Canning, Sangeeta, and Yazbeck 2015).

Second, it is important to expand female education, particularly secondary education, which is where education has a significant effect on fertility. Poor women and women with no education have the highest fertility rates across socioeconomic groups. In 2010, their fertility rates reached 6.9 and 6.8 births per woman, respectively. Malawian women with complete or incomplete primary educations have fertility patterns similar to women with no education. In contrast, women with secondary education or more have the lowest rates of fertility (3.6 births per woman).

This task will not be easy. In coming years, improvements in school retention along with growth in the school-age population will cause an unprecedented increase in both primary and secondary populations. In 2012, 50 percent of education sector expenditures were in primary education (World Bank 2013); secondary education accounted for only 14.8 percent. As a result, covering the needs of both subsystems will require significantly higher education spending. The government of Malawi recently increased public education spending to 8.1 percent of GDP, and education spending is growing faster than the general budget. Therefore, increasing education funding in the near future could be extremely challenging (World Bank 2013).

Third, it is important to increase access to family planning and reproductive health, especially among the poor, who report higher than desired fertility, and among adolescents, to curb child marriage and early childbearing (box 5.11). Improvements in these areas are desirable regardless of the potential economic payoffs, but they need to be given much higher priority than they are today. Controlling for socioeconomic and other characteristics, if Malawi were to eliminate early childbirth alone, the country's total fertility rate would decrease by 0.48 births (8 percent) (Onagoruwa and Wodon 2016). Likewise, based on data from the 2010 Demographic and Health Survey, postponing childbearing by one year would decrease a woman's expected number of children 4.5 percent, on average.

Box 5.11 Conditional Cash Transfers and Fertility Reduction among Teenage Girls in Rural Malawi

Cash transfer programs seem to be an effective intervention to reduce fertility among teenage girls in Malawi. Baird and others (2015) conducted an impact evaluation of a cash transfer program for teenage girls who dropped out of school in Malawi. The program, which provided conditional cash transfers to girls on the condition that they return to school, had large and long-term impacts on school completion, years of education, delayed marriage, and likelihood of bearing children. Two years after the program ended, the girls who were dropouts at the baseline but were offered cash transfers on the condition of returning to school were 10 percentage points less likely to be married and 4 percentage points less likely to have been pregnant; their school attainment was higher by six-tenths of a school year. The increased school attainment of women did not translate into better labor market outcomes because there were few income-generating opportunities available for them. Some women may be unable or unwilling to comply with conditions in such context of limited economic opportunities. Providing an unconditional cash transfer to adolescent girls to ensure some potential benefits around delaying early marriage and pregnancy topped up by conditional cash transfers for human capital accumulation and desired health behaviors may solve this tension (Baird, McIntosh, and Ozler 2016).

Summary

Reducing rural poverty in Malawi will require four elements: (a) stabilize growth that is consistent and strong; (b) raise the labor incomes of the poor by increasing the productivity of agriculture and facilitating movement into new, more remunerative nonfarm activities; (c) give larger and well-directed transfers to the poor by reforming existing safety net programs to help them to protect their incomes and assets against shocks; and (d) expand female secondary education and family planning, especially among poor adolescents, to reduce child marriage and early childbearing, to hasten the transition to smaller family size, and to generate the conditions for harnessing the income gains achieved through the other policies.

Notes

1. Cash-based subsidies are quite different from the current practice; therefore, caution is needed if they are to be introduced and rolled out. If cash-based subsidies are considered for rollout, the government of Malawi could start with a pilot, learn from it, and scale it up based on the lessons learned.

2. A thought experiment is a device for performing an intentional, structured process of intellectual deliberation in order to speculate, within a specifiable problem domain, about potential consequences for a designated antecedent (Yeates 2004).

3. COMSIP is a member-owned savings and investment institution created to provide financial services, especially savings mobilization and investment promotion, to the unserved and underserved periurban and rural communities. COMSIP Cooperative Union, which evolved from a component under the Malawi Social Action Fund, is implementing the savings and investment activities. It now has 135 cooperatives and is regulated by the Ministry of Industry and Trade under the Cooperative Society Act 1998.

4. See also table K.2 in appendix K for cross-country comparisons of overall changes in productivity and changes within and across sectors.

5. The type of model used to project future growth, called a computable general equilibrium model, captures the structural characteristics of and links between urban and rural areas. It includes the complex workings of the economy, including all interactions between producers, households, government, and the rest of the world.

6. A *biometric* is a measure of identity on the basis of a physiological (fingerprint, face, eye iris, or retina) or behavioral (speech or signature) characteristic. A biometric is an effective personal identifier because it is unique to and embodied in each person and cannot be forgotten, lost, or stolen. Recent advancements in recognition technology, coupled with increases in digital storage capacity and computer processing speed, have made biometric technology increasingly feasible in low-income and lower-middle-income country settings.

References

Ambler, K., A. de Brauw, and S. Godlonton. 2016. "Relaxing Constraints for Family Farmers: Providing Capital and Information in Malawi." IFPRI Working Paper, International Food Policy Research Institute, Washington, DC.

Angelucci, M., O. Attanasio, and V. Di Maro. 2012. "The Impact of Oportunidades on Consumption, Savings and Transfers." *Fiscal Studies* 33 (3): 305–34.

Baird, S., E. Chirwa, C. McIntosh, and B. Ozler. 2015. *What Happens Once the Intervention Ends? The Medium-Term Impacts of a Cash Transfer Programme in Malawi.* Grantee Final Report. New Delhi: International Initiative for Impact Evaluation.

Baird, S., C. McIntosh, and B. Ozler. 2016. "When the Money Runs Out. Do Cash Transfers Have Sustained Effects on Human Capital Accumulation?" Policy Research Working Paper 7901, World Bank, Washington, DC.

Beck, T., A. Demirgüç-Kunt, and R. Levine. 2007. "Finance, Inequality, and the Poor." *Journal of Economic Growth* 12 (1): 27–49.

Bianchi, M., and M. Bobba. 2013. "Liquidity, Risk, and Occupational Choices." *Review of Economic Studies* 80 (2): 491–511.

Blattman, C., and L. Ralston. 2015. "Generating Employment in Poor and Fragile States: Evidence from Labor Market and Entrepeneurship Programs." World Bank, Washington, DC.

Bruhn, M., and I. Love. 2014. "The Real Impact of Improved Access to Finance: Evidence from Mexico." *Journal of Finance* 69 (3): 1347–76.

Brune, L., X. Giné, J. Goldberg, and D. Yang. 2015. "Facilitating Savings for Agriculture: Field Experimental Evidence from Malawi." NBER Working Paper 20946, National Bureau of Economic Research, Cambridge, MA.

Caldés, N., D. Coady, and J. A. Maluccio. 2006. "The Cost of Poverty Alleviation Transfer Programs: A Comparative Analysis of Three Programs in Latin America." *World Development* 34 (5): 818–37.

Canning, D., R. Sangeeta, and A.S. Yazbeck, eds. 2015. *Africa's Demographic Transition: Dividend or Disaster?* Africa Development Forum Series. Washington, DC: Agence Française de Développement and World Bank.

Chirwa, E. W., and P. M. Mvula. 2014. "Malawi: Baseline Financial Literacy and Consumer Protection Household Survey." Reserve Bank of Malawi.

De Mel, S., D. McKenzie, and C. Woodruff. 2012. "One-Time Transfers of Cash or Capital Have Long-Lasting Effects on Microenterprises in Sri Lanka." *Science* 335 (6071): 962–66.

Dunga, S. 2014. "An Analysis of the Relationship between Access to Loans and District Poverty Rate in Malawi." *Mediterranean Journal of Social Sciences* 5 (13): 134–138.

Evans, D. K., and A. Popova. 2014. "Cash Transfers and Temptation Goods: A Review of Global Evidence." Policy Research Working Paper 6886, World Bank, Washington, DC. http://www.gsdrc.org/document-library/cash-transfers-and-temptation-goods -a-review-of-global-evidence/.

Flory, J. A. 2012. "Development Programs and General Equilibrium Effects: Experimental Evidence on Formal Savings and Informal Insurance in Villages." Working Paper, University of Chicago, Chicago, IL.

Gertler, P. J., S. W. Martinez, and M. Rubio-Codina. 2012. "Investing Cash Transfers to Raise Long-Term Living Standards." *American Economic Journal: Applied Economics* 4 (1): 164–92.

Goyal, A., and J. Nash. 2016. "Reaping Richer Returns: Public Spending Priorities for Pro-Poor Agriculture Growth in Africa." Africa Regional Study Flagship Series, World Bank, Washington, DC.

Grossman, J., and M. Tarazi. 2014. "Serving Smallholder Farmers: Recent Developments in Digital Finance." *Focus Note* 94.

Jacoby, H. 2016a. "Poverty and Distributional Implications of Reforms to Malawi's FISP." Note prepared for the Poverty and Social Impact Analysis of the Malawi Farm Input Subsidy Program. World Bank, Washington, DC.

———. 2016b. "Smart Subsidy? Welfare and Distributional Implications of Malawi's FISP." Working Paper, World Bank, Washington, DC.

Katengeza, S. P., J. J. Okello, E. R. Mensah, and N. Jambo. 2014. "Effect of Participation in ICT-Based Market Information Services on Transaction Costs and Household Income among Smallholder Farmers in Malawi." In *Technologies for Sustainable Development: A Way to Reduce Poverty*, edited by J.-C. Bolay, S. Hostettler, and E. Hazboun, 197–207. Berlin: Springer.

Ksoll, C., and R. F. Forskningsenhed. 2013. "Impact of Village Savings and Loans Associations: Evidence from a Cluster Randomized Trial." Rockwool Foundation Research Unit, Copenhagen.

McMillan, M. S., and K. Harttgen. 2014. "What Is Driving 'African Growth Miracle'?" NBER Working Paper 20077, National Bureau of Economic Research, Cambridge, MA.

Nsengiyumva, F., A. N. Peralta-Alva, N. Maehle, S. L. Ruiz, F. Wu, S. Banda, L. F. Almeida, and E. Rengifo. 2015. *Malawi Selected Issues*. IMF Country Report 15/346, International Monetary Fund, Washington, DC.

Onagoruwa, A., and Q. Wodon. 2016. "Early Childbirth and under Five Mortality in Malawi." Knowledge Brief. HNP (Health, Nutrition, and Population Global Practice), World Bank, Washington, DC.

Ricker-Gilbert, J. 2016. "Review of Malawi's Farm Input Subsidy Program in 2016 and Direction for Re-design." Report prepared for the Poverty and Social Impact Analysis of the Malawi Farm Input Subsidy Program. World Bank, Washington, DC.

Sharma, D., and G. Nagarajan. 2011. "Rural Finance Outreach in Central Malawi: Implications for Opportunity International Bank of Malawi." Financial Services Assessment, IRIS Center, University of Maryland, College Park.

Shaw, A., and G. Nagarajan. 2011. "Effects of Savings on Consumption, Production, and Food Security: Evidence from Rural Malawi." Financial Services Assessment, IRIS Center, University of Maryland, College Park.

Shimamura, Y. and S. Lastarria-Cornhiel. 2015. "Agricultural Microcredit and Household Vulnerability in Rural Malawi." *Journal of International Cooperation Studies* 22 (2): 363-83.

World Bank. 2013. "Malawi Public Expenditure Review 2013." Report 79865-MW, World Bank, Washington, DC.

———. 2015. *Global Monitoring Report 2015/2016: Development Goals in an Era of Demographic Change*. World Bank, Washington, DC.

———. 2016a. "Malawi CEM Background Note on FISP Reform." World Bank, Washington, DC.

———. 2016b. "Malawi Poverty Assessment." World Bank, Washington, DC.

———. 2016c. "Malawi Urbanization Review: Leveraging Urbanization for National Growth and Development." World Bank, Washington, DC.

———. 2016d. *World Development Report 2016: Internet for Development*. New York: University of Oxford Press.

Yeates, L.B. 2004. *Thought Experimentation: A Cognitive Approach*. Graduate Diploma in Arts (By Research) dissertation, University of New South Wales.

Official Development Assistance and Government Expenditures for Education and Health

The commitment of Malawi's government and donor community to health and education is evident from the resources allocated to these sectors. In 2011, Malawi received a total flow of official development assistance (ODA) of US$0.8 billion, equivalent to 15 percent of its national income. The distribution of the assistance reflects the donors' priorities. The largest proportion (41.5 percent) of ODA was allocated to health, and the third largest proportion (8.6 percent) was allocated to education (figure A.1).

In 2011, the allocation of government expenditures to various sectors was in line with the ODA allocation. The education sector received the largest share of public funds, followed by agriculture, health, and transport infrastructure in that order.

Figure A.1 Gross Official Development Assistance to Malawi and Distribution of Government Expenditures, by Sector

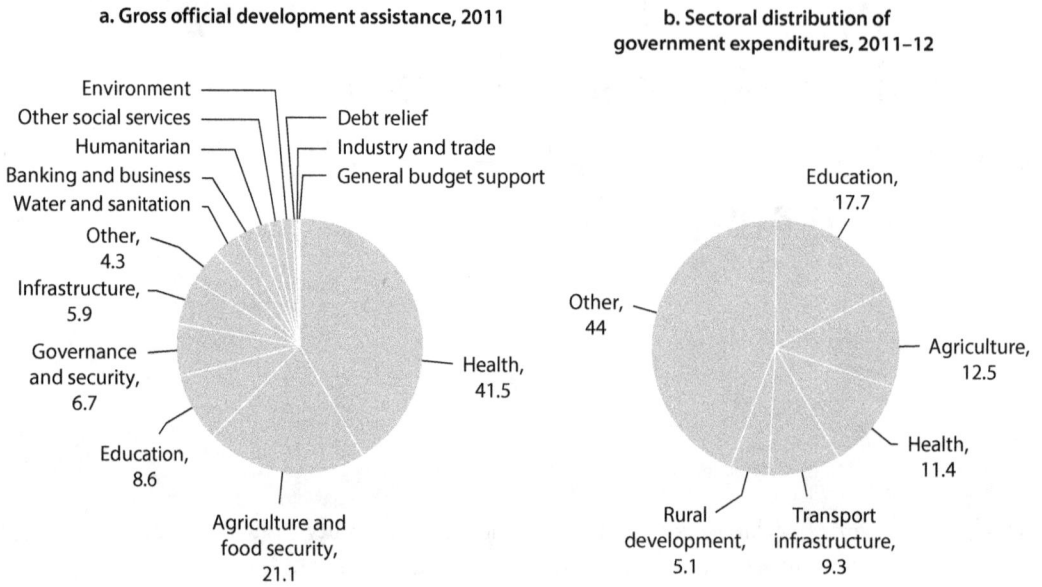

a. Gross official development assistance, 2011

b. Sectoral distribution of government expenditures, 2011–12

Environment
Other social services
Humanitarian
Banking and business
Water and sanitation
Debt relief
Industry and trade
General budget support
Other, 4.3
Infrastructure, 5.9
Governance and security, 6.7
Education, 8.6
Health, 41.5
Agriculture and food security, 21.1

Education, 17.7
Other, 44
Agriculture, 12.5
Health, 11.4
Rural development, 5.1
Transport infrastructure, 9.3

Sources: Coppard, Randel, and German 2013; World Bank 2013.
Note: Values were not available for some sectors.

References

Coppard, D., J. Randel, and T. German. 2013. "Investments to End Poverty: Real Money, Real Choices, Real Lives." Report, Development Initiatives, Bristol, United Kingdom.

World Bank. 2013. "Malawi Public Expenditure Review 2013." Report 79865-MW, World Bank, Washington, DC.

Daily Caloric Consumption per Capita of the Rural Poor

Figure B.1 depicts the average caloric intake per capita in rural areas of Malawi in 2004, 2010, and 2013. To allow for comparability with estimates for 2013, the values presented depict only the daily caloric consumption per capita during the nonlean season (March to November); they do not include the months spanning the lean season. Comparisons between poor and nonpoor households in rural areas reveal that the poor have significantly lower daily caloric consumption per capita than nonpoor households. A poor person consumes, on average, approximately 1,250 fewer kilocalories per day than a nonpoor person. The average caloric intake per capita of the poor also falls below a daily threshold of 2,100 kilocalories per capita. On average, poor individuals consume at least 367 fewer calories than the threshold.

Over time, caloric intake per capita in rural areas has not improved. The fact that the rural poor consume, on average, fewer than 2,100 kilocalories per person per day suggests the presence of prolonged food insecurity.

Figure B.1 Daily Caloric Consumption per Capita in Malawi, March–November, 2004–13

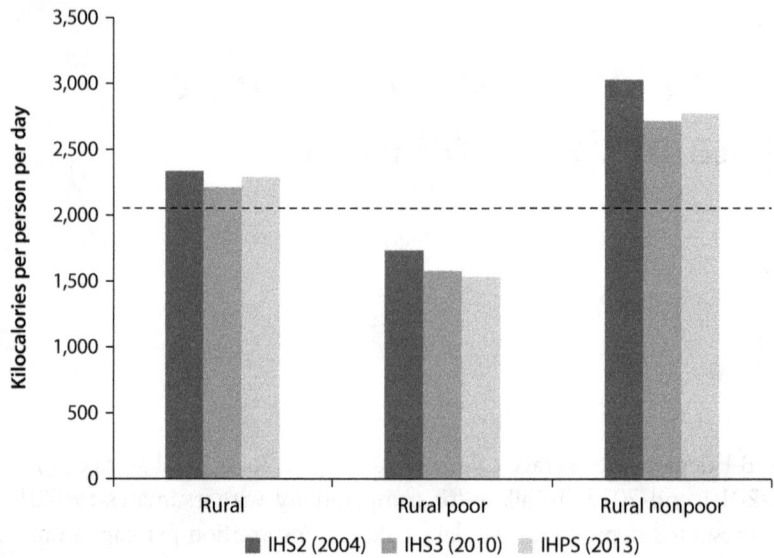

Source: World Bank 2016, based on IHS2, IHS3, and IHPS data.
Note: Dashed line denotes 2,100 calories/person/day, the minimum value for food security and nutritional stability (World Food Programme 2005). IHS2 = Second Integrated Household Survey; IHS3 = Third Integrated Household Survey; IHPS = Integrated Household Panel Survey.

References

World Bank. 2016. "Malawi Poverty Assessment." World Bank, Washington, DC.

World Food Programme. 2005. *Emergency Food Security Assessment Handbook*. 1st ed. Rome, Italy: World Food Programme.

Correlation between Price Inflation of Maize and Food Insecurity

It is typically recognized that sharp increases in food prices often lead to increases in food insecurity among persons without access to farmland or credit. In rural Malawi, analysis of household panel data confirms that higher maize prices can result in a higher level of food insecurity (table C.1). A one-unit increase in the inflation rate of maize prices increases the probability of experiencing food insecurity over the past 12 months, or of worrying about food in the past 7 days, by 8.0 and 5.3 percent, respectively. Individuals who face a one-unit increase in the rate of inflation of maize prices experience an additional 0.37 months of food insecurity, on average (Jolliffe, Seff, and de la Fuente 2016).

Table C.1 Maize Price Inflation and Experiential Food Insecurity in Rural Malawi

	Food insecure in the past 12 months	Number of months of food insecurity in the past 12 months	Worried about food in the past 7 days
Maize price 12 months ago (month 1)	0.003***	0.017***	0.004***
	(0.001)	(0.005)	(0.001)
Change in inflation rate of maize (past 12 months)	0.079***	0.371***	0.053**
	(0.016)	(0.077)	(0.022)
Food consumption score	−0.003***	−0.019***	−0.004***
	(0.001)	(0.005)	(0.001)
Daily per capita calorie consumption (thousands)	−0.006	0.083	−0.010
	(0.016)	(0.062)	(0.014)
Annual per capita expenditure (kwacha)	−0.000*	−0.000*	−0.000
	(0.000)	(0.000)	(0.000)
Number of observations	16,788	16,788	16,788
Adjusted R^2	0.066	0.074	0.048

Source: Jolliffe, Seff, and de la Fuente 2016.
Note: All models control for individual fixed effects and are estimated using OLS regressions. Observations are weighted to be representative of rural areas. Standard errors (in parentheses) are clustered at the EA level. EA = enumeration area; OLS = ordinary least squares; R^2 = coefficient of determination.
$*p < .1, **p < .05, ***p < .01$.

Reference

Jolliffe, D., I. Seff, and A. de la Fuente. 2016. "Food Insecurity and Rising Food Prices: What Do We Learn from Experiential Measures?" Unpublished, World Bank, Washington, DC.

Variability of Food Staple Prices in Malawi and Comparator Countries

Price variability or volatility has two components, a stochastic and a deterministic part. For food crops, the deterministic part largely corresponds to the seasonal movement in prices, following the seasonal nature of the agricultural production cycle. A systematic study of food price movements across a series of countries in Africa shows that food price seasonality is particularly high in Malawi (Gilbert, Christiaensen, and Kaminski 2016). At 50.6 percent on average (table D.1), maize price seasonality is particularly striking in Malawi. Put differently, maize prices are on average 50.6 percent higher during the peak (hunger) season than during the trough (postharvest).

Households in Malawi appear to suffer a double seasonality impact—the main staple food is maize, which has the highest seasonal gap among the cereals (33.1 percent on average across the countries studied), and there is a large country effect (34 percent). Moreover, seasonality in Malawi's food prices only explains 20 percent of overall food price volatility in Malawi. The prevalence of high seasonal gaps throughout Malawi together with the sharp drop in the gap as one moves north into Tanzania[1] suggests that the high Malawian gaps are the results of political or institutional factors specific to the country rather than agroeconomic factors. To that extent, it should be possible to reduce some of the more extreme instances of seasonal price variation in Malawi, including by facilitating cross-country trading, which would also benefit Tanzania. From this perspective, the specific attention in the seasonality literature to maize price seasonality and volatility in Malawi does not surprise—see, for example, Manda (2010), Chirwa, Dorward, and Vigneri (2011), and Ellis and Manda (2012).

Table D.1 Seasonal Gap Estimates in Select African Countries
price variability (%)

	Burkina Faso	Ethiopia	Ghana	Malawi	Niger	Tanzania	Uganda
Bananas (sweet)	–	9.10	48.60	–	–	–	–
Beans	–	–	–	27.70	–	23.20	28.10
Cassava	–	–	19.20	26.60	–	–	20.10
Cowpeas	–	–	14.50	–	47.50	–	–
Eggs	–	14.30	7.20	–	–	–	–
Maize	26.90	19.80	38.00	50.60	20.10	29.40	31.10
Matoke/plantains	–	–	61.50	–	–	–	28.80
Millet	23.40	–	9.20	–	–	20.20	19.00
Oranges	–	21.00	33.60	–	–	–	–
Rice	–	–	18.40	19.90	–	19.90	12.50
Sorghum	24.70	13.60	11.80	–	–	14.50	22.60
Teff	–	10.30	–	–	–	–	–
Tomatoes	–	36.30	98.00	–	–	–	–

Source: Gilbert, Christiaensen, and Kaminski 2016.
Note: The seven African countries were those in which Living Standards Measurement Study – Integrated Surveys on Agriculture (LSMS-ISA) project was administered. The table reports averages of the seasonal gap estimates for each country-commodity pair in wholesale markets irrespective of statistical significance using the preferred gap estimates. Ethiopia: teff refers to white teff. Ghana: rice refers to locally produced rice; plantain is ap'tu plantain; bananas are ap'em plantain. – = price data obtained.

Note

1. Gilbert, Christiaensen, and Kaminski (2016) show that maize price seasonality can change dramatically when crossing borders despite similar cultivation and meteorological conditions. They find that Mbeya, which is the capital of the Tanzanian region (*mkoa*) of the same name contiguous with the border with Malawi, exhibits a maize seasonal gap of 22.8 percent. Chitipa, Karonga, and Misuku, on the other hand, the closest locations along the Malawian border with time series market information at 143 km, 161 km, and 180 km from Mbeya, have seasonal maize price gaps of 48.3, 74.8, and 71.6 percent respectively.

References

Chirwa, E., A. Dorward, and M. Vigneri. 2011. "Seasonality and Poverty—Evidence from Malawi." In Devereux, S., R. Sabates-Wheeler, and R. Longhurst, eds. *Seasonality, Rural Livelihoods and Development.* London: Routledge.

Ellis, F., and E. Manda. 2012. "Seasonal Food Crises and Policy Responses: A Narrative Account of Three Food Security Crises in Malawi." *World Development* 40: 1407–1417.

Gilbert, C. L., L. Christiaensen, and J. Kaminski. 2016. "Food Price Seasonality in Africa: Measurement and Extent." *Food Policy.* Forthcoming. http://dx.doi.org/10.1016/j .foodpol.2016.09.016.

Manda, E. 2010. *Price Instability in the Maize Market in Malawi.* Saarbrücken, Germany: Lambert Academic.

Agricultural Productivity, Public Spending, and Poverty Reduction

Figure E.1 Agricultural Productivity in Malawi and Selected Other Countries, 2013

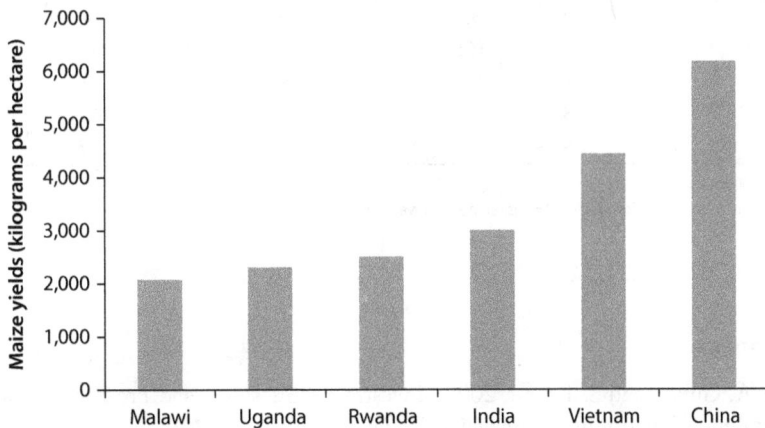

Source: FAOSTAT data 2013.

Table E.1 Shares of Agricultural Public Spending in Malawi, 2007–11

Component	Percent
Crop production (FISP)	52
Crop production (non-FISP)	11
Institutional support	8
Technology generation and dissemination	7
Irrigation	6
Livestock	2
Other	14

Source: World Bank 2013.
Note: FISP = Food Input Subsidy Program.

Table E.2 Contribution of Investments and Subsidies to Agricultural Growth and Poverty Reduction in India, 1960–2000

Indicator	1960s Returns	1960s Rank	1970s Returns	1970s Rank	1980s Returns	1980s Rank	1990s Returns	1990s Rank
Returns in agricultural GDP (Rs produced per Rs spent)								
Road investment	8.79	1	3.80	3	3.03	5	3.17	2
Educational investment	5.97	2	7.88	1	3.88	3	1.53	3
Irrigation investment	2.65	5	2.10	5	3.61	4	1.41	4
Irrigation subsidies	2.24	7	1.22	7	2.28	6	—	8
Fertilizer subsidies	2.41	6	3.03	4	0.88	8	0.53	7
Power subsidies	1.18	8	0.95	8	1.66	7	0.58	6
Credit subsidies	3.86	3	1.68	6	5.20	2	0.89	5
Agricultural R&D	3.12	4	5.90	2	6.95	1	6.93	1
Returns in rural poverty reduction (decrease in number of poor per million Rs spent)								
Road investment	1,272	1	1,346	1	295	3	335	1
Educational investment	411	2	469	2	447	1	109	3
Irrigation investment	182	5	125	5	197	5	67	4
Irrigation subsidies	149	7	68	7	113	6	—	8
Fertilizer subsidies	166	6	181	4	48	8	24	7
Power subsidies	79	8	52	8	83	7	27	6
Credit subsidies	257	3	93	6	259	4	42	5
Agricultural R&D	207	4	326	3	345	2	323	2

Source: Fan, Gulati, and Thorat 2008.

Note: — = not available; GDP = gross domestic product; R&D = research and development.

References

Fan, S., A. Gulati, and S. Thorat. 2008. "Investment, Subsidies, and Pro-Poor Growth in Rural India." *Agricultural Economics* 39 (2): 163–170.

World Bank. 2013. "Agricultural Public Expenditure Review 2000–2013 Malawi." World Bank, Washington, DC.

Determinants of Agricultural Productivity in Malawi, 2010–13

A household fixed-effects model is used to account for household-specific unobservables. Agricultural productivity is measured as quantity of maize produced per hectare. The model is specified as follows:

$$InY_{ph} = InX_{ph}\beta + Z_{ph}\beta \ \alpha_p + u_{ph,} \qquad (F.1)$$

for $p = 1, ..., P$ and $h = 1, ..., H$, where Y_{ph} is agricultural productivity observed for plot p belonging to household h. X_{ph} and Z_{ph} are vectors of variables that affect agricultural productivity, which are classified into physical inputs, human capital, asset ownership, and household and geo-variables, α_p is the unobserved household-invariant individual effects, and u_{ph} is the error term. For variables in X_{ph} (such as inorganic fertilizer, family labor, hired labor, and exchange labor) that have zeros, the Malawi Poverty Assessment team followed Bellemare, Barrett, and Just (2013) and D'Souza and Jolliffe (2013) and used the inverse hyperbolic sine transformation (IHST) instead of the log transformation. IHST is a logarithmic-like transformation that enables negative as well as zero-valued observations and enables the coefficients to be interpreted as elasticities. The estimates of the other independent variables change only slightly in magnitude when this transformation is used. The regression results are presented in table F.1.

Table F.1 Determinants of Agricultural Productivity in Malawi (Maize Yield)

Variable	Coefficient	Standard error
Log rate of inorganic fertilizer application (kilograms per hectare)	0.050***	0.009
More than 10% below recommended rate of fertilizer application (1 = yes)	−0.106*	0.057
More than 10% above recommended rate of fertilizer application (1 = yes)	−0.009	0.061
Basal fertilizer was applied within seven days after planting (1 = yes)	0.073*	0.042

table continues next page

Table F.1 Determinants of Agricultural Productivity in Malawi (Maize Yield) *(continued)*

Variable	Coefficient	Standard error
Intercropped (1 = yes)	0.102***	0.038
Applied organic fertilizer (1 = yes)	0.087**	0.043
Log seed rate (kilograms per hectare)	0.027***	0.010
Planted hybrid variety (1 = yes)	0.026	0.029
Log plot size (hectares)	−0.362***	0.068
Log plot size squared	0.001	0.023
Log family labor (days)	0.096***	0.022
Log hired labor (days)	0.056***	0.013
Log exchange labor (days)	0.010	0.043
Good or fair soil quality (1= yes)	0.154***	0.042
Soil quality index	−0.098**	0.040
Little or no slope (1 = yes)	−0.005	0.031
Soil type is between sandy and clay soil	0.029	0.034
Managed by female (1 = yes)	−0.128**	0.055
Age of plot manager (years)	0.003	0.002
Education of plot manager (years)	0.004	0.009
Household size	0.008	0.016
Dependency ratio	0.000	0.000
Household owns livestock (1 = yes)	0.131***	0.041
Household participates in off-farm income-generating activities (1 = yes)	0.041	0.047
Household earns agricultural and/or nonagricultural wage (1 = yes)	−0.060	0.037
Distance to district boma (kilometers)	−0.001	0.001
Agroecological zone fixed effects	Yes	
Durable assets index	0.056***	0.018
Log of total annual rainfall (millimeters)	2.433*	1.329
Log of average annual temperature (× 10° Celsius)	−0.712	1.348
Household received extension service for production (1 = yes)	−0.053	0.036
Household had access to credit (1 = yes)	0.025	0.042
Year (1 = 2013)	0.100**	0.041
Constant	−7.095	12.988
Number of observations	4,326	
R^2	0.699	

Source: World Bank 2016, based on IHS3 and IHPS data.
Note: Standard errors are in parentheses. IHS3 = Third Integrated Household Survey; IHPS = Integrated Household Panel Survey.
*$p < .1$, **$p < .05$, ***$p < .01$.

References

Bellemare, M. F., C. B. Barrett, and D. R. Just. 2013. "The Welfare Impacts of Community Price Volatility: Evidence from Rural Ethiopia." *American Journal of Agricultural Economics* 95 (4): 877–99.

D'Souza, A., and Jolliffe, D. 2013. "Food Insecurity in Vulnerable Population: Coping with Food Price Shocks in Afghanistan." *American Journal of Agricultural Economics* 96 (3): 790–812.

World Bank. 2016. "Malawi Poverty Assessment." World Bank, Washington, DC.

Characteristics of the Rural Poor and Nonpoor

Figure G.1 Select Characteristics of the Rural Poor and Nonpoor in Malawi, 2010 and 2013
percent

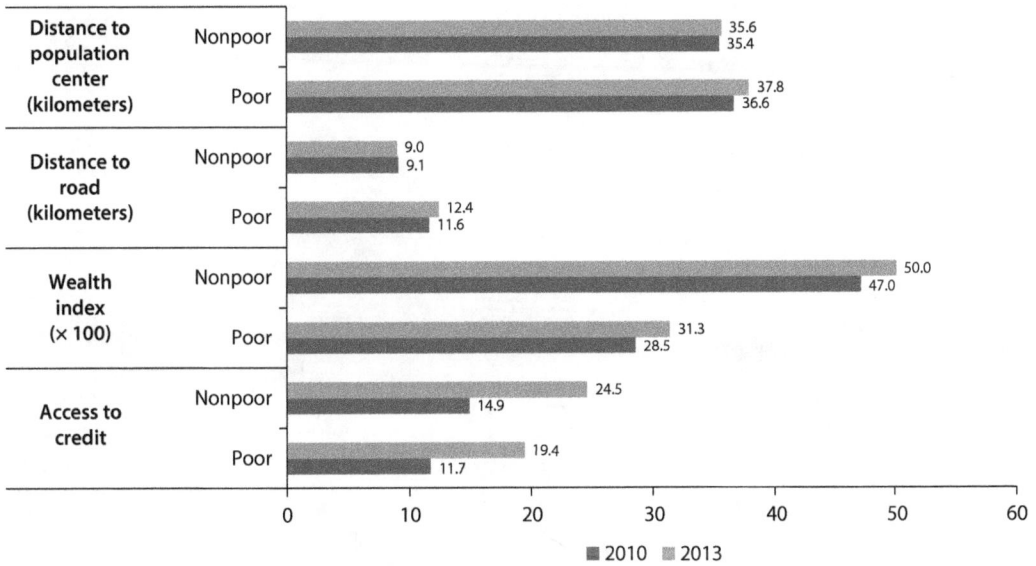

Source: World Bank 2016, based on IHS3 panel and IHPS data.
Note: IHS3 = Third Integrated Household Survey; IHPS = Integrated Household Panel Survey.

Reference

World Bank. 2016. "Malawi Poverty Assessment." World Bank, Washington, DC.

Review of Public Work Programs in Low-Income and Lower-Middle-Income Countries

Table H.1 Characteristics of Public Work Programs in Low-Income and Lower-Middle-Income Countries

Country	Total amount paid per year (PPP)	Working days per year	Target	Timing	Other supports	Impacts
Malawi	0.62	48	Targeted to poor households	Planting and harvest	Subsidized fertilizer	No significant impact
Ethiopia	15.44	120	Targeted to chronically food-insecure households	Mainly in lean season; additional food and cash assistance provided when there is unpredicted shock	Food, job training	When combined with agricultural support, (+) food security, technology adoption, nonfarm business
Ghana	169.48–225.97	57	Self-targeting, but household needs to be "extremely poor"	Agricultural off-season	—	(+) paid employment, food consumption, school attendance
Liberia	4.31	40	Voluntary participation open to community members ages 18 years	No specific season	—	21% decline in the poverty gap
Sierra Leone	0.04	50	Youth in poor and vulnerable communities	Rotation	—	(+) income, starting business, asset accumulation of livestock
Tanzania	0.48–1.44	65	Self-targeting	Rotation	—	
Bangladesh	1.33–2.22	120	Ultra-poor in food-insecure areas, vulnerable households in disaster-prone areas	Public work from January to June, job training in other months	Food, skill training	(+) income, number of income-generating activities
India	12.67	100	Not specifically targeted to the poor; guarantees employment for anyone needing a job	Guarantees employment for anyone needing a job or hit by idiosyncratic shocks	—	(+) nutritional intake, accumulation of nonfinancial assets such as land

Sources: Andrews and others 2011; Beegle, Galasso, and Goldberg 2015; Davis and Handa 2015; Handa and others 2013; Hoddinott and others 2012; Imbert and Papp 2015; Rosas and Sabarwal 2014; World Bank 2014.

Note: PPP = purchasing power parity.

References

Andrews, C., P. Backiny-Yetna, E. Garin, E. Weedon, Q. Wodon, and G. Zampaglione. 2011. "Liberia's Cash for Work Temporary Employment Project: Responding to Crisis in Low-Income, Fragile Countries." SP Discussion Paper 1114, World Bank, Washington, DC.

Beegle, K., E. Galasso, and J. Goldberg. 2015. "Direct and Indirect Effects of Malawi's Public Works Program on Food Security." Policy Research Working Paper 7505, World Bank, Washington, DC.

Davis, B., and S. Handa. 2015. "How Much Do Programmes Pay? Transfer Size in Selected National Cash Transfer Programmes in Sub-Saharan Africa." The Transfer Project Research Brief 2015-09, University of North Carolina, Carolina Population Center, Chapel Hill, NC; UNICEF, Florence.

Handa, S., M. J. Park, R. O. Darko, I. Osei-Akoto, B. Davis, and S. Diadone. 2013. "Livelihood Empowerment against Poverty Impact Evaluation." Carolina Population Center, University of North Carolina, Chapel Hill.

Hoddinott, J., G. Berhane, D. O. Gilligan, N. Kumar, and A. S. Taffesse. 2012. "The Impact of Ethiopia's Productive Safety Net Programme and Related Transfers on Agricultural Productivity." *Journal of African Economics* 21 (5): 761–86.

Imbert, C., and J. Papp. 2015. "Labor Market Effects of Social Programs: Evidence from India's Employment Guarantee." *American Economic Journal: Applied Economics* 7 (2): 233–63.

Rosas, N., and S. Sabarwal. 2014. "Opportunity and Resilience: Do Public Works Have It All? Evidence from a Randomized Evaluation in Sierra Leone." World Bank, Washington, DC.

World Bank. 2014. "Bangladesh—Employment Generation Program for the Poorest Project." World Bank, Washington, DC.

Household Participation Rates in the Malawi Farm Input Subsidy Program, by Landholding and Poverty Status

Figure I.1 FISP Participation in Malawi, by Landholding, 2013

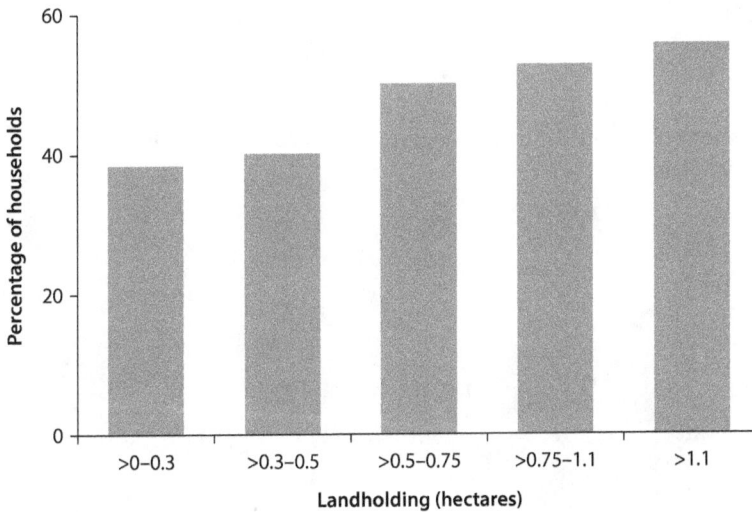

Source: Estimates are based on IHPS data.
Note: IHPS = Integrated Household Panel Survey.

Figure I.2 FISP Participation of Poor Households in Malawi, by Landholding, 2013

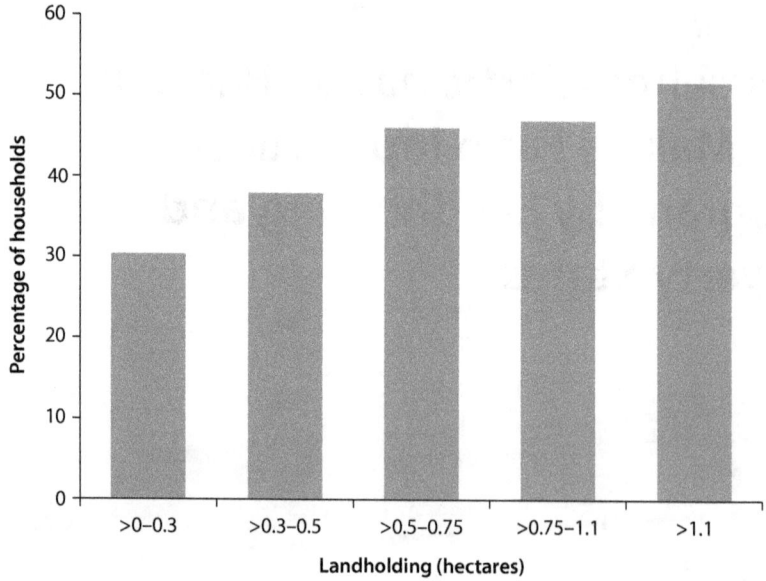

Source: Estimates are based on IHPS data.
Note: IHPS = Integrated Household Panel Survey.

Figure I.3 FISP Participation of Nonpoor Households in Malawi, by Landholding, 2013

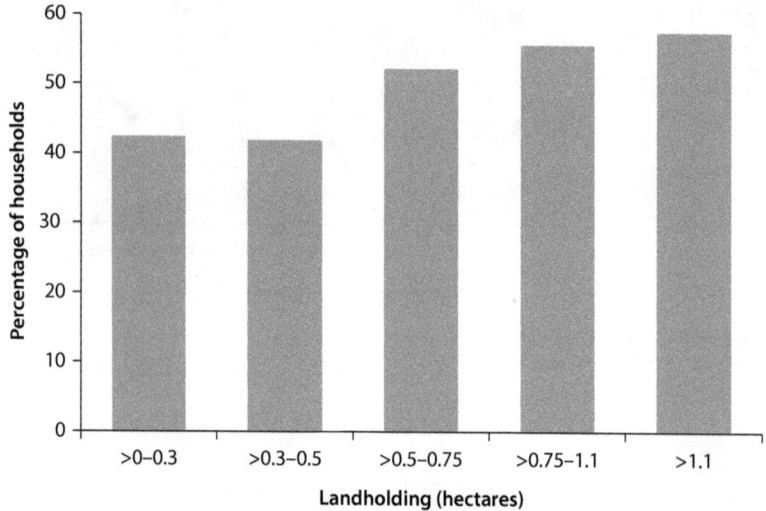

Source: Estimates are based on IHPS data.
Note: IHPS = Integrated Household Panel Survey.

Effects of a Cash (Instead of an In-Kind) Transfer on Poverty in Malawi, 2010

Figure J.1 Effects of a Cash (Instead of an In-Kind) Transfer on Poverty in Malawi, 2010

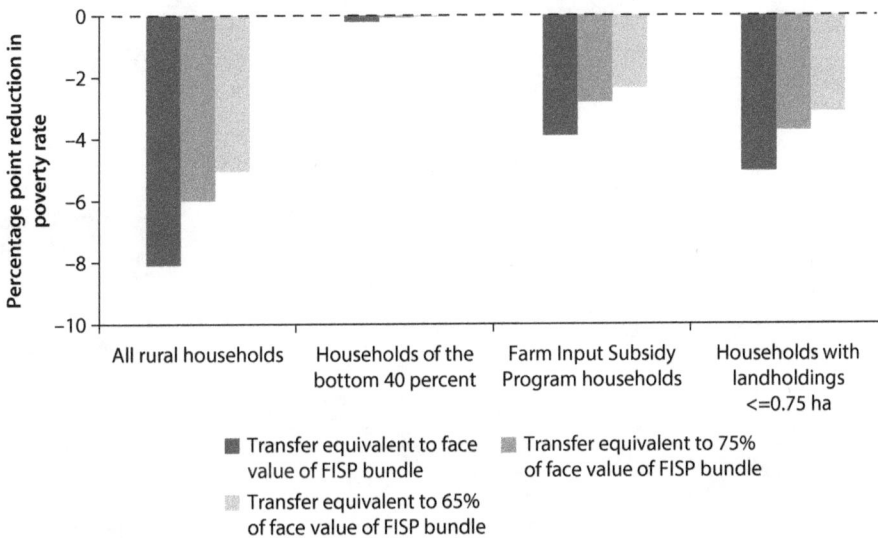

Transfer equivalent to face value of FISP bundle

Transfer equivalent to 75% of face value of FISP bundle

Transfer equivalent to 65% of face value of FISP bundle

Source: Estimates are based on IHS3 data.
Note: FISP = Farm Input Subsidy Program; IHS3 = Third Integrated Household Survey.

Cross-Country Decompositions on Sectoral Employment and Productivity

Table K.1 Changes in Sectoral Share of Employment in Africa, 2000–10

Country	Agriculture	Mining	Manufacturing	Tertiary
Angola	−12.55	−0.28	0.15	12.69
Cameroon	−5.23	−0.11	5.49	−0.15
Ethiopia	−8.59	0.34	2.67	5.58
Ghana	−11.02	−0.41	−0.19	11.62
Kenya	−21.56	0.00	7.19	14.37
Malawi	−10.90	−0.04	1.44	9.50
Mali	−3.76	0.01	1.41	2.34
Mauritius	−3.91	−0.28	−8.62	12.80
Mozambique	−0.92	−0.69	3.94	−2.34
Nigeria	−6.92	0.15	0.99	5.78
Rwanda	−10.55	0.48	2.48	7.58
Senegal	−6.54	0.14	2.97	3.43
South Africa	−7.84	−2.47	−0.12	10.42
Tanzania	−11.54	0.20	1.49	9.85
Uganda	−11.19	0.12	1.22	9.86
Zambia	−0.03	0.12	0.33	−0.43
Simple average (excluding Mauritius, North Africa, and South Africa)				
Simple average	−8.61	−0.16	2.10	6.67
Weighted average	−8.35	−0.06	1.87	6.54

Source: McMillan and Harttgen 2014, table A.3.

Table K.2 Decomposition of Productivity Growth in Africa, Post-2000
percent

Country	Labor productivity growth	Of which	
		Within sector	Structural
Angola	5.68	5.29	0.39
Cameroon	−2.61	−3.08	0.46
Ethiopia	2.09	2.06	0.03
Ghana	3.63	3.66	−0.03
Kenya	0.57	0.29	0.27
Malawi	−1.73	−1.80	0.08
Mali	2.81	2.29	0.52
Mauritius	2.29	1.82	0.46
Mozambique	4.91	3.98	0.94
Nigeria	3.77	0.96	2.81
Rwanda	3.96	−0.16	4.12
Senegal	0.79	−0.37	1.16
South Africa	2.47	2.10	0.38
Tanzania	3.17	0.76	2.41
Uganda	1.78	−0.88	2.65
Zambia	1.30	1.23	0.57
Africa (unweighted)	2.18	1.31	0.87
Africa (weighted)	2.87	2.07	0.80

Source: McMillan and Harttgen 2014, table 5.
Note: The Africa averages (weighted and unweighted) also include three North African countries: Algeria, the Arab Republic of Egypt, and Morocco.

Reference

McMillan, M. S., and K. Harttgen. 2014. "What Is Driving 'African Growth Miracle'?" NBER Working Paper 20077, National Bureau of Economic Research, Cambridge, MA.

History of Malawi's Farm Input Subsidy Program

Malawi's initial input subsidy program in the wake of structural adjustment was the Starter Pack. In place during the 1998/99 and 1999/2000 agricultural seasons, the Starter Pack grew out of the recommendations of the Malawi Maize Productivity Task Force, which had been established to explore policy options for addressing the country's chronic national food shortages (Harrigan 2008). The task force identified declining soil fertility and maize productivity as two major contributors to food shortages. The Starter Pack entitled all Malawian smallholder farm households to 15 kilograms of inorganic fertilizer, 2 kilograms of hybrid maize seed, and 1 kilogram of legume seed for free; the maize inputs were sufficient to plant approximately 0.1 hectare of maize (Druilhe and Barreiro-Hurlé 2012; Harrigan 2008). The original objectives of the program were to raise agricultural productivity by introducing farmers to "best-bet" technologies in a risk-free way, to kick-start agricultural development, and to achieve national food self-sufficiency (Harrigan 2008; Levy 2005), not social protection (Chirwa and Dorward 2013).

National maize production increased markedly in Malawi in the years of the Starter Pack (likely due in part, but not entirely, to the program), but the program was unpopular with donors, who highlighted its high fiscal cost, negative effects on the development of private sector input markets, and late delivery, among other challenges (Harrigan 2008). Donor opposition, including pressure from the International Monetary Fund to reduce expenditures on the Starter Pack, eventually led to its scaling down and transformation into the Targeted Inputs Program (TIP).[1] Under TIP, emphasis shifted from raising agricultural productivity and food self-sufficiency to providing a safety net for poor smallholder farm households.[2]

Targeted Inputs Program, 2000/01–2004/05

TIP was essentially a "targeted version of the Starter Pack" (Druilhe and Barreiro-Hurlé 2012, 18). Its scale varied over time, with 1.5 million free input packs distributed in 2000/01, 1 million in 2001/02, 2.8 million in 2002/03 (following the

2002 food crisis), 1.7 million in 2003/04, and 2 million in 2004/05; this is in contrast with the 2.8 million input packs distributed in each year of the Starter Pack (Harrigan 2008). In its last year (2004/05), the size of the TIP input pack increased to 25 kilograms of fertilizer, 5 kilograms of open-pollinated variety (OPV) maize seed, and 1 kilogram of legume seed.[3]

Farm Input Subsidy Program, 2005/06–Present

Malawi's present-day input subsidy program, the Farm Input Subsidy Program (FISP), was established in 2005/06. The program's core objectives are raising household and national food security, food self-sufficiency, and incomes by improving resource-poor smallholders' access to improved agricultural inputs (Chirwa and Dorward 2013; Kilic, Whitney, and Winters 2015; Lunduka, Ricker-Gilbert, and Fisher 2013).

The number of smallholder farm households that FISP has aimed to reach has varied over time, but has been 1.5 million per year during the three most recent agricultural years (2012/13 through 2014/15) (Logistics Unit 2015). Other key features of the program, including the total quantity of subsidized inputs distributed and the fertilizer subsidy rate, are summarized in table 4.1 in chapter 4. As of 2014/15, beneficiary farmers were to receive vouchers for fertilizer, maize seed, and legume seed:

- Two fertilizer vouchers: one for a 50-kilogram bag of NPK (nitrogen, phosphorus, and potassium) fertilizer as basal dressing and one for a 50-kilogram bag of urea as top dressing. When redeeming their vouchers, farmers had to pay a top-up fee of MK 500 per 50-kilogram bag.
- One maize seed voucher for 5 kilograms of hybrid maize seed or 8 kilograms of OPV maize seed for free, although seed companies could apply a discretionary top-up fee of MK 100 on the voucher.[4]
- One legume seed voucher for 3 kilograms of soybean seed or 2 kilograms of other legume seed (beans, cowpeas, pigeon peas, or groundnuts) for free (Logistics Unit 2015).[5]

In August 2015, the Malawian government announced that the farmer contributions would increase to MK 3,500 per 50-kilogram bag of fertilizer, and MK 1,000 and MK 500 for the above-mentioned quantities of maize and legume seed, respectively (*The Daily Times*, Malawi, August 7, 2015, p. 1). This is equivalent to a fertilizer subsidy rate of approximately 70 percent— much lower than the 90–95 percent subsidy rates that have prevailed in recent years.

Beneficiary farmers redeem their fertilizer coupons at government-run outlets—Agricultural Development and Marketing Corporation (ADMARC) and Smallholder Farmers Fertilizer Revolving Fund of Malawi (SFFRFM) locations— and their seed vouchers at registered, private agro-dealers' shops (Kilic, Whitney, and Winters 2015; Logistics Unit 2015). That is, fertilizer for FISP is distributed through government, not private sector, channels.[6] Until 2013/14, all FISP coupons were paper, but an electronic voucher (e-voucher), scratch-card-based system was piloted for seed in six extension planning areas (EPAs) in 2013/14 and expanded to 18 EPAs in 2014/15. Fertilizer e-vouchers were piloted in 2014/15 in the six EPAs where seed e-vouchers had been piloted in 2013/14 (Logistics Unit 2015). The fertilizer e-voucher is to be expanded to eight districts and used to distribute 30,000 metric tons of the 150,000 metric tons of fertilizer intended for the 2015/16 FISP (*The Daily Times*, Malawi, August 7, 2015, p. 1).

FISP beneficiary selection and coupon allocations occur as follows (Kilic, Whitney, and Winters 2015; Wanzala-Mlobela, Fuentes, and Mkumbwa 2013; Lunduka, Ricker-Gilbert, and Fisher 2013). First, the Ministry of Agriculture and Food Security allocates coupons to districts in proportion to their number of farm households. Second, within each district, the district commissioner, in conjunction with the district agricultural development officer, traditional authorities, nongovernmental organizations, and religious leaders determine how to allocate the district's coupons to EPAs within the district and to villages within the EPAs. And third, within each village, beneficiaries are selected through community-based targeting in open forums. In general, FISP beneficiaries are to be full-time smallholder farmers who cannot afford one or two bags of fertilizer at commercial prices. Priority is given to resource-poor households (for example, those with elderly, human immunodeficiency virus/acquired immune deficiency syndrome (HIV/AIDS)–positive, female, child, orphan, or physically challenged household heads or household heads who are taking care of elderly or physically challenged individuals) (Kilic, Whitney, and Winters 2015).

Notes

1. See Levy (2005) and Harrigan (2008) for further details on the Starter Pack.

2. According to Harrigan (2008, 245), "These objections [to the Starter Pack] coincided with an evolution of donor food security policies toward a more holistic livelihoods approach as well as an elevation of the social safety net program in Malawi. Hence, donors were willing to endorse a scaled-down free inputs program and to recast it in the light, not of a production-enhancing technological transfer, but as one of many targeted social safety nets, albeit not necessarily the most effective."

3. See Levy (2005) for a discussion of the other key differences between the 2004/05 program and previous years.

4. Maize seed quantities have varied over time. For example, in the early years of the program, seed coupons were for 2 kilograms of hybrid seed or 4–5 kilograms of OPV seed (Lunduka, Ricker-Gilbert, and Fisher 2013).

5. As discussed in Dorward and Chirwa (2011), in the early years of the program, FISP included maize and tobacco fertilizers and OPV maize seed (but no hybrid or legume seed). Hybrid maize seed was added in 2006/07; legume seed as well as cotton seed and chemicals were added in 2007/08; and fertilizers for tea and coffee and storage

chemicals for maize were added in 2008/09. Tobacco, cotton, tea, and coffee inputs were subsequently phased out. See Dorward and Chirwa (2011) for a summary of other program changes from 2006/07 through 2008/09.

6. In 2005/06, both fertilizer and seed vouchers had to be redeemed at ADMARC and SFFRFM outlets. In 2006/07 and 2007/08, seed vouchers were redeemable at private seed retailers, while fertilizer vouchers were redeemable at private fertilizer retailers and at ADMARC and SFFRFM outlets. But since 2008/09, fertilizer vouchers are only redeemable at ADMARC and SFFRFM outlets (Dorward and Chirwa 2011; Logistics Unit 2015). Government selects, via a tender process, companies to import and deliver fertilizer to SFFRFM and ADMARC locations (Wanzala-Mlobela, Fuentes, and Mkumbwa 2013).

References

Chirwa, E., and A. Dorward. 2013. *Agricultural Input Subsidies: The Recent Malawi Experience*. Oxford, U.K.: Oxford University Press.

Dorward, A., and E. Chirwa. 2011. "The Malawi Agricultural Input Subsidy Programme: 2005–06 to 2008–09." *International Journal of Agricultural Sustainability* 9(1): 232–247.

Druilhe, Z., and J. Barreiro-Hurlé. 2012. "Fertilizer Subsidies in Sub-Saharan Africa." ESA Working Paper 12–04, Agricultural Development Economics Division. Rome, Italy: Food and Agriculture Organization of the United Nations.

Harrigan, J. 2008. "Food Insecurity, Poverty and the Malawian Starter Pack: Fresh Start or False Start?" *Food Policy* 33 (3): 237–49.

Kilic, T., E. Whitney, and P. Winters. 2015. "Decentralized Beneficiary Targeting in Large-Scale Development Programs: Insights from the Malawi Farm Input Subsidy Program." *Journal of African Economies* 24 (1): 26–56.

Levy, S. (ed.). 2005. *Starter Packs: A Strategy to Fight Hunger in Developing and Transition Countries? Lessons from the Malawi Experience, 1998–2003*. Wallingford, UK: Centre for Agriculture and Bioscience International.

Logistics Unit. 2015. "Final Report on the Implementation of the Agricultural Inputs Subsidy Programme, 2014–15." Lilongwe, Malawi: Logistics Unit.

Lunduka, R., J. Ricker-Gilbert, and M. Fisher. 2013. "What Are the Farm-Level Impacts of Malawi's Farm Input Subsidy Program? A Critical Review." *Agricultural Economics* 44 (6): 563–79.

Wanzala-Mlobela, M., P. Fuentes, and S. Mkumbwa. 2013. "NEPAD Policy Study: Practices and Policy Options for the Improved Design and Implementation of Fertilizer Subsidy Programs in Sub-Saharan Africa." Midrand, South Africa: New Partnership for Africa's Development Planning and Coordinating Agency.

Environmental Benefits Statement

The World Bank Group is committed to reducing its environmental footprint. In support of this commitment, we leverage electronic publishing options and print-on-demand technology, which is located in regional hubs worldwide. Together, these initiatives enable print runs to be lowered and shipping distances decreased, resulting in reduced paper consumption, chemical use, greenhouse gas emissions, and waste.

We follow the recommended standards for paper use set by the Green Press Initiative. The majority of our books are printed on Forest Stewardship Council (FSC)–certified paper, with nearly all containing 50–100 percent recycled content. The recycled fiber in our book paper is either unbleached or bleached using totally chlorine-free (TCF), processed chlorine-free (PCF), or enhanced elemental chlorine-free (EECF) processes.

More information about the Bank's environmental philosophy can be found at http://www.worldbank.org/corporateresponsibility.

green
press
INITIATIVE

www.ingramcontent.com/pod-product-compliance
Lightning Source LLC
Chambersburg PA
CBHW080424270326
41929CB00018B/3152